Ovid before Exile

Publication of this volume has been made possible in part through the generous support and enduring vision of WARREN G. MOON.

Ovid before Exile

Art and Punishment in the *Metamorphoses*

Patricia J. Johnson

THE UNIVERSITY OF WISCONSIN PRESS

The University of Wisconsin Press
1930 Monroe Street, 3rd Floor
Madison, Wisconsin 53711-2059
uwpress.wisc.edu

3 Henrietta Street
London WCE 8LU, England
eurospanbookstore.com

Printed in the United States of America

Library of Congress Cataloging-in-Publication Data
Johnson, Patricia J. (Patricia Jane)
Ovid before exile : art and punishment in the Metamorphoses / Patricia J. Johnson.
p. cm.—(Wisconsin studies in classics)
Includes bibliographical references and index.
ISBN 0-299-22400-7 (cloth : alk. paper)
1. Ovid, 43 B.C.–17 or 18 A.D. Metamorphoses. 2. Ovid, 43 B.C.–17 or 18 A.D.—Criticism and interpretation. 3. Epic poetry, Latin—History and criticism. 4. Art and state—Rome. 5. Freedom and art—Rome. I. Title. II. Series.
PA6519.M9J64 2007
873′.01—dc22 2007011820

ISBN-13: 978-0-299-22404-2 (pbk.: alk. paper)

matri patrique et fratribus carissimis
filiis delectis
et sine quo nihil
marito optimo

Contents

Acknowledgments

A first book is something of a tenth-month child, and its author as a result benefits from the prenatal care of a long list of midwives, both individual and institutional. I can acknowledge by name only a handful of those who have helped me along the way. The Boston University Department of Classical Studies has provided a stimulating and supportive environment for my research over the past decade; I single out Ann Vasaly and Jay Samons from among many wonderful colleagues for their insightful readings and frank advice. The Boston University Humanities Foundation and its director, Katherine O'Connor, provided me with two Junior Fellowship years at the foundation, in whose collegial seminars two of the book's chapters were enriched; I am particularly indebted to Peter Hawkins for his wisdom about the writing process. A delightful sojourn as a visiting scholar at the American Academy in Rome in spring 2004 brought the book to completion in the inspiring atmosphere of Ovid's beloved *urbs.* Various chapters began their lives as talks for the Classics Departments at Brown, Michigan, and SUNY Buffalo, whose presiding Latinist and editor of *Arethusa,* Martha Malamud, first convinced me to take on the *Metamorphoses* in graduate school at the University of Southern California; I have enjoyed her support ever since. I am grateful for the gracious and thoughtful readings of earlier drafts by Bruce Redford and Michael Putnam. The University of Wisconsin Press and its anonymous readers made excellent observations and suggestions. As a non-anonymous reader for the Press, Elaine Fantham provided a reading both expansive and detailed that sharpened and improved every chapter. The manuscript was made presentable in a timely fashion by the acute editing of Sophie Klein. I owe a special debt of gratitude to the Greek and Latin literature editor for the Wisconsin

Studies in Classics series, Patricia Rosenmeyer, without whose assistance, on everything from content and style to the logistics of publishing, the book would never have seen the light of day. It goes without saying that all remaining *errores* are entirely my own responsibility.

A project of this length demands a great deal not only of the author but also of her family, to whom I dedicate this book. My sons, Andreas and Alexander Viglakis, grew up with this project and will probably be as relieved as I to see it in print. The same is doubtless true of my husband, Jeffrey Henderson, whose affection and support have been my staff of life during the book's gestation.

Ovid before Exile

Introduction

Problems and Approaches

Saepe etiam audacem fugat hoc terretque poetam,
quod numero plures, virtute et honore minores,
indocti stolidique et depugnare parati,
si discordet eques, media inter carmina poscunt
aut ursum aut pugiles; his nam plebecula gaudet.

[Even the bold poet is terrified and sent running when the uneducated dolts in the audience, greater in number but inferior in virtue and rank, call for a bear or boxers in the middle of the songs, ready to fight with the knights if they disagree; for these things please the mob.]

Horace *Epist.* 2.1.182–86, 13 BC

a! ferus et nobis nimium crudeliter hostis,
delicias legit qui tibi cumque meas,
carmina de nostris cum te venerantia libris
iudicio possint candidiore legi.

[How vicious was he, an enemy too cruel, who read for you my racy verses, while other poems from my books, praising you, could be read, to elicit a more glowing review.]

Ovid *Tr.* 2.77–80, 9 AD

It is one of the fascinating coincidences of ancient literary history that two of the greatest poets of the Augustan era, Ovid and Horace, each composed a long verse letter to the emperor Augustus toward the end of their respective careers on the subject of poetry, filling the entirety (Ovid) or more than half (Horace) of the second volume of a substantial collection of poetry, Ovid's *Tristia* 2 and Horace's *Epistles* 2.[1] Composed at opposite ends of the emperor's long reign, *Epistles* 2 in perhaps 13 BC, *Tristia* 2 in 9 AD, the poems are worlds apart in many ways. Horace seeks the support of Augustus for modern Latin poetry books, in the course of a general review of the rather daunting conditions for poetic performance in Rome, while Ovid seeks the emperor's pardon for the licentious poetry of his youth, supplying all the while a vigorous defense of his life and poetic career. Horace, in 13 BC, is safely at Rome in the good graces of his patron Maecenas and *his* patron Augustus; Ovid, in 9 AD, has been sent by personal command of Augustus to a troubling exile on the Black Sea. The poems and their authors occupy distant poles both politically and geographically.

Yet the poems share a pressing concern about working conditions for poets, presenting what Feeney calls, regarding *Epistles* 2.1, "a politically informed investigation of the social status of poetry"[2] and the (potentially negative) impact of audiences on their work.[3] Horace laments a combination of declining taste and worsening behavior in the theater, where poetic recitations are yielding to (and poets are fleeing from) a popular appetite for spectacle. Augustus is capable of righting this wrong by virtue of his great authority:

Verum age et his, qui se lectori credere malunt
quam spectatoris fastidia ferre superbi,
curam redde brevem, si munus Apolline dignum
vis complere libris, et vatibus addere calcar,
ut studio maiore petant Helicona virentem.

[Indeed, give some care to those who would rather entrust themselves to a reader than endure the scorn of the arrogant spectator, if you want to fill that worthy gift to Apollo [i.e., the new Palatine Library] with books, and to spur the poets to aspire with greater enthusiasm to springlike Helicon.]

Epist. 2.1.214–18

By the time of Ovid's exile, according to the scenario sketched in *Tristia* 2, this authority has transformed Augustus, in the absence of Maecenas and with the passing of the years, into the only poetic audience of any real importance, by whom public opinion is guided (*Tr.* 2.88, *est vultus turba secuta tuos*, 'the crowd follows your expression').[4] Unfortunately, Ovid claims, the emperor has been deliberately misled by one of the poet's enemies, who drew Augustus's attention to the most salacious sections of the *Ars Amatoria*. So while in 13 BC the disapproval of theater audiences is driving poets away from the stage *(fugat)*, and only

Augustus can remedy it by supporting nonperforming poets, in 9 AD the disapproval of Augustus alone has driven Ovid into an exile he regularly refers to as a *fuga.*

Conditions for poetic composition were a concern of Latin poets long before the Augustan period, of course. Terence expresses high anxiety about criticism of his plays for being too innovative in the prologue to *Women of Andros,* for example, and reports in the prologue to *Phormio* that in their last performance the cast had been driven off the stage by a rowdy and unappreciative audience. The ability of Vergil's Tityrus to continue his singing and composition in *Eclogues* 1 is dependent on the kindness of a Roman benefactor, apparently the young Octavian, while Meliboeus's lands are confiscated for distribution to soldiers; this is a political process that, in *Eclogues* 9, poetry has failed to stop. Apart from the above-cited *Epistle,* according to which, as Feeney observes, "the history of Roman literature . . . is for all intents and purposes coextensive with the history of the state's regulation of it,"[5] Horace expresses concern in *Epistles* 1.13 that the delivery of a copy of the *Odes* to Augustus take place when the emperor is receptive and not otherwise engaged. This same anxiety is reflected in Ovid's much longer *Tristia* 1.1 (lines 69–104, especially 93–96).

It is the premise of this book that conditions for the production of poetry changed dramatically in the years between Horace's *Epistles* and the end of Ovid's career at Rome, and that Ovid frequently reflects upon those changes in his *Metamorphoses.* I begin by proposing that acknowledgment of Ovid's *distance* from the Rome of Vergil, Horace, Propertius, and Tibullus is necessary for a proper understanding of the *Metamorphoses,* particularly of its treatments of artists at work. Ralph Johnson suggests in *Darkness Visible* that "it is possible to see in Vergil's time not an age of faith but the beginning of the age of anxiety," and the stirrings of "intuitions of a terrible dualism";[6] by the time Ovid was writing the *Metamorphoses* and *Fasti* these are no longer intuitions but realities. The literary-historical evidence of Ovid's own works, discussed below, suggests a drop in first-rate poetic production during these years at Rome, which I argue is the result of a decline in the freedom afforded poets by the emperor, parallel to the well-documented decline in the republican arts of oratory and rhetoric. The attrition of the great poets of the Vergilian generation, the death of Maecenas in 8 BC, and the exposure of Augustus's daughter Julia on charges of immorality in 2 BC all contributed significantly to a changed atmosphere for creative writing in Ovid's final decade in Rome.

Rather than advance a new theoretical approach to Ovid's poem, this study combines formal analysis of the episodes of artistic performance, particularly regarding Ovid's deployment of epic ekphrasis, with exemplary close readings, guided by a long-standing belief that individual poets can and often do respond to and comment upon their own artistic circumstances in their poetry, particularly where art and its creation are the subject. My approach has been informed and improved by a number of recent approaches to the *Metamorphoses.* For example, while I read Ovid's often dizzying narrative levels as indications of his interest in the poet/artist's control of art and audience generally, my discussion is nonetheless indebted to Stephen Wheeler's close attention to narrators, narrative structures, and audiences in his *Discourse of Wonders,* which reveal to him a poem composed for public performance (very much in line with the philosophy of David Raeburn's recent Penguin translation).[7] Similarly, Philip Hardie's framing of "ecphrastic universes" in the poem opens the door for my broadened definition of Ovidian ekphrasis.[8]

Most influential for my conclusions about the sociohistorical importance of the episodes have been modern evaluations of Augustan poetry in the light of Augustus's ideological program, discussed in more detail below. From a perspective grounded in the circumstances of the late Augustan period, I offer here a fresh evaluation of the most substantial examples of Ovid's treatment of artistic creation and reception in the poem: the poetic contest between the Emathides and Muses in book 5, the weaving contest between Arachne and Minerva in book 6, and the two songs of Orpheus in book 10. The episodes are striking in isolation, but even more so as a group. In dialogue as always with his literary predecessors, Ovid provides an ekphrastic description of each work as it takes shape, set within an often elaborate sketch of the human background of its creation: the emotions that motivate the artworks, the social contexts of the performances, their (intended and unintended) audiences, and finally the effects of the artworks on both audience and artist. For these expansive descriptions of both visual and verbal art I employ the term 'performative ekphrasis' (chapter 1). The remainder of the book is devoted to a discussion of the interplay between artist and performance conditions in the episodes themselves. The settings and audiences of the songs of the Emathides and Muses in book 5 (chapter 2) motivate specific performance strategies for each group of singers. Within both narrative frames crafted by Ovid (the original poetic contest on Mount Helicon, and its reprise at a later date to Minerva), the song of the Emathides is flawed by a fatal miscalculation of their audience and judges, while the Muses devise a poetic strategy that succeeds in gaining approval. Minerva will move directly to provoke a weaving contest with Arachne at the opening of book 6 (chapter 3), where the goddess's looming presence will inspire Arachne to produce a surpassingly beautiful but strategically ill-advised artwork. Orpheus (chapter 4) is the only mortal artist of the group who lives to sing another day. His first song in the underworld is a masterpiece of political strategy, but not of art; his second, freed, as he thinks, from the constraints of a demanding audience, will explore the limits of X-rated mythological love stories. Like his colleagues in the previous episodes, however, he is mistaken about the audience for his second song, and like them will suffer a terrible, indeed in his case, the ultimate, transformation.

The time seems right for such a reappraisal of the *Metamorphoses,* and of particular relevance to an American critic. The post-Vietnam era, whose popular and academic cultures prided themselves on both their challenges to and transcendence of social and artistic boundaries, was the beginning of an American age which has in many ways resembled the Ovidian. Like the citizens of the early Roman empire, Americans issued a collective sigh of relief at the end of a war that inflicted painful damage on the home front, and have not endured a military draft since; a period of unprecedented economic prosperity followed, accompanied by a declining commitment to traditional values; most recently the United States, like Rome of the Augustan period, has been thrust, only half-willingly, into citizenship with a large, unfamiliar, and rather hostile world. The send-up of traditional romance in the *Amores,* the satire and open eroticism of the *Ars Amatoria,* the fantastic sound-bite episodes of the *Metamorphoses,* the often-journalistic complaints of the exile from the edge of the world, all have resonated for late-twentieth- and early-twenty-first-century American readers.

Ovid's new relevance has been evident both within and without academia in the west. In the arts, homage to his innovative *Metamorphoses* has often been paid in the last thirty years in the form of adaptations for the stage, and in vivid translations, novels, and poems inspired by his life, his art, or his subject matter. In academic circles, many of what Stephen Hinds called in 1987 the "ageing generalisations"[9] about Ovid's poems (that they were, inter alia, emotionally shallow, mannerist and rhetorical, overly explicit, politically escapist, sycophantic, or lacking in seriousness) have been confronted and, if not entirely discarded, at least have been subjected to vigorous debate and discussion.[10] Brooks Otis's

Ovid as an Epic Poet launched a generation of studies that undertook a reevaluation of the *Metamorphoses'* status as epic, including Hinds's watershed 1989 study of the poetic contest, *The Metamorphosis of Persephone;* a fresh appreciation of the poem's structure, models (especially Alexandrian), and generic characteristics and innovations has continued to this day. These studies initiated in turn a new era of Ovidian *Quellenforschung,* which replaced the search for superior 'originals' for aspects of Ovid's epic with the discovery of the complex and playfully allusive relationships the poem establishes with its poetic predecessors in Rome, Alexandria, and Athens. Frederick Ahl's 1985 *Metaformations* unveiled a seemingly impossible parade of puns and wordplays in the *Metamorphoses* that dispensed once and for all with the poem's reputation as a careless compendium of Greek myth, and inspired a generation of close readings of Ovid's language.[11] Gender and sexual politics in the *Metamorphoses* were finally addressed as openly by modern critics as they were in the poetry itself, in the work of Leo Curran, Amy Richlin, and their numerous successors.[12] In this period Ovid has also for the most part been freed from his characterization as the apolitical man-about-town by an often-heated controversy over the poet's pro- or anti-Augustanism.[13] From this debate a more nuanced definition of 'Augustanism' has emerged that speaks more of a complex engagement with the politics and culture of the Augustan principate than rigid support or opposition for the new emperor and his policies.[14] This discussion was revolutionized by Zanker's *Power of Images in the Age of Augustus,* which detailed for the first time the use Augustus made of cultural material (myth, literature, the arts) to promote his political power and (primarily moral) agenda. Critics have developed, as a result of studies like Ahl's landmark reconsideration of the literary strategies of Augustan and Flavian poets,[15] a more sophisticated notion of ideology in the Augustan period, the better to evaluate the ways in which the content and very structure of the *Metamorphoses* engages with and challenges its Augustan context. The essays by Denis Feeney, Duncan Kennedy and Philip Hardie in *Roman Poetry and Propaganda in the Age of Augustus*[16] testify to the benefits of politically astute study of Ovid's poems, while the issue of free speech in antiquity has itself found new life in the second 2002 *Penn-Leiden Colloquium on Ancient Values* and its now-published proceedings.[17] In brief, we have learned not to take Ovid or his *Metamorphoses* so lightly.[18]

Renaissance has inevitably been followed by canonization; Ovid's poetry is as a result now back on the scholar's library shelf where it belongs, alongside those Augustan poets acknowledged to be Rome's greatest, including Vergil, Horace, Propertius, and Tibullus. Yet no one would dispute that Ovid is somehow *different* from this Augustan peer group; his difference, after all, was what originally brought about the isolation of his work from the approved grand masters of Roman poetry for all those years. There is first of all Ovid's unmistakable tone: his irreverent and almost adolescent playfulness, often jarringly intermingled with moments of pathos and seriousness, divides and perplexes Ovid's fans and detractors both.[19] All would agree, however, that his vast range of tone is unique and unimaginable in a poet of the earlier Augustan period. Ovid's approach to genre is similarly idiosyncratic. While Gallus, Propertius, and Tibullus defined and refined amatory elegy, Ovid loaded his *Amores* with provocative eroticism and an irony frequently venturing into parody. In the *Heroides* Ovid blended elements from a variety of poetic genres to create a wholly new form, which gives voice to a host of mythological heroines and their lovers.[20] Similarly the *Fasti* represents an uneasy marriage of the antiquarian, aetiological elegy of the Alexandrian Callimachus with the ultra-Roman, and ultra-ideological, calendrical tradition.[21] The generic *comparanda* for the *Ars Amatoria,* ironically listed by Ovid himself in *Tristia* 2.471–90 (handbooks on games, table settings, and handicrafts) cannot begin to account for his masterfully subversive satire of Roman sexual mores. With the *Metamorphoses,* Ovid threw out the rule book provided by his epic predecessors in Latin and eclectically reformulated Greek and Latin epic poetry. Elements of Callimachus's *Aitia,* perhaps Nicander's *Heteroeumena,* and Hesiod's *Theogony* are all blended into a famously deft but often problematic mix of craftsmanship, humor, and ominous seriousness.[22] Although generic experimentation was characteristic of the arts of earlier Augustan Rome, the boldness of the *Metamorphoses* still stands apart; this episodic, unheroic, mythological epic has sparked a century-long debate over its very classification as epic and its relationship to Ovid's elegiac works.[23]

Ovid's poesis therefore actively departs in several important respects from the practice of the Augustans. In their well-intentioned eagerness to reclaim Ovid for the golden age of Latin literature, critics have naturally tended to emphasize continuity with the past, tracing the allusions Ovid regularly makes to the Augustans, and to downplay the discontinuities that are the trademark of his distinctive contribution. The result has been an elision of, and general puzzlement over, Ovid's brilliant difference. Many would consider this a reasonable sacrifice, after so long a relegation of Ovid's poems to the realm of the second-rate. But classification of Ovid's *Metamorphoses* as simply an 'Augustan' work, as Gordon Williams long ago acknowledged,[24] is problematic.

Ovid's reputation as a poet is now more secure than ever before in the modern period: appreciative studies of Ovid's relationship with his Augustan predecessors are now in the mainstream. It seems safe, therefore, to cautiously review and question some of the assumptions invoked to support that relationship, while clarifying the historical position of Ovid and his great *Metamorphoses*. This study concurs with the simple principle expounded by E. J. Kenney twenty-five years ago regarding the *Metamorphoses'* more incredible tales: "In reading the story of Pygmalion (10.242–97) we forget that in the real world statues do not come to life; we know only that if they did this is how it would be."[25] If mortal singers were to challenge the Muses on Helicon, if Arachne were to compete with Minerva, if we were present for the legendary songs of Orpheus in the underworld or Thrace, this, to the cynical and perhaps rather discouraged Ovid of the late Augustan period, is how it would be.

Tempora Ovidiana

sed vereor, ne te mea nunc fortuna retardet,
  postque meos casus sit tibi pectus iners.
dum licuit, tua saepe mihi, tibi nostra legebam,
  saepe tui iudex, saepe magister eram;
aut ego praebebam factis modo versibus aures,
  aut, ubi cessaras, causa ruboris eram.
forsitan exemplo, quo me laesere libelli,
  tu metuis poenae fata secunda meae.
pone, Perilla, metum; tantummodo femina nulla
  neve vir a scriptis discat amare tuis.

[I worry that my fate now may be holding you back, that after my calamity your heart may have turned away from your art. While I could, I often read your work to myself, and mine to you; often I was your critic or your teacher. Sometimes I lent an ear to the verses you had just written, or if you had stopped writing, I made you feel ashamed. Perhaps you are now afraid of suffering a fate like mine, harm caused by the books I've written. Set aside your fear, Perilla; just let no woman or man learn how to love from your writing.]

Tr. 3.7.21–30

Ovid's verse epistle to the young Perilla, thought to be his stepdaughter, was written early in the poet's relegation, soon after his arrival in

Tomis, in perhaps 9–10 AD. It is interesting both for what it does and does not say. Composed to encourage Perilla to continue her work as a poet, Ovid expresses concern that his unfortunate exile will stifle her creativity, for two reasons, one implied and one explicit. The implication, treated at more length (23–26), is that since Ovid is in exile, he can no longer play the roles of *iudex* and *magister* to her budding talent; we are to understand from *tibi nostra* that he in turn will no longer benefit from her feedback on his work. His explicit worry is that she will be afraid *(metum)* of suffering a similar fate as a result of her own *libelli* (27–28). The solution he proposes is direct and simple: she will be fine as long as she refrains from advising lovers in her poetry, in effect, by censoring her subject-matter: *tantummodo femina nulla / neve vir a scriptis discat amare tuis* (29–30). We might have expected him to put her mind at ease by claiming that his *error,* rather than his *carmen,* was the decisive reason for his exile, as critics generally infer from the long delay between the publication of the *Ars Amatoria,* in 2 AD at the latest, and Ovid's relegation in 8 AD. But as he has presented the case to Perilla, the *Ars* and its immoral content were the primary cause of his relegation by Augustus, and he offers a warning to the young poet on the conduct of her career.

Presented with the fact of Ovid's relegation and evidence like *Tristia* 3.7 in its aftermath, we tend to divide Ovid's career in two parts, before and after 8 AD. The pre-exilic Ovid was the embodiment of Augustan free expression, the carefree and popular composer of the outrageous *Ars Amatoria* and the innovative *Metamorphoses.* The post-exilic Ovid, reduced to issuing laments and making pleas from exile in the *Tristia* and *Epistulae Ex Ponto,* was living proof of the Roman emperor's intolerance of artistic free speech. The author of the *Fasti* falls somewhere in between these two poles, the *auctor* of a work begun at Rome but bearing clear indications of its revision during exile.[26]

There is no question that a shift in Ovid's poesis accompanied his geographic shift to the Black Sea: from exile until death his poetry focuses almost exclusively on securing his return to Rome, or at least a more hospitable place of exile. It is also evident, however, that Ovid's poetic production shows signs of change in the years before his departure for Tomis. Most critics acknowledge a decline in these years in the forms of literature specifically linked to the ruling elite and its old political freedoms, in particular oratory and history, but the effect this same atmosphere must have had on the work of poets has not been much explored. In particular, there has been scarce discussion of the specific historical context of the composition of the *Metamorphoses* apart from studies evaluating its redeployment of myth and genre in the context of Augustan ideology.[27] The *Metamorphoses,* with its surreal, timeless atmosphere and easily digestible surface, has seemed to betray few clear signs of its origins in a period of dramatic change in the principate and in conditions for literary composition. Ahl successfully captures Ovid's dilemma: "He stands on the perilous brink between what we take to be the simple 'classical' world of Augustan poetry and the complex obscurity of the 'Silver Age.' His admirers pull him safely into the classical fold by showing he is simple and thus classical; his detractors push him out to join Seneca and Statius in mannered obscurity."[28]

Ovid's own characterization of his poetic career indicates that a rigid demarcation at the moment of exile is misleading; he instead records a change in poetic direction after the publication of the *Ars Amatoria.* As he makes his appeal for a recall from exile in *Tristia* 2, Ovid distinguishes the different stages of his career: *ne tamen omne meum credas opus esse remissum,* 'You mustn't think that all my work is dissolute' (2.547–62), claiming to have embraced a new respectability, which according to his apology begins while he is still in Rome (2.63–66). As we might expect in a plea for the emperor's mercy, Ovid regrets the scandalous elegiac poetry of his youth, in particular the *Ars: at cur in nostra nimia est lascivia Musa / curve meus cuiquam suadet amare liber?,* 'Why is my Muse so scandalous, and why does my book advise anyone to love?' (2.313–14). The bulk of *Tristia* 2 is devoted to reiterating that the *Ars* was responsible for his exile, for its instruction on the conduct of illicit love affairs: *altera pars superest, qua turpi carmine factus / arguor obsceni doctor adulterii,* 'The other part of the charge remains, that I am said to have become a teacher of obscene adultery by writing a base poem' (2.211–12). Augustus's investment in reform of the morals of the Roman elite had by this time been substantial, from the passage of still-unpopular legislation penalizing adultery and rewarding marriage in 18 BC *(Leges Juliae)* to the surrender of his daughter Julia to its statutes in 2 BC. Ovid's *Ars* is a frontal assault on the values that Augustus made the centerpiece of his reign.

Ovid claims to have turned over a new leaf after the *Ars* with the composition of more 'important' works with *grandia vela,* 'grander sails': these include the *Fasti,* still underway; his tragedy, *Medea,* now lost; and the incomplete *Metamorphoses,* which he twice urges the emperor to read (*Tr.* 2.63–66, 555–62). The date of the tragedy is early in his career,[29] but the other two works are certainly the product of Ovid's last years in Rome, and, Ovid claims, signal a conscious departure from the *lasciva Musa,* particularly of the instructional variety. We tend to dismiss Ovid's construction of his career in this poem, as his characterization serves his self-defense so well. But in fact Ovid did turn away from erotic elegy after the *Ars.* With the *Fasti* Ovid began a new elegiac project on the Roman calendar, a subject of particular interest to the princeps, dedicated to Augustus before his death, and to the prince Germanicus afterwards. It marks a significant departure from the indecent erotic elegy that was both his glory and his downfall, focusing on Roman history and religion and incorporating a healthy dose of explicit praise for the emperor and his family. In the epic *Metamorphoses* Ovid signals a full retreat from the genre of amatory elegy on the one hand, and from the scandals of contemporary Rome on the other, turning to the more removed and far less controversial field of Greek mythology.

I therefore agree with Williams that Ovid devises a new artistic strategy after the publication of the *Ars Amatoria,* although I would not characterize it as a retreat into irrationality as he does,[30] or, as Otis once argued, a decision to pander to the emperor's wishes.[31] As recent criticism has demonstrated, Ovid's *Fasti* does not avoid engagement with Augustan values, but rather undertakes a more subtle relationship with them, maintaining a "hermaneutic alibi" that leaves the text open to both encomiastic and resistant readings.[32] Ovid undermines Julian modifications of the Roman festival calendar by a series of textual strategies, what Harries[33] calls "counter-effects": incongruous juxtaposition, omission, and the unreliability of Augustan narrators, including the gods.[34] In the *Metamorphoses* Ovid's explicit linkage of the Roman elite with the marauding Olympians in book 1 anchors the poem's twisting narrative with what Ahl has called "motifs of tyrannical power and its abuse,"[35] which detail the inevitable violence and silencing suffered by those who unwittingly find themselves in the presence of the powerful. Critics have perceived even sharper critiques of the Augustan regime in Ovid's handling of the Augustan 'sacred cows': his slight treatment of the foundation of Rome (the so-called little *Aeneid* in books 13–15), and the undignified portraits of Jupiter, Apollo, and Venus, the gods dearest to the princeps.

What historical factors triggered Ovid's change of strategy? The cultural atmosphere of Ovid's last ten years at Rome, the time of the composition of the *Metamorphoses,* is a gray area, a less-documented span of years between the often-discussed cultural accomplishments of the 'high' Augustan period and the reign of Tiberius.[36] The testimony of ancient historians regarding the nonmilitary particulars of this period is limited and compounds the difficulty of evaluating it. Critics have consequently arrived at dramatically different conclusions about the degree of autocracy exercised by Augustus and its possible effects during the final lap of the Augustan era. While Fantham characterizes these years as the onset of Augustus's "anxious and almost paranoiac old age," and cites Seneca the Elder's account of the burning of speeches and repression of free speech by Augustus, Galinsky's discussions of the literary scene in this period argue that it was in fact a time of less anxiety, of "refinement, elegance and sophistication" under the *pax augusta*.[37]

Galinsky's argument rests on an optimistic reading of Suetonius's portrait of the emperor's clemency, which provides a list of the political enemies whom Augustus had forgiven.[38] Although their offenses are primarily verbal (libel or verbal challenge), and therefore bear some similarity to artistic free speech, treatment of political opponents is a much different matter in Roman society than the treatment of writers.[39] The history of the late Republic and early Augustan period is filled with stories of enemies turned overnight into friends or even in-laws; clemency toward today's political foes is therefore a sensible virtue for any Roman politician. Suetonius's testimony is also suspicious because here and elsewhere in the *Life* he suppresses Augustus's worst offences against the freedom of expression familiar from other sources, including the exile of Ovid in 8 AD.

By contrast, Tacitus paints a grim picture of political freedom lost in his brief discussion of the end of the Augustan period in *Annales* 1.2, despite his overall preference for Augustus over Tiberius. He records the aspiring autocrat's success at persuading the Romans to abandon republican freedoms for monarchy: *militem donis, populum annona, cunctos dulcedine otii pellexit,* 'he compelled the army with bonuses, the people with free grain, and the rest with the sweetness of leisure/peace,' a picture filled with scorn for both the seducer and the seduced. Tacitus concludes with a description of the princeps's gradual absorption of all republican political offices without opposition, *nullo adversante,* 'as the boldest men had died in the proscriptions or in battle, while the rest of the nobility were bribed . . . and therefore all the more ready for slavery [*servitio promptior*].' While Galinsky rejects this testimony as displaying "the narrowest of biases," Syme's *Roman Revolution* and *History in Ovid* both make a strong case on the basis of the Tacitean evidence for an expanding Augustan autocracy and corresponding reductions in the freedom of literary expression in the principate beginning, in his framework, in about 13 BC.[40]

Personal events in the life of the emperor surely played a role in "the atmosphere of gloom and repression that clouded the last decade of the reign," according to Syme, who focuses on the effect of personal, natural, and military disasters on the aging Augustus.[41] Augustus's rage and embitterment over the behavior of his daughter Julia was the result, in Fantham's view, of "extraordinary emotional imbalance," which would only have been deepened by the loss of his last consanguineous heir, Gaius, in 4 AD.[42] Knox argues that the shift in atmosphere was caused not so much by a change in attitude of Augustus himself as by his increasing weakness and a corresponding transfer of power to Tiberius, whose intolerance of free speech is well documented: "In his years as emperor Tiberius showed himself sensitive in the extreme to any writing that could be interpreted as critical of himself."[43]

Whatever may have been its cause, from perhaps 2 BC to 8 AD, the princeps, and the atmosphere in his capital, underwent changes for the worse. As Feeney observes in response to Galinsky,[44] "rampant" free speech is hardly reflected in many of the measures taken by the princeps in these years. Titus Labienus, nicknamed 'Rabienus,' is charged with treason for his libelous histories, which Seneca reports were the first works of literature to be burned at the orders of the state, an act he describes as *saevitia,* 'savagery' committed by madmen, *dementissimi homines.*[45] Labienus commits suicide, most likely to avoid execution. Cassius Severus's sharp slander of members of the Roman elite incited the extension of the laws of *maiestas* to cover speech acts, as well as his own relegation to Crete, in perhaps 8 AD, as Knox suggests.[46] Fantham adds the fate of the Greek historian Timagenes, once favored by Augustus, and concludes that "the peace in the last years of Augustus' principate was that of absolute power and diminishing tolerance."[47] The relegation of Ovid in 8 AD for, in part, the writing of the *Ars Amatoria,* was the culmination of several stressful years for Augustan writers.

The earliest major changes in the literary atmosphere in Augustus's Rome, however, were very likely wrought by natural attrition: the aging, disappearance, and death of the great 'golden' generation of Augustan poets, and the failure or inability of the Roman elite to ensure that they would be replaced. The Augustan poets composed and recited in the salons of the early Augustan world under the gaze of a small but supportive group of wealthy patrons with literary interests and the power to promote them. For this world Ovid expresses tremendous nostalgia. When he boasts, in *Tristia* 4.10, *tulerint magnos cum saecula nostra poetas,* 'our age has produced great poets,' he does not list his recent contemporaries; the kindred spirits from line 41 on all date from the early years of the principate. Sadly, and significantly, all were dead or inactive by the time of the publication of the *Ars Amatoria.* Gallus, mentioned seven times in Ovid's poetry, was the longest-gone, when as the first prefect of the new province of Egypt he had a political run-in with Augustus and committed suicide in 27/26 BC, when Ovid would have been only sixteen or seventeen years of age.[48] Vergil died in 19 BC, after which his great epic was edited and published, by all accounts against his wishes; Fantham identifies this as Augustus's first literary intervention, an omen of things to come.[49] Tibullus followed soon after; Ovid comments *nec avara Tibullo / tempus amicitiae fata dedere mihi,* 'and the greedy fates gave Tibullus no time for friendship with me' (*Tr.* 4.10.41–42). The latest datable reference in the elegiac poetry of Propertius is 16 BC;[50] although the date of his death is unknown, he was certainly not active after the mid-teens BC. Aemilius Macer, a writer on naturalist themes and the subject of Tibullus 2.6.1, was gone by 16 BC. Horace and Maecenas, the longest-lived of the group, died in close succession in 8 BC. A change in the literary atmosphere was already visible in the more socially conscious, patriotic and frequently encomiastic strategy of much of the late Horace (*Carmen Saeculare, Odes* 4, *Epistles* 2). Although Horace responds to a great deal more than political matters in *Odes* 4, as Putnam amply demonstrates in his consideration of the poem's movement from private to public,[51] there is some truth to Syme's comment that "the wishes of Caesar and the poet's response are in concordance" in many of the poems.[52] The poetry, lives, and deaths of two other poets of the *convictus* or group of *sodales* mentioned in *Tristia* 4.10, Ponticus (epic) and Bassus (probably iambs), are known to Propertius and Ovid but unknown to us.[53]

Other possible survivors of the 'golden era' leave little trace in the historical record.[54] The poetic activity (beyond the poems in the manuscripts of Tibullus) and life spans of Lygdamus[55] and Sulpicia, the other documented members of the circle of Messalla Corvinus, are unknown. There are in fact no details of Messalla's patronage of the arts after Tibullus, although Ovid acknowledges his early support in several letters to his sons from exile. Syme is surely right to date Messalla's death before the relegation of Ovid in 8 AD on the evidence of *Epistulae Ex Ponto* 1.7 and *Tristia* 4.4; Messalla's last recorded act was his nomination of Augustus for the title *pater patriae* in the Senate in 2 BC.[56] If Pliny's account of his failing memory denotes a chronic condition (*Naturalis historia* 7.24), Messalla's withdrawal from public life may well have had a medical cause.

After the loss of so many giants of the Augustan cultural scene, the ranks do not seem to have been reconstituted. The need for the kind of cultural legitimacy bestowed by poetry and noncivic arts on the early reign of Augustus seems to have diminished with the passage of time; the princeps's own tastes leaned toward mime. Knox argues that Tiberius, whose intolerance of free speech is well-documented during his own reign, was decisive in the changing atmosphere;[57] Syme doesn't relieve Augustus of responsibility in this way, but acknowledges that Tiberius's devotion to contemporary *Greek* poetry and scholarship, perhaps a reaction against early Augustan support for the *Latin* literary arts, may have played a role in the poetic dry spell after the death of Augustus.[58]

In the poetic genres in particular, Ovid's *Metamorphoses, Fasti,* and the exilic works are the only poems of the major genres confidently dated to this period to survive antiquity intact. I realize this is an argument *ex silentio.* But let us consider Ovid's own appraisal of his contemporaries. A catalogue of over thirty contemporary poets in *Epistulae Ex Ponto* 4.16, his last extant poem, includes twenty-nine names or easily deciphered hints at names.[59] Ovid optimistically (perhaps ironically?) precedes the catalogue with the comment *famaque post cineres maior venit,* 'greater fame is earned after death'; it is a sobering fact that, of the twenty-nine, at least twelve are entirely unknown to us now, and apart from the elusive Grattius, whose *Cynegetica* is extant, most are only identified to posterity by references in Ovid's letters and fragments.[60]

The list includes all five poets to whom Ovid addressed letters from exile, which cluster in his final book of *Epistulae Ex Ponto,* composed between 13 and 16 AD. Albinovanus Pedo, called *sidereus* in 4.16, was a close friend of Ovid's, although directly addressed only once (*Pont.* 4.10, autumn of 14 AD). Pedo was an epigrammatist who also composed a *Theseis* and a historical epic on a campaign of Germanicus (of 16 AD, in which he participated as prefect), of which twenty-three rather over-stuffed lines are preserved by Seneca the Elder; Seneca the Younger dubs him *fabulator elegentissimus,* evidently for his clever gossip about Sextus Papinius.[61] Cornelius Severus, to whom Ovid addresses *Epistulae Ex Ponto* 4.2, also composed a historical epic whose subject is variously described: Ovid calls him *vates regum,* a poet of kings (*Pont.* 4.2.1), while the poem's subject is either described as *res Romanae* (Probus fr. 1) or *bellum Siculum* (Quintilian, *Institutio oratoria* 10.1.89). He also wrote a poem on the death of Cicero, which is quoted in Seneca *Suasoriae* 6; Seneca calls him a better verse-maker than poet. Carus (*Pont.* 4.13), the tutor of Germanicus's children, was a recent friend, from the time of Ovid's relegation if *Tristia* 3.5 is also addressed to him. Ovid considers him worthy of tackling the theme of Germanicus's impending triumph, so perhaps he too is an historical epicist.[62] Tutica-nus, who may have been Ovid's oldest friend (*paene mihi puero cognite paene puer,* 'whom I knew as a boy when he was still a boy,' 4.12.20), receives two letters, 4.12 and 4.14, in which Ovid mentions his *Phaeacis,* of which no fragments survive; his Latin paraphrase of the *Odyssey* is mentioned only by Ovid. The evidence is slim, but it is still worth noting that these authors all worked on subjects Ovid explicitly defines as 'safe' in *Tristia* 2.313–23: *Troia* (2.318, traditional martial epic), *Thebas* (2.319, tragedy), and *bellatrix Roma* (2.321, Roman military historical subjects, especially, says Ovid, the *meritis multis* of Caesar, or panegyric, 2.323).

The names most familiar to us from the remainder of Ovid's list do not conjure a late Augustan literary environment comparable in either sodality or achievement to the early Augustan age. The epigrams of the poet Domitius Marsus were much admired by Martial, who also attributes to him an (epic?) *Amazonis* (4.28). But his latest datable fragments address the death of Tibullus shortly after Vergil's in 19 BC; most of the fragments, and his poetic activity, seem to concentrate in the 30s BC. L. Varius Rufus, the old friend of Vergil, was praised for his *forte epos* by Horace (*Satires* 1.10.44–45) and by all for his *Thyestes,* most likely performed in 29 BC, but nothing is heard about him after his revision of Vergil's *Aeneid* for Augustus in 19 BC; he disappears from the record at about the same time as Marsus. Some "wretched fragments," as Conte calls them,[63] of Rabirius's epic on Antony were long ago uncovered at Herculaneum; he is praised alongside Vergil by Velleius (2.36.3), not the most discerning critic, but is less appealing to Seneca (*De benefciis* 6.31, where one line of the epic is quoted) and Quintilian (*Institutio oratoria* 10.1.90). C. Melissus is well known from Suetonius's *Lives of the Grammarians* 21 as the freedman of Maecenas who was asked by Augustus to head the famous library in the Porticus Octaviae at some point after 23 BC, but his equestrian *togatae* have not survived. All we can be sure of regarding the *Iliacus Macer* of *Epistulae Ex Ponto* 4.16 is that he is *not* Aemilius Macer; he may be the Macer of 2.10, a close friend of Ovid's from his youth and a writer on Trojan themes. Sempronius Gracchus was far better known for his alleged adultery with Julia, the daughter of Augustus, than for his tragedies. The astronomical *Aratea* and the learned *Prognostica* of Germanicus postdate Ovid's exile, probably composed during the early reign of Tiberius; Manilius's *Astronomica* is very likely from the same period, exhibiting the influence of Ovid's hexameter and possibly referring in one place to the beginning of Tiberius's reign.[64]

The undistinguished nature of this list of poets, particularly in the context of their often disappointing fragments, cannot be entirely accounted for in my view as an accident of survival or transmission. Many of these writers earn only the barest mention by their contemporaries, historians of their period, poets of the following generation, later grammarians or commentators. As Fantham observes, "It is an extraordinary fact that no other voice [than Ovid's] is extant from this last decade to comment on the state of intellectual freedom or suppression. Those who were writing at this time, like Livy, kept to the neutrality of their subject matter. This silence, after the unbuttoned social and literary reflections of Horace's *Satires*, is almost shocking."[65]

Whatever explanation we offer for it, the evidence suggests that poets of great talent and major poems of high quality and/or controversial subject matter were in short supply in the later Augustan period. As a result, while the publication of the *Ars Amatoria* at the turn of the millennium increased Ovid's public following and visibility, the traditional picture of these years as carefree must be adjusted. Ovid laments the loss of the sodality of earlier Augustan writers in *Tristia* 4.10,[66] where he expresses professional nostalgia not for the literary world he left behind in Rome in 8 AD, but for the poets who had left *him* behind many years earlier, who were like gods to him: *quotque aderant vates, rebar adesse deos* (*Tr.* 4.10.42). The *Metamorphoses* was begun at a time when those gods had been all but gone for more than a decade, without noteworthy replacement. Ovid clearly had a large circle of friends (although judging from the poet's frequent reprimands from exile and his remark at *Tristia* 1.3.15–16, the loyalty of many was not reliable), but he was by that time the only poet of exceptional talent working in Rome. He was not the only great *writer* in Rome, of course; Livy and others were working in history and in oratory. But in verse, as Galinsky observes, only the dramatic genres (the princeps's favorites) were truly flourishing,[67] and although these have a measurable influence on Ovid's epic, the distance, both historical and intellectual, between the *Metamorphoses* and the *Fasti* and these minor genres is evident. After Ovid, Rome would not see another poet of lasting reputation until Lucan, some forty-five years later; truly outstanding poetic production, apart from Ovid's, slowed to a crawl. Whether Augustus silenced other writers of whose subjects or lifestyles he disapproved with relegation or threats, or merely isolated those who were unfriendly or useless to his principate, or simply chose not to patronize (as chief patron of the Roman state) certain poets and genres, the result was the same: few patrons and fewer poets of distinction in the waning years of his reign.

The most compelling piece of evidence against a hospitable reception for art in late Augustan Rome is of course the relegation of Ovid to the Black Sea at the personal command of the emperor for *carmen et error,* a poem and a mistake. Despite the surprise that Ovid registers in his exile poems at the princeps's decree, it must have been the alacrity of his punishment, not its possibility, that stunned him. The reduced ranks of literary figures in this period suggest to me that Augustus's willingness to use political muscle to banish a well-known literary figure did not surface overnight, and that a shift toward autocracy must have had a chilling effect on aspiring poets well before Ovid's relegation. Late Augustan Rome, from the death of Horace (and perhaps more importantly, the death of Maecenas) until the death of the princeps, was not a welcoming venue for the performance and production of major groundbreaking poetry.

Thus when Ovid describes the scope of his poem in its proem with the words *ad mea tempora* ('down to my own day,' *Met.* 1.4), I think he not only defines the chronological sweep of the epic *ab origine mundi,* 'from the beginning of the world,' but also opens the poem to a reading against the circumstances of his own day, and even the circumstances of his own life in particular.[68] The changes in the literary atmosphere of late Augustan Rome left their mark on the *Metamorphoses,* in particular, I will argue, on its mythological accounts of artists. Ovid depicts artists at work far more often than any of his predecessors, Greek or Latin, in any poetic genre. His favorite setting for them is the traditional meeting place for the forces of power and art in his own world, the performance. I hope to show below how Ovid's episodes of artistic performance, always fraught with stress and danger for artists, establish a universal formula for successful art in the *Metamorphoses:* the accurate calculation and fulfillment of the expectations of powerful audiences. The audiences range from the divine (the Muses, Minerva, and Pluto and Persephone) to the semi-divine (the nymphs of Helicon) to mortals (the Thracian women), whose power variously resides in their territorial authority, their capacity for violence, or simply their vote, in the case of the nymphs. Each of the artists designs a particular strategy for success with their audience within a particular performance context: those who please their audiences succeed, while those who fail to do so, whether by miscalculation or deliberate insolence, are destroyed with their artworks. Ovid's artists shrewdly shape their own narratives, though not always successfully; the realism of their performances in the *Metamorphoses* explodes the myth of the inspired, vatic mission of art established by such figures as Demodocus and Orpheus in earlier epic. In the pages below, I evaluate each of these episodes as a peculiarly late-Augustan Ovidian meditation on the realities of artistic creation, a meditation writ large on Ovid's mythological canvas.

1

Ovid's Artists

Artists at Work

in nova fert animus mutatas dicere formas
corpora; di, coeptis (nam vos mutastis et illa)
adspirate meis primaque ab origine mundi
ad mea perpetuum deducite tempora carmen.

[I am moved to tell about forms changed into new bodies; Gods, inspire the beginnings of my work, for you have changed even these, and lead down/spin out a continuous song from the first beginning of the universe to my own time.]

Met. 1.1–4

Artists and their artworks have always been the colorful fellow-travelers of Greek and Roman epic and epyllion.[1] Well before Ovid's *Metamorphoses,* Daedalus, Hephaestus, and other craftsmen, named and anonymous, delighted the epic heroes in their company with sculptures, paintings, and shields and cups of metal,[2] while Demodocus, the Sirens, Orpheus, and Iopas enchanted them with cosmogonic and martial lays;[3] Helen, Penelope, Minerva, and the anonymous artist behind the extraordinary ekphrasis of Catullus 64 created narratives for and about the heroes in woven and embroidered cloth.[4] The depth and detail of such representations of artworks and artists in ancient epic vary considerably; examples range from the briefest of allusions to an artist to full-scale ekphrastic descriptions of works of art.[5]

With transformation as the *Metamorphoses'* central theme, it is not surprising that displays of creative activity of one sort or another, in which material is transformed or translated into another medium, are a regular feature of the action of the poem. It opens, as promised in its third line, with the original metaphor of artistry from the natural world, the creation of the universe. The world's first artist, the pointedly unnamed *mundi fabricator*, 'craftsman of the universe,'[6] is styled at various points in the opening narrative as a sculptor, a weaver, and even a Vulcan-like metallurgist, whose universe, shaped out of chaos, shares many features with the world as depicted on the shield of Achilles in *Iliad* 18.[7] With such a creative and transformative opening, the epic certainly can be and has been read, by Barkan most notably, as expressing an "art of continuous changes, radiant with multiplicity but confounding clear definition," reflecting "a reality in the universe that is similarly fluid."[8]

Human creativity is similarly one of the epic's most persistent motifs, a mortal complement to its physical and psychological metamorphoses motivated by a host of cosmic, divine, and other mysterious forces. A range of arts and skill-levels are represented, from the folkloric and mythographic narratives of Ovid's countless storytellers, epitomized by the bored and restless Minyeides in book 4, to the most sublime forms of artistry. In book 6, the imprisoned Philomela so subtly weaves her tragic story into a web that it is decipherable only to its recipient, her sister. The craftsman Daedalus, already well-known to Roman epic audiences from Vergil's description in *Aeneid* 6 of the elaborate gates he decorated for the Temple of Apollo, leaves Crete behind in *Metamorphoses* 8 on a machinery of wings he designed and constructed for himself and his son. In book 10, Pygmalion sculpts an ideal female companion, whom Venus animates at his request. Polyphemus's long travesty of a pastoral lament in book 13 throws Ovid's mini-*Aeneid* off its already-tottering heroic balance.[9] Even the famously warlike Perseus is figured artistically in the epic; as he petrifies his enemies with the Gorgon Medusa's head, he creates an impromptu sculpture garden of their marble *imagines* in book 5.[10] Such episodes document Ovid's fascination with the potential (both positive and negative) inherent in human creativity and expression, and highlight the aetiological role (usually unintentional) of human behavior in the great coming-into-being of his metamorphic universe.

It is indicative of Ovid's special interest in artists, their products, and particularly the conditions under which those artworks are created that he dedicates four lengthy episodes in the *Metamorphoses* to the stories of five literary and fabric artists, or groups of artists, in the process of creating six different artworks. *Metamorphoses* 5 and 6 are bridged by a pair of competitions, the first in song, the second in weaving. At the outset of book 5, Minerva has come to Mt. Helicon to see the new Hippocrene spring, and hears an account of a recent singing contest between the Muses and a group of mortal singers called the Emathides. One of the Muses briefly summarizes the challenge and song of the Emathides,[11] then offers a verbatim narration of Calliope's responding contest entry. When the nymphs of Helicon vote in favor of the Muses' song, the Emathides protest insolently and are transformed by the Muses into magpies. At the opening of book 6, the story of the contest between Minerva and the mortal weaver Arachne follows directly on, and from, the poetic contest. Minerva visits Arachne in disguise to incite a competition in weaving; the organization, themes and aesthetic qualities of the competing tapestries are described by Ovid in detail. Although (or perhaps because) Arachne's tapestry wins the day, Minerva destroys it, and then thwarts Arachne's ensuing suicide attempt by transforming her into a spider.

In book 10 the two best-known performances of the legendary Orpheus, in the underworld and in Thrace, are presented by Ovid in full. In the first, he sings to the gods of the underworld to persuade them to release his dead wife, Eurydice. He succeeds, but loses Eurydice a second time when he turns to gaze at her on the way out of the underworld. After this disappointment, Orpheus, in self-imposed isolation from humanity in general and women in particular, addresses a second song on a variety of erotic subjects to an audience of animated trees, beasts, and birds. While his audience is enthralled by the performance, an unseen group of Thracian women is less so, and in anger at his rejection of heterosexual love they attack and dismember him, scattering the audience.

These four scenes stand out from Ovid's ongoing preoccupation with mortal creativity in several ways that recommend their separate consideration. They are prominently placed at the one- and two-thirds points of the fifteen books of the poem, a symmetry particularly striking in a work whose fundamental structure has proven so elusive.[12] It is a demonstration of the poem's rejection of a traditionally tidy epic narrative framework that the division of the *Metamorphoses* into pentads, or even into books, has been hotly contested, and a variety of intricate structures within the work have been proposed by various critics.[13] In favor of a triple-pentad structure for the poem is the fact that Ovid was very fond of multiples of three in his pre-exilic works (after exile, Ovid's poetry books were shaped by other considerations): three books of *Amores,* at least two of which contain fifteen poems; very likely fifteen

Heroides; three books of the *Ars Amatoria;* six books of *Fasti;* and fifteen books of the *Metamorphoses.* Contemporary examples of universal or annalistic history, such as Cornelius Nepos's *Chronica* and Livy's history (the former divided into thirds, and the latter into pentads)[14] are particularly relevant to the *Metamorphoses,* since the poem is arranged in a roughly chronological sequence like a universal history, 'from the first beginning of the universe to my own day.' Within that vast expanse of time the poem moves forward fluidly through its chosen narratives (if we imagine a swift, meandering brook rather than a broad and slow-moving river) making ample use of such standard epic narrative devices as flashback and recollection, and loosely joined by one or another of Ovid's enterprising collection of linkage devices deployed in accordance with the poet's sometimes inscrutable logic.

However we might choose to divide the poem, the poetic and weaving contests and the performances of Orpheus anchor the epic at two important narrative moments. Before the contests of books 5 and 6, the poem's temporal frame is the creation of the world and its original divine and mortal inhabitants. In Ovid's universe this era includes numerous sexual assaults upon mortal women by the Olympians, and the exploits of their resulting offspring,[15] the earliest generation of Greek heroes: the Theban house of Cadmus, the new worship of Dionysus, and the adventures of the Argive Perseus, from whose side Minerva has just departed at the outset of the account of the poetic contest.[16] Between the contests (framed by the rise and final fall of Cadmean Thebes) and the songs of Orpheus in book 10, Ovid proceeds to the next generation of Greek heroes and the adventures of Tereus (the Thracian savior of Athens), Erectheus, Jason, Theseus, and Hercules; Orpheus, to ancient poets, is arguably the most important hero of this generation, and his adventures close the second pentad. After Orpheus, Ovid turns immediately from Greek mythical history to the origins of Rome with the Trojan cycle, and the consequent founding and rise of Rome under the Julian descendants of Aeneas, with whom he concludes the poem. The four scenes of artists-in-performance preside, Janus-like, over the transitions from each of these broadly conceived universal eras to the next.[17]

These episodes are also exemplary and provide particularly fertile ground for analysis in the overall creative atmosphere of the poem, because they are full portraits of working artists in performance, whose status as such assumes thematic priority. There are other candidates for this role in the epic, and critics cast the net of artistry in the *Metamorphoses* more widely[18] or more narrowly[19] according to various criteria.

Leach includes among Ovid's artistic performances the stories of the daughters of Minyas in book 4, for example.[20] But despite their imaginative and exotic tales, the Minyeides are characterized above all as semicomic Ovidian housewives, whistling while they work.[21] Their final transformation has nothing to do with their storytelling, but rather with their refusal to observe the festival of Bacchus. Another performer in the epic is Polyphemus, who serenades the nymph Galatea with a travesty of a pastoral love song (13.789–869). But he is clearly cast as an untalented novice. Several well-known artists of Greek myth make appearances in the epic, including Philomela, Pan, Marsyas and Daedalus. Each provides an interesting angle on the question of artistic freedom. The creations of Philomela and Daedalus are both direct responses to tyrannical power. Philomela has been imprisoned and sexually assaulted by her sister's husband, who then cuts out her tongue to silence her. Philomela's weaving secretly and successfully communicates her circumstances to her sister (6.571–86). Daedalus, more in his role as craftsman than as artist, constructs wings for himself and his son to escape from the tyranny of King Minos of Crete (8.189–95). Unfortunately Ovid only provides the barest of descriptions of their products (Philomela's web is purple and white, and Daedalus's wings are like panpipes). Pan and Marsyas both undertake musical competitions with Apollo. Ovid limits himself to a graphic record of the flaying of Marsyas (6.385–91). Pan's competition with Apollo is an abbreviated version of a music contest along the lines of the weaving contest, incited by Pan's slight of Apollo. Unfortunately, his song is only briefly characterized as 'barbaric' (11.162–63), while Apollo's is even more succinctly described as possessing 'sweetness' (11.170).[22] By contrast, the episodes discussed in this book are conspicuous for their presentation of the performances and artworks, in full for the first time in extant ancient literature, of legendary artists of greater (Muses, Orpheus, Minerva) or lesser (Emathides, Arachne) renown in Greek and Roman myth.[23] The performers are portrayed as celebrities who are proud of their far-reaching artistic reputations, often to their own, or their opponents', misfortune, and the circumstances in which they sing and weave bear all the marks of professional performance.

Ovid's artists therefore stand apart from other creative individuals in the *Metamorphoses* as professionals like himself, whose difficult position in the face of power or violence is regrettably constant over the course of the universal history he constructs. Ovid shapes their stories to provide a remarkably clear line of sight, from the point of view of a late Augustan artist, into the entire artistic process as it was then conceived: the motivation or compulsion to create, the development of theme and structure of a composition, and the moment of presentation of the artwork, including its audience and their response. It can fairly be said that the artistic condition receives such careful consideration nowhere else in all of ancient poetry. In Ovid's mythical world, the circumstances and protagonists of these public performances are cosmic in scale and power: the most famous artists, the most dangerous gods and patrons, and the most legendary performances, settings, and artworks to be found in Greek mythology are his subjects. Each episode eloquently explores the difficult and often dangerous relationship between power and art, the powerful and the artist, and the occasion that conventionally joins them, the artistic performance. The effect of the reception of the artworks on the artists themselves forms the climax of each episode and provides a sharp commentary upon the relationship between art, artists, and audiences in Ovid's own time.

Performative Ekphrasis

I coin the term *performative ekphrasis* to describe these episodes, in which a detailed representation of the conditions of artistic performance is combined with descriptions of the art produced under those conditions.[24] It will refer in this study not only to the tapestries of Minerva and Arachne in book 6, the fullest examples of conventional ekphrasis in the *Metamorphoses*,[25] but also, more controversially, to the songs of the Emathides and Calliope in the preceding poetic contest, which complement and mirror the tapestries, and the pair of songs of Orpheus in book 10, which structurally balance and allude to the pair of songs in book 5.[26] Each of these 'performative ekphrases' is in essence a double narrative, comprising an ekphrastically described artwork and a narrative of the moment and circumstances of its creation.

The ekphrasis occupies a privileged place in epic poetry; next to the catalog, it is the king of epic literary devices, and Ovid's deployment of an innovative form of it in these episodes signals their importance. Michael Putnam provides an elegant working definition of a conventional Vergilian ekphrasis:

> Ekphrasis, the topos of "speaking out" in order to describe a person or animal or landscape or, most usually, a work of art, inevitably generates a pause in the narrative when art looks at and continues art, and when the artisan of

> words, who works on our imaginations by his own verbal constructions, manufactures artifacts within his text for us to see with our mind's eye. As art describes art, we linger, not to escape the story's flow but to deepen our understanding of its meaning, to watch metaphor operating on a grand scale where epic text and one of its grandest synecdoches work as didactic complements to each other.[27]

While this description captures much of the effect of Ovid's performative ekphrases, the device plays a rather different role in the *Metamorphoses* than Putnam has described for the *Aeneid*. Ovid's emphasis upon the artists themselves and his visualizations of the way they work, for example, is fairly unusual in ekphrasis,[28] in which objects are typically either unattributed, like the coverlet in Catullus 64 or the temple of Juno in *Aeneid* 1, or completed long before the time of the narrative, like Daedalus's temple of Apollo at Cumae in *Aeneid* 6.[29] This lack of attribution frees the artistic object from its context and allows it to be contemplated in isolation, enhancing its more abstract, metaphoric qualities, and opening the ekphrasis to a broader range of interpretations by the reader. By contrast, Ovid contextualizes these ekphrases by embedding them within the circumstances of performance. This has the effect of 'directing' the reader's interpretation of the Ovidian ekphrasis to a greater degree than does the conventional form.[30]

The contemplative nature of the ekphrasis, facilitated by its suspension of the main narrative, is further complicated in this poem both by the episodic nature of Ovid's epic (what constitutes an interruption is often a matter of critical debate), and by the elaboration of the circumstances of the artwork's creation, which ties the ekphrasis closely to its narrative context. Rather than suspending the narrative, the performances are themselves mini-narratives within the epic and, apart from the song of the Emathides,[31] unfold in 'real time.' As a result, they do not have the traditional ekphrastic quality of arresting, and rising above, the narrative.

Nonetheless, Ovid's ekphrases share with Putnam's models an undiminished ability to encourage the reader to linger and reflect upon the artwork's symbolic relationship to the whole. The artworks just as surely evoke, in an allegorical or metaphorical way, the themes of the local narratives in which they are found, while their narratives similarly reflect many of the themes of the poem as a whole. At the same time, the performative aspect deliberately draws attention to the subject of its own narrative (the artist, the performance, and the artwork) and encourages consideration of the conditions under which art comes into being in the world. As a result, Ovid's ekphrases grant art qua art an even greater significance than in traditional epic ekphrases, where the relatively isolated artwork has a distant, symbolic nature in relation to the main narrative, and in some sense 'serves' it.[32]

Ovid's interest in the process of artistic creation leads to a deployment of ekphrasis that transcends its traditional use and poses questions about the practice of art itself. His portraits of artists at work involve the reader, with powerful immediacy, in all the complexity of the moment of artistic creation. To varying degrees the reader is made privy to the creator's state of mind, motivation, and methods, as well as to the evolution of the artwork itself as it takes shape; we even observe the responses of an attentive audience. In each instance we catch a glimpse of the life of one artist as imagined by another, and consequently we can discern a reflection of the poet's own musings on the creation of art.

Performative Predecessors

THE WEAVING CONTEST

While the descriptions of the tapestries of Minerva and Arachne in book 6, long considered the great masterpieces of Ovidian ekphrasis, suit the conventional definition of this rhetorical device as a description of an artwork or other visual object within a narrative, their emergence before our eyes from the hands of their producers, within a narrative of their motivation and production, sets them apart from the majority of ekphrastic descriptions of art. Ovid's autopsy of artistic creation follows in the venerable footsteps of a tradition established by Homer's description of the creation of the shield of Achilles in *Iliad* 18, a tradition continued in Vergil's description of the shield of Aeneas in *Aeneid* 8.[33] The three epic episodes reveal a special interest, beyond the aesthetics of the artwork depicted in ekphrasis, in the creator of the artwork and the development of his motivation.

In a narrative of almost one hundred lines, Homer portrays Thetis's cautious approach to Hephaestus for the creation of Achilles' new armor after the death of Patroclus in *Iliad* 18. The episode appears at the long-awaited turning point of the epic, as Achilles finally emerges from his self-imposed isolation to make amends to Agamemnon and avenge the death of his friend; but Achilles' armor has been stripped from the body of Patroclus by Hector. Thetis arrives at the home of Hephaestus and

Charis (18.369–92) to find the smithy hard at work, ἱδρώοντα, sweating (18.372), with cunning skill, ἰδυίῃσι πραπίδεσσι (18.380). Her host and hostess graciously observe that her visit is highly unusual: πάρος γε μὲν οὔ τι θαμίζεις, 'Before this you have not been used to come,' (18.386, repeated at 425). Even before greeting her, Hephaestus recalls to his wife his long-standing debt to Thetis for saving him when his 'dog-faced' mother Hera threw him from heaven because he was lame;[34] Thetis and Eurynome nursed him for nine years (18.394–409).

Hephaestus's earlier debt is combined by Homer with an account of Thetis's current suffering to provide a powerful motivation for the creation of the shield. After summarizing the action of the *Iliad* thus far, Thetis recalls the grief she, like Hephaestus, has suffered at the hands of the Olympians, in her case, Zeus (18.428–61). She reminds her hosts of her powerlessness to save Achilles, who is 'doomed to a speedy death' (υἱεῖ ἐμῷ ὠκυμόρῳ, 18.458); she only seeks to maximize his glory before the inevitable occurs. Hephaestus quickly agrees, and claims he would save Achilles from death (as Thetis and Eurynome had saved him) if he could: αἲ γάρ μιν θανάτοιο δυσηχέος ὧδε δυναίμην / νόσφιν ἀποκρύψαι, ὅτε μιν μόρος αἰνὸς ἱκάνοι, 'And I wish that I could hide him away from death and its sorrow / at that time when his hard fate comes upon him' (18.464–65). In a moment of graceful reciprocal exchange (a system whose failure among mortals is a central theme of the epic, and whose antithesis is embodied by the quarrelling Achilles and Agamemnon), the shield is a work of gratitude, and its glorious workmanship reflects the great value of the original debt, the life of Hephaestus himself. Hephaestus orders his magical bellows to blow as he casts the numerous metals for its manufacture, then turns to his anvil to hammer out the shape and figurative design. The ekphrasis itself is framed by active verbs of manufacture: ποίει, ἔτευζ', ἐτίθει, even ποίκιλλε, just as Ovid's account of the tapestries will deploy verbs of manufacture: *pingit, inscribit, facit, simulat, designat.* The gratitude of Hephaestus is driven home with every blow of his hammer. The ekphrasis of the shield's images unfolds as he works, representing a world balanced by the very rules of social relations that inspired its construction. The social context of the shield's manufacture and the intent of the artist at work provide us with an aspect of the significance of its design: the relationship between Hephaestus and Thetis provides an exemplary model from the social order, depicted on the shield, which lies in ruins about them in the epic itself.

In *Aeneid* 8 Vergil similarly grants almost as much emphasis to the motivation of the craftsman Vulcan by the persuasion of Aeneas's mother Venus (8.370–406), and to the conditions and process of actual manufacture by the Cyclops (8.407–53), as he does to the ekphrasis of the shield itself (8.608–728). Again the power of persuasion is at work, this time in a private and erotic rather than a public and social setting, as Venus urges her husband, Vulcan, to create armor for a son fathered by another (albeit mortal) man. She alludes to Thetis's successful request in *Iliad* 18 (*te filia Nerei / te potuit lacrimis . . . flectere,* 'the daughter of Nereus could sway you with tears,' 8.383–84) and reminds him that she had asked for no help for the Trojans during the war, *non arma rogavi* (8.376). The weakness of Venus's appeal only serves to highlight the fact that Vulcan's obligation to her is marital only, not a reciprocal sense of duty as in Thetis's case. The motivation in this scene will instead be Eros, the irresistibility of Venus, marking a shift from the *Iliad*'s concern with μῆνις, anger, and its impact on society, to the *Aeneid*'s preoccupation with the impact of *amor* on *Roma.* The couple's consequent lovemaking and sleep, long a scandal among critics,[35] is followed by the endearing image of Vulcan rising in the early morning to set to work, like a housewife busy about her husband's home (8.407–15). The shield is in this case a labor of lust, and as Scully has argued, figures as the sole product of an otherwise sterile union.[36] Its representation of Rome's generations and triumphs, seen in this context, is a celebration of Eros and fertility. But it likely also expresses Vulcan's bitter perspective on the fertility of Venus with a mortal man, Anchises, whose descendants through their son Aeneas are the subject of the shield's design.

Although directly descended from *Iliad* 18, Vergil's episode is a less fitting model for Ovid's tapestries than Homer's, for he delays the actual ekphrasis of the shield itself for some 175 lines until it is presented to Aeneas by Venus. It is therefore not revealed at the moment of its production, as are the artworks in Homer and Ovid. Vergil purposely severs the shield's content from its motivation and its creator, transferring responsibility for its interpretation onto the mortal for whom it was created, Aeneas, and away from either the poet himself, the narrator, or the shield's creator, whose view of its subject matter may well have been ironic. The interpretive onus is thus shifted onto Aeneas, whose inability to comprehend what is represented (*ignarus,* 8.730), much less his stepfather's irony, is part of the hero's striking inability to perceive his place in history throughout the epic.

The *Metamorphoses* episode depicting the creation of tapestries by Minerva and Arachne is clearly indebted for its structural frame and focus to this epic ekphrastic tradition. In each, a description of the artist(s) is followed by a scene presenting the motivation for the creation of the artwork, which in the *Metamorphoses* comprises a jealous provocation of Arachne by Minerva in disguise, and Arachne's unwitting challenge in response, which will result in the weaving contest. In all three episodes, the poets go to some lengths to contextualize the artwork socially: Homer's shield of Achilles is the product of a setting of civilized exchange and reciprocity, while Vergil's is conceived in a marriage bed. Ovid's tapestries likewise have their origin in a familiar social space, the public square, and under familiar social conditions, the artistic competition. All three poets supply a host of technical details, in the descriptions of Hephaestus's/Vulcan's workshop, and of the setup of the weavers' looms. Verbs of creation abound in all three accounts, focusing our attention upon the artistic process. Finally, the relationship between the themes of the artworks and the vexed circumstances from which they emerge that are evident in the *Iliad* and the *Aeneid* will also figure prominently in Ovid's tapestries, discussed in detail in chapter 3 below.

THE POETIC EKPHRASES

The imposing figure of Minerva connects the weaving contest and its pair of tapestries at the opening of book 6 to the preceding poetic contest and its pair of songs at the end of book 5. Having heard the Muses describe their sweet revenge upon their rivals, and hungry for her own, Minerva passes swiftly from Mount Helicon, at the conclusion of the account of the poetic contest, to Asia Minor and her rival Arachne. She is the pivot upon which Ovid symmetrically balances the two artistic contests, one in song and one in fabric: each contest features divine and mortal protagonists, includes a detailed description of the artworks, and concludes with the demise of the mortal artists. We are clearly expected to see the contests and their artworks as a matched set. By means of this linkage Ovid stretches the traditional definition of the appropriate ekphrastic subject, exemplified by the tapestries of Minerva and Arachne, to include the *carmina* in the singing contest that precedes them.

Such an extension of the ekphrastic device to include nonvisual art should not surprise us. Horace had declared the unity of the arts of painting and poetry years before (*ut pictura poesis, Ars Poetica* 361 ff.).

His view is confirmed by Ovid's own unique description of Philomela's weaving as a *carmen* in *Metamorphoses* 6.582.[37] Leach finds Ovid's poetry particularly closely related to the visual arts, and reminds us that the mythological subjects of the songs of the Emathides and Muses were regularly represented in the visual arts in the ancient world; she argues that such visual representations may have influenced Ovid's descriptive passages throughout the epic.[38] Hardie observes that Ovid "elides the formal division between narrative and description that characterizes ecphrasis."[39] It seems to me a short step for Ovid to treat the performed songs in which those myths are found as artworks worthy of ekphrasis themselves. This expansion of the boundaries of ekphrasis has the remarkable effect of elevating poetry and its performance to the status of other art forms deserving of ekphrastic treatment. Most important, the ekphrastic presentation signals the reader to attend carefully to the framed description as if it were a free-standing product, a meta-poem. Ovid invites us to consider poetic artworks as equally worthy of the distinctive emphasis of ekphrastic treatment.

It goes without saying that modern critics do not generally consider poetic works embedded within narratives to be technically 'ekphrastic,' but regard the very essence of the device to lie in the translation—of an artwork or other visual object such as a landscape or a building—from the visual to the verbal medium. Current thinking often shies away from even this broad a definition; as Vincent observes, "Since Leo Spitzer's 1955 study on Keats' 'Ode on a Grecian Urn,' the tendency in critical writing has been toward the narrower definition," that is, "a representation of a work of plastic art, real or imagined, in a literary text."[40] Although Heffernan's original definition more broadly conceives that ekphrasis "represents representation," he too explicitly rejects a definition that would include literary texts: "My own definition of *ekphrasis* rests on what I believe to be a fundamental distinction between writing about pictures and writing about texts."[41] He sees a kind of competition underway in ekphrases between the object and the language struggling to describe it. Krieger's much broader definition concentrates upon the device's effects, "wherever the poem takes on the 'still' elements of plastic form," but does not include literary objects, because they do not participate in this kind of 'stillness' but, on the contrary, move the narrative forward.[42] In his view, most descriptions of landscape and architecture within ancient epic would be ekphrastic; such settings in fact comprise the majority of minor examples in the *Metamorphoses* and other Greek and Roman epics, and they conform to the most fundamental ancient definition of ekphrasis or *enargeia,* a description that renders its subject vividly to 'the eyes of the mind' (Quintilian, *Institutio oratoria* 8.3.62).

But what happens to such a device in a non-narrative, or rather a multi-narrative epic such as the *Metamorphoses,* which so regularly twists in new directions as to render the notion of 'narrative pause' almost meaningless? As with so many of the literary tools he inherits from his elegiac and epic predecessors, Ovid uses the epic ekphrasis to represent and draw attention not simply to visual objects, but to art itself, as it is being produced. Reversing what Genette has described as the "ever-submissive, never-emancipated" slavery of description to narrative,[43] the poetic ekphrasis displaces the narrative and focuses our attention upon the poet, and poetry itself, as a nearly physical object. With the inclusion of the performance context, Ovid transforms the verbal artwork into a visual one, a tableau of artistic creation.

Each of the poetic performance episodes retains the basic elements of traditional ekphrasis. Ovid clearly marks the onset of the descriptive passages in each episode, for example, and establishes a break from the main narrative. In book 5 the events leading up to the original singing contest provide a long introductory frame, setting it off from the larger episode of Minerva's visit to Helicon; to introduce the songs themselves, the nymphs are selected as judges and take their seats according to convention. A specific introduction to the Emathides' song is precluded by their rudeness: they begin their performance without drawing lots. But their song is formally framed at its close, *hactenus ad citharam vocalia moverat ora,* 'thus far had she sung along with the cithara' (5.332). Active verbs of creation fill the description of the song of the Emathides (5.319–31: *canit, ponit, extenuat, narrat, dixit*), evoking the language of the creation of the Homeric and Vergilian shields. The song of Calliope receives a lengthy introduction, including an elaborate demurral, expressing reluctance to waste Minerva's time (*sed forsitan otia non sint / nec nostris praebere vacet tibi cantibus aures,* 5.333–34), the singer's outfit, and finally the first notes of her cithara. In this half of the contest, the song is presented verbatim, in direct discourse, for 320 lines. It too closes formulaically: *finierat doctos e nobis maxima cantus,* 'and so the greatest of us had come to the end of her learned song' (5.662).

Ekphrastic framing elements are also provided for the songs of Orpheus in book 10, which are also represented in full in direct discourse. The first, in the court of the underworld, is prefaced by a swift introduction: he enters, strikes the strings, and begins (*sic ait,* 10.17). The end of his brief song is clearly demarcated as well, *talia dicentem nervosque ad verba moventem,* 'speaking and accompanying his words with the cithara' (10.40). For his second song Orpheus takes his place in the countryside, tunes his instrument, and lifts his voice in song (*hoc vocem carmine movit,* 10.147); the song ends together with the tenth book, connected to the gruesome events that follow in book 11 by *carmine.* Ekphrastic framing, direct representation of the artwork, and even a degree of narrative suspension are therefore elements of all four poetic passages.

But there is no denying that the ekphrastic representation of song is highly unusual in ancient poetry. Poets before Ovid were understandably wary of reproducing verbatim the work of legendary poets like Orpheus and the Muses; to express the inexpressibly lovely, or to make concrete that which has been for centuries intangible and therefore magical, might well seem an arrogant enterprise, doomed to failure.[44] Apollonius and Vergil are hesitant to undertake it; the beauty and magic of Orpheus's songs at *Argonautica* 1.494–511 and *Georgics* 4.453–84 and 507–15 are only alluded to via paraphrase. And while the Muses are ubiquitous in ancient literature from Hesiod forward as the direct inspirers of all human poetry, their own creations are not directly recorded outside the *Metamorphoses.*[45] True to his reputation in Quintilian and elsewhere,[46] Ovid is unhampered by the appearance of arrogance or any anxiety of influence, and leaps at the opportunity to use these legendary singers to offer a construction of the realities of poetic performance, while no doubt relishing the chance to draw them down to earth.

The two best-known and most substantial poetic performances presented in ancient epic prior to the *Metamorphoses* are performed by Demodocus at the court of the Phaeacians in *Odyssey* 8, and by Orpheus in *Argonautica* 1.494–511.[47] These episodes share with Ovid's their representation of poets of mythical stature at work. But in neither case is the song represented verbatim, a fact that highlights Ovid's desire to demonstrate the relationship of a specific artwork to the context of its production. Apollonius provides a description of the context for Orpheus's song, a drunken argument between Idas and Idmon incited by Jason's depression on the eve of the journey to obtain the golden fleece. The song, a cosmogony detailing the powers of the gods, could be seen as a corrective to the impiety of Idas. But in fact the song stops short of praising the reign of Zeus, whom Idas had specifically insulted, concluding with ὄφρα Ζεὺς ἔτι κοῦρος, ἔτι φρεσὶ νήπια εἰδώς, 'Zeus still a boy, still thinking childish thoughts' (*Argon.* 1.508). Cosmogony was the predictable subject of any Orphic song by the Hellenistic period. Segal rightly observes that for Apollonius the magical effects of the song upon the drunken crew are its most important feature, making a more general philosophical point about the civilizing power of poetry and music over nature and human impulses rather than providing a commentary on the poet's role in society.[48]

Demodocus's dual performance is quite another matter. The requirements of Greek ζεινία surround the songs of Demodocus in *Odyssey* 8 as the Phaeacians offer their hospitality to the stranger in their midst, Odysseus, much as considerations of guest-friendship infuse the scene in *Iliad* 18 between Hephaestus and Thetis discussed above. Alkinoös insists on a feast with entertainment, and the blind Demodocus is summoned. His first song, inspired by the Muse (and, we suspect, Alkinoös, who has his own suspicions about the identity of his guest) recounts the quarrel of Odysseus and Achilles that signaled to Agamemnon that the time had come to launch the expedition to Troy. Demodocus pauses and begins again several times in response to his enthusiastic audience, but Alkinoös perceives Odysseus's grief at the recollection of the war and moves his guests on to participate in athletic competitions. Demodocus's performance is coyly shaped by the (suspected) κλέος of the guest of honor in the first instance, and then as the song progresses, by the desires of the gathering and the demands of his patron. Its failure to please their guest functions as yet another reminder of the vast gulf that has opened between the worlds of the *Iliad* and the *Odyssey;* to recall the war is a depressing matter for its heroes in the aftermath.[49] After the mixed response to his first song, Demodocus aims to satisfy all three groups with his second attempt. In a move that Callimachus himself might have appreciated, and Ovid certainly would have, Demodocus turns from 'heroes and kings' (historical, martial epic) to an amusing account of the ambush of the lovers Ares and Aphrodite by her husband Hephaestus, a performance both humorous and full of wit. The shift from martial epic to erotic myth mirrors shifting postwar sensibilities, from public to private, which are arguably the *Odyssey*'s principal theme. Demodocus's pair of performances depicts, as no other sort of narrative could, the impact of the post–Trojan War world on poetic themes, and on poets themselves who seek to bridge the two worlds. Heroic commemoration, once a source of delight, is now a source of grief, and Homer shows how deftly the poet Demodocus adapts to the new conditions.

While Ovid's performative ekphrases share an interest in the circumstances of performance with the examples from Homer and Apollonius, they are clearly distinguished by their reproduction in full of a nonvisual artwork. Ovid is not the first to incorporate into ekphrases objects experienced by senses other than the eyes, of course; the limits of epic ekphrasis are pushed in this direction most notably by the ekphrasis of the wedding coverlet of Peleus and Thetis in Catullus C. 64.50–264, on which appears the abandonment of Ariadne by Theseus. Although it could be argued that Catullus's reproduction of Ariadne's long lament (64.132–201) is not technically part of the ekphrasis of the coverlet, from which Catullus digresses after line 70, the poet does not formally close the ekphrastic frame until line 249, with the woven image of Ariadne gazing out *(prospectans);* his description of the rest of the tapestry continues for fourteen more lines. Ariadne and the Bacchic throng who rush to greet her all speak, move, play instruments, and cry out vividly from within the ekphrasis of a single, magical artwork. It is an extension of Quintilian's formulation, that ekphrasis should render what is described to the eyes of the mind, to include the ears of the mind as well. Part of what Laird calls the "disobedience" of the ekphrasis of Catullus's C. 64 is precisely its violation of traditional ekphrastic media boundaries, because Catullus does not limit the ekphrasis "to the description of what can be consistently visualized."[50]

Catullus's ekphrasis incorporates voice but not song or poetry, which might have provided us with a direct model for Ovid's practice. However, Catullus's delightful and ironic predecessor, Theocritus *Idylls* 15, revels in ekphrastic poetic description. As in Ovid's epic, Theocritus closely associates an ekphrasis of a tapestry with a representation of a publicly produced song, stretching the definition of the ekphrasis to include a verbal artwork. The auditors, two middle-class Sicilian women, pause to describe the queen's lovely tapestries in terms similar to Ovid's in book 6: ὡς ἔτυμ' ἑστάκαντι καὶ ὡς ἔτυμ' ἐνδινεῦντι, ἔμψυχ', οὐκ ἐνύφαντα, 'how like one standing, and one walking about, alive, not woven' (*Id.* 15.82–83) ≈ *verum taurum, freta vera putares,* 'you would have thought the bull, the waves, were real' (*Met.* 6.104). A singer well-known to the women from other festivals then performs a hymn to Aphrodite, which itself includes an ekphrastic description of scenes on a woven coverlet on the couch of Adonis; it is therefore strikingly similar to Catullus 64. Like the hymn to Ceres sung by Calliope in *Metamorphoses* 5, which is followed directly by the ekphrases of Arachne's and

Minerva's tapestries, Theocritus's hymn to Aphrodite, preceded by the ekphrastic presentation of the palace weavings, is clearly meant to be attended to in the same way as the conventional ekphrases that it follows.

A final likely inspiration for Ovid's extension of the ekphrasis to poetic art are the pastoral poems of Theocritus and his successors, with their frequent and direct representations of song. To an ancient reader, any literary representation of a poetic performance would have immediately called to mind pastoral poetry. Relevant to the structure of Ovid's episodes in particular are the pastoral song contest (for book 5) and the pastoral lament (for Orpheus's second song). These are best known in Greek from Theocritus, the genre's inventor, and in Latin from Vergil's *Eclogues,* whose debt to Theocritus is evident.[51] Ovid's lengthy parody of the song of Polyphemus in *Metamorphoses* 13.789 ff. indicates that he found in Theocritus (in particular, *Id.* 11) a poet whose ironic distance from the idealized rural landscape of his poetry he could appreciate.[52] In the song episodes of books 5 and 10, Ovid adopts from pastoral the verbatim representation of poetry in poetry and the apparently idyllic rural setting, which will be discussed in chapter 2 below; the singing competition of book 5 most closely parallels the non-amoebaean *Idylls* 6 and 7, and *Eclogues* 5 and 8. But the similarities end there. The professionalism of the artist-protagonists in Ovid's episodes is a fundamentally urban construct; both the artists and their creative situations depart sharply from the relaxed rural atmosphere that surrounds Theocritean pastoral song, which in any case, as Segal has demonstrated,[53] almost always signals a setting for danger and violence in the *Metamorphoses.* Like Ovid's Polyphemus, the Theocritean shepherd is (however disingenuously) depicted as an amateur, competing for a goat or a cup; songs performed or recalled remain in the innocent domain of the idealized countryside. One does not encounter an Orpheus or a Calliope in these settings, nor the threatening atmosphere of the poetic contest with its life-or-death stakes, nor the violent reprisals of Thracian women. In its Roman incarnation pastoral song departs from its *locus amoenus* to confront (Roman) reality, most pointedly in Vergil's *Eclogues* 9, where songs were reputed to but could not in the end save the farm of the shepherd-poet Moeris; he bitterly comments, *sed carmina tantum / nostra valent, Lycida, tela inter Martia quantum / Chaonias dicunt aquila veniente columbas,* 'In wartime our songs are about as effective as Chaonian doves are said to be in battle with an eagle, Lycidas' (*Ecl.* 9.11–13). Ovid's ultimately fatal pastoral settings are even less propitious for song than Vergil's; the powerful prevail in the singing contest, while Orpheus's seemingly safe pastoral performance venue will become the site of his dismemberment.

Conclusions

In Ovid's episodes of performance, the ekphrasis is molded to the service of a different priority from that of either the rhetorical tradition (primarily ornament and vividness) or the literary tradition (narrative pause or relief). Rather than slowing or halting the narrative for a moment of contemplation of an extra-narrative visual object, more or less independent of its context and often sublime in its symbolic relationship to the outer narrative, Ovid grounds his artworks firmly in their corresponding narrative context, to capture the moment of artistic creation as well as the artwork. In this respect Ovid's performative ekphrases conform to one important aspect of Heffernan's stricter definition: they are all artworks, and their presence is intended to problematize art, to define what qualifies as art, and what inspires and shapes it.

Portraying the difficult relationship between art and artists and their social context emerges as the poet's primary consideration. As "an artisan of words," in Putnam's phrase, Ovid depicts other such artisans in the creation of verbal artifacts in epic meter under the special and dangerous conditions of performance. Ovid's concerns are shared by a number of other poets in the ancient tradition, but he differs from his predecessors in his interest in the artistic product, which emerges from the circumstances of its production, and the artist, always irretrievably transformed by the performance in Ovid's poem.

In my view, the unusual ekphrases of the *Metamorphoses* reflect the anxieties of artistic production present, as I argued in the introduction, in the *tempora Ovidiana,* during which the great patrons and protectors of art were either dead or largely inactive, and the great community of Augustan poets, which possessed tremendous authority and prestige, had dwindled to a smaller and less distinguished group of which Ovid was the evident but most provocative star. The potential for danger faced by late Augustan and early imperial poets in performance is the background against which Ovid's episodes of artistic performance must be read. They reveal a socially conscious view of the artist working within an often destructive social context, within a claustrophobic web of ineffective artistic patronage, indentured artists, and compromised artworks—a world in which brutal power relationships typical of the political world seem to have invaded the sphere of art. The chapters that follow examine Ovid's mythical exploration of the dangers of this world.

2

The Poetic Contest

Metamorphoses 5

Setting and Audience

LOCUS (IN)AMOENUS: THE SETTING OF THE POETIC CONTEST

The songs of the book 5 poetic contest are performed within a narrative of unusual complexity, even by *Metamorphoses* standards.[1] In the outermost frame, the Muses on Mount Helicon are paid a visit by Minerva; her presence here links the contest to the preceding battle narrative in book 4, where she had assisted her brother Perseus in a war against his new bride's jilted fiancé.[2] Minerva arrives on Helicon as a tourist to see the already-famous Hippocrene ('Horse-spring'), created by a hoof-blow of Pegasus, whose birth from the neck of the decapitated Medusa she had recently witnessed (*vidi ipsum materno sanguine nasci,* 'I saw him born from his mother's blood,' 5.259). After an exchange of greetings, and the Muses' account of their near-assault by the mortal king Pyreneus (5.273–93), Minerva hears the voices of magpies, the now-transformed Emathides, in the branches above. Their complaints (*sua fata querentes,* 'protesting their fate,' 5.298) prompt one of the Muses to recount the story of the Emathides' challenge of the Muses and their ensuing poetic competition. This account of the contest forms the inner narrative frame of the episode. The Muse quickly sketches the outlines of the Emathides' song of the rout of the Olympians by the monster Typhoeus, while the long text of Calliope's responding song is reported verbatim: the rape of Proserpina by Pluto, the wanderings of her mother, Ceres, in search of her, and the ultimate reconciliation of Jupiter and Ceres. The episode, and book 5, ends with the victory of Calliope's song and the transformation of the Emathides into magpies, which closes the inner narrative frame. Ovid returns to the outer narrative only at the opening of book 6, where Minerva admires both the song and the punishment decreed by the Muses (*carminaque Aonidum iustamque probaverat iram,* 'She had approved the song and righteous anger of the Aonian Muses,' 6.2) and immediately departs to exact similar vengeance from a mortal rival of her own, the weaver Arachne: *laudare parum est, laudemur et ipsae / numina nec sperni sine poena nostra sinamus,* 'It's a small thing to praise; let me be praised, too, for not allowing her to scorn my divinity without punishment' (6.3–4).

Both the inner narrative of the poetic contest and the outer narrative of Minerva's visit are located by Ovid on venerable Mount Helicon, the original *locus poeticus* within the mythical geography of Hellenic poetry and its origins. Helicon's role as the source and signifier of all poetry provides the starting point for Hinds's meticulous study of the contest, which opens with a discussion of the importance of this setting for Ovid's highly literary concerns in the episode.[3] Hinds demonstrates that Mount Helicon signals a special engagement with literary issues, including an entire complex of punning allusions to Ovid's Hellenistic and Roman literary predecessors.[4]

For those in Ovid's audience who might be knowledgeable in Latin poetry but less so in the finer points of literary aesthetics, Mount Helicon sets the episode in one of the best-known literary landscapes in Augustan poetry, the *locus amoenus* or 'pleasant place,' conjured by poets since Hesiod as a safe, restful haven for poets and poetic composition and/or lovemaking.[5] In Augustan poetry this type of setting frequently finds its way into the lyrics of Horace (esp. *Odes* 1.1, 1.17, 3.4, 3.13, 3.25, 4.2),[6] and even into the elegies of the urban sophisticate Propertius, for whom it provides a safe place to express his grief early in his collection (*hic licet occultos proferre impune dolores,* 'here I may voice my private grief without consequences,' 1.18.3); later he will regain his vocation as a poet of love on Helicon itself (3.3).[7] The most celebrated of these settings, however, for the Augustans and for all time, are the country retreats of Vergil's *Eclogues,* adapted in turn from the *Idylls* of Theocritus. Vergil's shepherds sing and love in an idyllic landscape, which, however threatened by politics and war, is known for the pleasant groves, grasses, shade, springs, caves, and breezes it provides for the composing poet.[8] The pastoral genre, the only Greco-Roman literary form dedicated to the verbatim presentation of song and song contests, provides an evident literary ancestry for Ovid's poetic contest.[9]

Ovid's Mount Helicon shares many characteristics with the idyllic countryside haunts of Vergil's Daphnis and Damoetas;[10] indeed, the pleasantness of the Muses' home is the first topic of conversation between Minerva and the Muse early in the episode. The mountain itself is described as 'virginal' (5.254), in Latin literature only here and *Metamorphoses* 2.219, emphasizing the purity of both the landscape and its resident Muses.[11] While inspecting the new spring, Minerva casts her eye about to take in groves of ancient trees, caves and meadows filled with flowers, *silvarum lucos circumspicit antiquarum / antraque et innumeris distinctas floribus herbas* (5.265–66), all conventional elements of the *locus amoenus.*[12] Special attention is drawn to this description and its noble pedigree by the unusual solemnity of line 265 (five spondees, including the fifth foot); the *silvae* of Helicon are clearly *antiquae* both in cosmic and literary time. This lovely setting is directly linked with the practice of poetry by Minerva's subsequent comment: *felicesque vocat pariter studioque locoque / Mnemonidas,* 'and she calls the daughters of Mnemosyne (Memory) fortunate in both their vocation and their location' (5.267–68). As the account of the contest begins, Minerva will settle in to hear Calliope's song in the light shade so often sought by the Roman pastoral shepherd: *nemorisque levi consedit in umbra* (5.336).[13] The locale powerfully evokes the pastoral tradition and its poetic contests.

We are further alerted to the presence of the bucolic tradition in the episode by the lineage of the rival Emathides. The father of these challengers of the Muses is Pieros of Pella;[14] their patronymic would therefore be *Pierides,* a name elsewhere in Latin applied to the Muses themselves, from the district of Pieria in northern Greece where Mount Olympus is located. Ovid capitalizes here upon the multiplication of Muse genealogies in the Roman world. Cicero records two possible origins for a group of nine Muses: they were either the Heliconian daughters of Mnemosyne and Jupiter, as in *Metamorphoses* 5.268, *Mnemonidas,* or the daughters of Pieros and Antiope, *quas Pieridas et Pierias solent poetae appellare,* 'whom the poets usually call the Pierides or the Pierians' (*De natura deorum* 3.54); this latter group would of course be mortal. So the Emathides would, according to at least one ancient writer, be none other the Muses themselves. Although Ovid does not directly refer to this tradition by applying the Pierid patronymic to his Muse-challengers (he calls them *Emathides,* after the district of Emathia just north of Pieria and Olympus), the identification of their father as Pieros opens up the possibility that either group of singers in the contest could conceivably lay claim to the title of 'the Muses' and the possession of Helicon. The Pierid Muses certainly have a prominent place in the works of the Latin poets. Although the application of patronymics by Ovid's contemporaries is notoriously sloppy, most of the appearances of *Pierides* as a patronymic for the Muses are found in or evoke a rural context.[15] And in Vergil's far more careful practice, the name is exclusively reserved to address the Muses of the *Eclogues* (3.85, 6.13, 8.63, 10.70–72). These pastoral associations of the rival Emathides' Pierid ancestry heighten the contest's bucolic flavor.

So it is not surprising that the structure of the *Metamorphoses* contest and its songs largely replicates the structure of a pastoral song contest. The Emathides swiftly issue their challenge (5.309–10), set the stakes (5.311–14), select the nymphs as judges (5.315), and begin. They do not draw lots, to the consternation of the Muses: *tunc sine sorte prior, quae se certare professa est / bella canit superum,* 'Then without drawing lots, one who announced she would compete sang the battles of the gods' (5.318–19). The Emathides' failure to follow proper procedure is part of their arrogance, in the eyes (and reprise) of the narrating Muse, although the drawing of lots is not required by bucolic protocol: while it is mentioned in Theocritus's *Idylls* 8, *Idylls* 6 explicitly rules that the challenger must sing first: πρᾶτος δ' ἄρξατο Δάφνις, ἐπεὶ καὶ πρᾶτος ἔρισδε (6.5). In agreement with this same convention, the judge of *Eclogues* 3 commands Damoetas the challenger to sing first and Menalcas to respond (3.58). So, despite the Muses' complaints to the contrary, the Emathides sing first in accordance with the established pastoral tradition.

The sustained compositions of Ovid's contestants also reflect a particular type of bucolic practice. The shepherds of Theocritus and Vergil often compete in short, hexametric, amoebaean stanzas, quite unlike the songs found here (e.g., *Id.* 5, *Ecl.* 3 and 7).[16] But in *Eclogues* 8, Damon and Alphesiboeus each present a long series of quatrains that allow a greater development of theme, inspired, as Coleman suggests,[17] by *Idylls* 8's unusual elegiac couplets. Damoitas and Daphnis in *Idylls* 6 also present longer, self-contained poems. The thematic responsion so evident in the songs of the *Metamorphoses* contest is also characteristic of many bucolic songs; in *Eclogues* 3, for example, Menalcas responds to the themes and views expressed in each of Damoetas's stanzas (Jupiter vs. Apollo, Galatea vs. Amyntas, etc.). In Ovid's episode Calliope actually completes the song of the Emathides, which had been deliberately ended to exclude the ultimate triumph of the Olympians, before she proceeds with her own theme, the rape of Proserpina.[18] Finally, all bucolic song contests end with the passing of judgment and the award of a prize, just as Ovid's episode ends with the decision of the nymphs and the punishment of the Emathides (5.662–78).

As is so often true in this poem, however, similarities between the *Metamorphoses* passage and its models only highlight the innovations of Ovid's practice. Above all, the imbalance of power of the participants in Ovid's contest, so often seen in mortal/immortal relationships in the *Metamorphoses*, violates the traditionally collegial spirit of the bucolic contest. The poetic competitors of Theocritus and Vergil are roughly equals, and typically judgment is passed and the agreed-upon prize presented in what is perceived by all to be a fair process with a minimum of grousing. Ovid's protagonists, in contrast, do not compete on level ground. The Muses are immortals, the Emathides mortals, and as is usually the case in the *Metamorphoses*, the gods cannot lose. Even if the competition were genuine, the jury is stacked: the contest's judges are the Muses' own local nymphs. And so in contrast to the balanced presentations of earlier bucolic songs reported in reprise form, namely *Idylls* 6 and *Eclogues* 7, where each contest entry is faithfully reproduced, Ovid's Muse raconteur negatively summarizes (for Minerva and Ovid's reader both) most of the song of the Emathides, presenting only a few final lines in direct discourse. Like Minerva in the weaving contest, the victors control the contest's, and the Emathides', subsequent history;[19] and so the contest concludes unfairly. Finally, after the nymphs have declared for Calliope, and the Emathides protest the injustice, the Muses decide to collect far more than was arranged by the original stakes of the contest. We assume that they seize the Emathides' territory pledged at the outset of the contest; they also punish them with transformation for daring to propose the contest in the first place, and for lamenting its outcome:

. . . convicia victae
cum iacerent, 'quoniam' dixit 'certamine vobis
supplicium meruisse parum est maledictaque culpae
additis et non est patientia libera nobis,
ibimus in poenas et, qua vocat ira, sequemur.

['When the losers hurled insults,' [Calliope] said, 'Since it is not enough that you have earned punishment for the contest, and since you add insult to injury, and since our patience is not infinite, we will proceed to exact punishment, following where our anger leads us.']

Met. 5.664–68

The result is the transformation of the Emathides into magpies *(picae)*, birds who like parrots can raucously imitate human speech (as heard by Minerva at the opening of the episode) but have no poetic ability. Thus the typically good-natured pastoral poetic competition becomes in Ovid's hands an unfair match between unequal participants, and with a largely predetermined outcome that silences the defeated once and for all.

Ovid's revision of the bucolic contest in the episode is very much in keeping with his deployment of the pastoral setting generally in his poetry.[20] Hinds has recently observed that "a sense of threat" is arguably a feature of this landscape tradition,[21] but in fact the threat is typically external (however close by). Horace's *locus amoenus* could offer the poet Tyndaris a retreat ideal for poetic composition, safe from the sexual violence of Cyrus (*ne male dispari / incontinentis iniciat manus,* 'lest he lay his immoderate hands on you, who are hardly his match in strength,' *Odes* 1.17.26–27). And Vergil's pastoral sanctuary, despite the devastating effect of Rome's political upheavals upon its inhabitants, remains intact;[22] what changes is access to it, denied those whose land has been confiscated for redistribution to returning veterans. In the pages of the *Metamorphoses* the proverbial safety of rural retreats is revealed to be an illusion, and their appearance in the narrative only deepens a terrible foreboding of danger.[23] Daphne and Io are raped by Apollo and Jupiter in, respectively, 'the pathless woods' (*nemora avia,* 1.479) and 'the shade of the deep woods' (*umbras altorum nemorum,* 1.590–91); Mercury, in the guise of a singing goatherd, concludes his song with the murder of Argus (1.698 ff.); Callisto is raped by Jupiter in Arcadia (2.405 ff.), and Europa on the shore of Sidon, among the herds of her father's cattle (2.836 ff.). Several such landscapes appear within the song of Calliope in book 5; Hinds carefully examines the setting of the rape of Proserpina in Henna (5.385–92) in this light,[24] while Segal discusses the setting for the violation of the pool of Cyane (5.409–37) and the rape of Arethusa (5.587–91).[25] It is not only the subnarratives, however, that unfold in these settings, but the contest itself. In each case, the loveliness of the landscapes contrasts disturbingly with the violence they host.

So while Ovid's Helicon evokes a traditional pastoral landscape, it possesses none of the remove and freedom typical of it. The home of the Muses is at the center, not the periphery, of the exercise of divine power both in the realm of literature and in the context of the episode, and so entirely lacks the psychological qualities of an apolitical pastoral retreat. Helicon even lacks repose for the Muses themselves; the mountain is teeming with uninvited visitors in the episode, who bring with them various kinds of tension and conflict. The first (in narrative order) is Minerva herself, direct from the battlefield; the second is the mortal king, Pyreneus, whose attempted sexual assault is the subject of the Muse's lament in her opening exchange with Minerva; the last are the rival Emathides. Each encounter spoils the traditional pastoral splendor of Helicon, and contributes to Ovid's characterization of the poetic contest that takes place within its borders.

MINERVA PATRONA ET VIRAGO

The imposing figure of Minerva opens and closes the poetic contest and throws into relief the relationship of the narrating Muse with her powerful and important listener. Scholars rarely discuss the role of Minerva in Ovid's contest, despite the trouble the poet has clearly taken to put her there;[26] it seems to have been entirely Ovid's notion to extend the narrative levels of the contest one further step by placing it within a recapitulation by the Muse for Minerva. Ovid inverts the sequence of the only other extant account of the contest, from Nicander *Heteroeumena* 4 (summarized in *Antoninus Liberalis* 9). There, the beauty of the Muse's contest entry caused Mount Helicon to swell with pleasure; its consequent deflation by a kick of Pegasus's hoof created the Hippocrene spring. Minerva is entirely absent from this account. Ovid omits any cause-and-effect relationship between the contest and the spring; instead he places the creation of the spring in an earlier episode in book 5, outside the contest narrative, where it will motivate the all-important arrival of Minerva to see the results. The effect is a dramatic shift of emphasis. While Nicander's story was a theological myth about hubristic mortals and their just punishment, Ovid's episode turns toward the singers and their performances, and underscores the social dynamics of poetic production.

The battle-stained goddess cuts a striking figure among her gentle poetic colleagues on Mount Helicon. Minerva is not otherwise known for visits to the Muses or an interest in (un)natural phenomena (apart from her own olive tree in Athens), and her appearance directly following her gruesome work with Perseus is startling. Hers is an undeniably epic presence in a pastoral setting, and recalls the incongruity, as framed by the Augustan poets, of military and literary pursuits, of battlefields and pastoral or mountain retreats, of *officium* and *otium.* The stark differences between these worlds will actually be the subject of the opening conversation between Minerva and the Muses. In Augustan poetry the elegiac life of love and poetry is regularly offered up as an alternative to the traditional political and military lives of elite Roman men, whose achievements are properly recorded in epic and prose. Critics have suggested that Minerva's appearance alongside the pastoral Muses in the episode therefore constitutes a programmatic 'hint' that poses the question: will the product of this union be an epic, an elegy, or a hybrid?[27]

Minerva's interest in the Hippocrene is puzzling, but explained by a series of intratextual allusions. Her opening words to the Muses refer to the spring as a marvel:

fama novi fontis nostras pervenit ad aures
dura Medusaei quam praepetis ungula rupit.
is mihi causa viae; volui mirabile factum
cernere; vidi ipsum materno sanguine nasci.

['I've heard the story of a new spring, which the winged child of Medusa created with a blow of his hard hoof. This is the reason for my visit; I wanted to see this miraculous creation; I saw the child's birth from his mother's blood.']

Met. 5.256–59[28]

The matronymic of Pegasus, *Medusaei,* directs the reader back to the Perseus saga of books 4–5, where the adjective was most recently used just seven lines previously to describe Medusa's now-hideous face *(ore Medusaeo).* It happens that Minerva has every reason to express a special interest in the offspring of Medusa and Neptune. At the close of book 4, Perseus reports that Medusa, once a most beautiful maiden (*clarissima formā,* 4.794) with particularly lovely hair, was raped by Neptune in Minerva's temple. In a shocking expression of her strict virginity, Minerva herself effects the transformation of Medusa into a snaky-haired monster as punishment, *neve hoc inpune fuisset,* 'lest this go without punishment' (4.800). As she mentions in book 5, Minerva witnessed the birth of her offspring, the flying horse Pegasus, from his mother's blood, *materno sanguine.* She perhaps tactfully suppresses the fact that Pegasus was born quite literally of Medusa's blood, issuing from her neck when his mother was decapitated by Perseus.

The poetic contest therefore opens with a recollection of Minerva's Olympian lineage, her militarism, her strict chastity, and her justice against mortals, effected through transformation. The presence of this virginal, Olympian Minerva in the outer frame of the narrative is crucial to evaluating the Muses' behavior and song. In the coming episode, the Muses will practically cringe in the presence of their prestigious

Olympian visitor; the story of the unfortunate Medusa will foreshadow the thematic role of rape in the coming song of Calliope; and Minerva's treatment of Medusa will provide a model for the Muses in their transformation of the Emathides, as well as Minerva's ensuing transformation of her own artistic rival Arachne in book 6.

The difference in status between Minerva and the Muses is made painfully obvious throughout the episode. Urania follows Minerva's explanation for her visit with a polite and gracious rejoinder: *quaecumque est causa videndi / has tibi, diva, domos, animo gratissima nostro es,* 'Whatever the reason you've come to see our home, goddess, your presence is most welcome to our hearts' (5.260–61). Minerva's tour through the Heliconian grove is described in some detail (5.263–68). But the most telling evidence for Minerva's *auctoritas* among the Muses appears in a surprising piece of flattery without precedent in the mythological tradition. The unnamed Muse claims that Minerva would have made a fine member of their choir if her more important work hadn't called her away: *o, nisi te virtus opera ad maiora tulisset / in partem ventura chori Tritonia nostri,* 'Oh, if only virtue had not called you away to greater accomplishments, you could have been part of our choir, Tritonia' (5.270). The lines have a hymnic quality, with their invocation, their expression of the virtue of the goddess, and their dramatic delay of Minerva's Olympian patronymic *Tritonia* until the end of the second line. *Virtus* recalls Minerva's (masculine) military vocation, *maiora* her greater social contributions out in the (nonpoetic) world, *Tritonia* her international prestige. The suggestion that Minerva might have been a Muse herself is, on the face of it, absurd; Minerva is depicted as talented in poetry or music only here and in a perplexing reference in the *Fasti.*[29] The *Fasti* narrator's, and the Muse's, association of Minerva with song is an unabashed bit of flattery.

In fact, the terms of this piece of flattery surface elsewhere in Ovid's oeuvre, as Hinds observes.[30] Ovid will echo them in his praise of the prince Germanicus, the dedicatee of the *Fasti,* in *Epistulae Ex Ponto* 4.8: *quod nisi te nomen tantum ad maiora vocasset / gloria Pieridum summa futurus eras,* 'If your great name had not called you to greater things, you would have become the glory of the Muses' (*Pont.* 4.8.69–70). *O nisi te* is echoed in *quod nisi te, virtus* is replaced by *nomen, tulisset* becomes *vocasset,* while the nonliterary pursuits are called *maiora* in both passages. Germanicus and Minerva are both cast by Ovid as potential poets, talented enough for inclusion in the company of the Muses, had not the pressing business of *maiora* intervened, in both cases the affairs of war. I think the allusion helps complete our understanding of both passages. With Ovid's echo of the book 5 passage in the exile poem, Germanicus gains an aura of divinity from an association with Minerva; at the same time, Ovid's intentions in the book 5 passage are correspondingly clarified. Minerva is addressed as a patron of the arts like Germanicus, and the Muses are in some sense her clients, or at least her social inferiors.

This characterization of Minerva-as-patron is not limited to the *Metamorphoses;* she also appears in patronal guise in *Fasti* 3, where an apparently hesitant Mars is enjoined by Ovid to take time from his military labors to listen to poetry, on the model of Minerva:

Bellice, depositis clipeo paulisper et hasta,
   Mars, ades et nitidas casside solve comas.
forsitan ipse roges, quid sit cum Marte poetae:
   a te, qui canitur, nomina mensis habet.
ipse vides manibus peragi fera bella Minervae:
   num minus ingenuis artibus illa vacat?

[Warrior, set aside your shield and spear awhile; have a seat, Mars, take off your helmet and let down your shining hair. Perhaps you ask, what's Mars got to do with poetry? Well, the month I sing takes its name from you. You know how fierce wars are fought by the hands of Minerva; nonetheless, hasn't she time for the noble arts?]

Fasti 3.1–6

What Mars and Minerva have to do with poetry is nothing less than the traditional Roman relationship of the busy general and his worshipful poet: *Fasti* 3, on the month of March, is a poem in Mars's honor to which Ovid would have him attend. He is in good company in Ovid's oeuvre. Jupiter too is imagined basking in the warmth of his poet's praises in *Tristia* 2, where Ovid asks (begs?) Augustus to take note of the praises of him contained in the *Metamorphoses:*

fama Iovi superest: tamen hunc sua facta referri
   et se materiam carminis esse iuvat,
cumque Gigantei memorantur proelia belli,
   credibile est laetum laudibus esse suis.

[Jupiter has the lion's share of glory; still he loves to have his exploits told, to be the subject of a poem delights him, and when his battles with the Giants are recalled, you can believe he takes pleasure in the praise.]

Tr. 2.69–72

Horace similarly imagines Caesar at his ease after battle in *Odes* 3.4, now not with his poets but with the Muses themselves:

vos Caesarem altum, militia simul
fessas cohortis abdidit oppidis,
 finire quaerentem labores
 Piero recreatis antro.

[You, Muses, once the troops, battle-weary, have been tucked into towns, and great Caesar seeks an end to his labors, you refresh him in your Pierian cave.]

Odes 3.4.37–40

Ovid clearly identifies such services for a powerful (military) patron during his rare moments of leisure as anxious ones for the poet. In his dedication of the *Fasti* to Germanicus, he likens the opinion of his patron to that of Apollo himself:

da mihi te placidum, dederis in carmina vires
 ingenium voltu statque caditque tuo.
pagina iudicium docti subitura movetur
 principis, ut Clario missa legenda deo.

[If you are kindly to me, you will give strength to my poetry; its worthiness stands or falls by your expression. About to undergo the judgment of a learned prince, my page shakes as though sent to be read by Clarian Apollo.]

Fasti 1.17–20

To what degree do these examples reflect upon Minerva in the poetic contest? The flatteries of the Muses indicate their awareness of the goddess's superior authority. And while Minerva herself never intrudes upon the Muses' narratives in the course of the episode, editorial remarks remind us that the Muses know she is listening. At 5.280, the Muse notes parenthetically that Pyreneus recognized the Muses: *'Mnemonides,' (cognorat enim).* In the same passage, at 5.282, she includes a parenthetical weather report *(imber erat).* Finally, in the preface to Calliope's song appears a stock poetic demurral:[31] *sed forsitan otia non sint / nec nostris praebere vacet tibi cantibus aures?* 'but perhaps you haven't the leisure to lend an ear to our songs?' (5.333–34). By these means Minerva is kept firmly in view as an auditor of consequence until the onset of Calliope's song.

Minerva's characterization in the episode as a literary patron is complemented by her particularly virginal aspect in the aftermath of the Medusa episode, which also has a noticeable effect upon the course of the narrative. Early in the visit her chastity seems to motivate the very strange tale, unique to Ovid, of the attack on the Muses by Pyreneus (5.269 ff.). The Muse confides that the Muses would be happy on Mount Helicon if only they were safe, but 'now everything terrifies our virgin minds.' A bold local king, Pyreneus, invited the Muses into his home to escape the rain when they were traveling to Mount Parnassus.[32] When they attempted to leave, he tried to rape them *(vim parat);* when the Muses conveniently sprouted wings and flew away, he followed: *seque iacit vecors e summae culmine turris,* 'and the madman threw himself from the top of a tower.'[33] Before Minerva's reaction to this story can be registered, the Emathides are heard in the branches above and the subject of the conversation is changed, but we can only suppose she would have been sympathetic. The story seems designed to demonstrate how much the Muses have in common with their chaste visitor, and to draw them together as goddesses (their interchange is characterized shortly thereafter as 'goddess to goddess,' *deae dea* (5.300). Calliope's song strives to underscore this special relationship of chastity again and again; in addition to detailing the trials and tribulations of a number of innocent virgins, she will blame the rape of Proserpina on Venus, Minerva's arch enemy, who has declared war on those who devote themselves to chastity.[34]

So although Minerva maintains a low profile during the narratives of the Muses, she is cast as the central authoritative figure in the outer frame of this episode in a dual capacity, as the archetypal champion of chastity, and as an Olympian patron. Her presence has a powerful effect upon the Muses and the content of their report, including the songs of the Emathides and Calliope. As we will see below, the Muse seems to have selected and tailored the content of her account for Minerva, as the representative Olympian, in keeping with the Muses' traditional function, from Hesiod forward, of delighting the gods with song, particularly with songs glorifying themselves.[35] This role is not to be taken lightly, especially in the context of the *Metamorphoses,* where the immoderation and brutality of the Olympians when displeased or foiled is ruthlessly and repeatedly documented.[36]

Subverting Gigantomachy: The Song of the Emathides

The subject of the doomed Emathides' song, the battle between Jupiter and his competitors for the kingship of heaven, is at the heart of both Ovidian and modern critical controversy about their *poesis.* While the usual account of the gigantomachy, familiar from the art, literature and even philosophy of the Greek and Roman world, focuses upon the success and supremacy of the Olympians over the earth-born Giants and/or Typhoeus, the Emathides lionize Typhoeus, who emerges from the earth in 5.321 and terrifies the gods *(caelitibus fecisse metum),* who flee for sanctuary to the Nile.[37] As the Muses complain to Minerva, *falsoque in honore Gigantas / ponit et extenuat magnorum facta deorum,* 'she bestows false honor on the Giants and makes light of the deeds of the great gods' (5.319–20). In their unique version, the shameful transformations undergone by the Olympians to escape their enemy stand at the center of the account *(et se mentitis superos celasse figuris):* Jupiter becomes a ram, Apollo a crow, and so forth. The song comes to an abrupt end after the account of the transformations without an Olympian *aristeia;* with *hactenus . . . vocalia moverat ora* in line 332 the Muse announces its premature conclusion, a wrong she will rapidly set right in her subsequent revision of the battle's outcome.

Critics have largely ignored both the Emathides and their presentation of a Typhonomachy. Those who haven't typically second the opinion of the Muses, whose description of the song leaves little room for debate about their critical opinion (negative). Hofmann first suggested that the Muses might represent an Alexandrian literary viewpoint in the contest, with the Emathides as the champions of the epic *carmen perpetuum:* he pointed to the epic themes of the Emathides' song in lines 319–20, *bella canit superum* and *magnorum facta deorum,* as anti-neoteric flags.[38] Hinds's 1989 discussion, while similar in approach, is both more balanced and more complete. He acknowledges that the Muses disapprove of the song's "moral reprehensibility," that is, its impiety towards the gods, but argues that gigantomachy is more importantly "the very sternest kind of martial epic there is." He documents the Callimachean nature of the Muses' denunciation of the Emathides and their *poesis,* noting the images of crowds, massiveness, ignorance, and verbosity they employ to describe them: *turbam* in line 301, *intumuit* and *stolidarum* with *turba* again in 305, and at the episode's close, *garrulitas* and *studium inmane loquendi* in 678. On this basis Hinds cannot but concur with the Muses that the Emathides are impious, impolite, and lousy poets to boot.[39]

Several details in the passage, however, raise doubts about a reading that champions the Muses at the expense of the Emathides and their theme.[40] As Barchiesi and Rosati have observed, the very narrative structure of the contest calls into question the narrating Muse's objectivity.[41] It is difficult to establish the reliability of the narrating Muse, or of any of Ovid's narrators in the narrative maze of the *Metamorphoses*, for that matter. But the particularly intricate narrative layering of the book 5 contest (Ovid reports that the Muse reported to Minerva about a song sung in a contest some time earlier, by poets now transformed into magpies chattering in the trees above them) undermines our confidence in the Muse's version of events.

Furthermore, the honesty of the Muses is directly challenged by the pointed censure of the Emathides' challenge: *desinite indoctum vana dulcedine vulgus / fallere,* 'Stop deceiving the uneducated crowd with empty sweetness' (5.308–9). According to the Emathides the Muses' poetry is both aesthetically superficial *(vana dulcedine)* and ethically dishonest *(indoctum vulgus, vana, fallere)*. The charge is not entirely without precedent. It calls to mind most vividly Hesiod's Muses in the *Theogony*, who sharply chide their initiate, ἴδμεν ψεύδεα πολλὰ λέγειν ἐτύμοισιν ὁμοῖα, / ἴδμεν δ' εὖτ' ἐθέλωμεν, ἀληθέα γηρύσασθαι, 'We know how to speak falsehoods as though they were true, but we know how to speak the truth, when we want to' (*Theog.* 27–28). The possibility that Calliope's song in book 5 might be only a *fama,* and possibly *mentita,* is echoed later in the *Metamorphoses* by the sole external mention of the song, Orpheus's rhetorical comment to Proserpina and Pluto at 10.28: *famaque si veteris non est mentita rapinae,* 'if the story of the ancient rape (of Proserpina) is not a lie.' And in book 5 itself, we can simply observe one instance where the narrating Muse seems to slip. While she claims to quote verbatim the conclusion of the song of the Emathides at 5.327, her interjected *dixit* spoils the hexameter and puts the lie to a direct quotation *('duxque gregis' dixit 'fit Iuppiter: unde recurvis')*. The temptation to align our own and Ovid's loyalties with these Muses and to condemn the Emathides outright should be moderated by these caveats.[42]

The second modern charge against the Emathides, that their theme of gigantomachy renders their song un-Callimachean and therefore 'bad poetry,' requires a closer look at gigantomachy in Latin poetry. Given the tremendous range of representations in both Greece and Rome of the battles of the gods and giants, I think it is an oversimplification to characterize the theme of gigantomachy as an anti-Alexandrian faux pas. The theme's metaphoric potential had appealed to artists ever since the famous equation of the Greek defeat of the Persians with the Olympian victory over the Giants on the Parthenon metopes.[43] We find lengthy treatments of this type in a number of eminent non-epic Greek poets.[44] Roman poets also exploit the theme for its political implications. Feeney has identified an early Roman political use of gigantomachy in Naevius *Bellum Poenicum* fragment 8, for example, which identifies the Roman forces in the Punic War with the Olympians, while the Carthaginians lurk behind their gigantic challengers.[45] Critics concur that Naevius probably had in mind as his model the gigantomachy from the temple of Zeus Olympius at Acragas, a relief that originally symbolized the Sicilian *Greeks'* struggle against the barbarian Carthaginians. Such a redeployment of the image in the service of Rome demonstrates how easily the theme could be made to conform to a changing political climate.

In Augustan poetry, the Giants and Typhoeus do not only, or even usually, appear in *recusationes* as an example of undesirable subject-matter for poets of a Callimachean bent, but are used to great advantage in a variety of literary contexts. For example, in Vergil's account of Jupiter's opponents at *Georgics* 1.276–83, we find that the figure of Typhoeus provides a complex bridge between the realms of nature and politics. His attempt to overthrow the prevailing order is commemorated on his birthday with an ill-omened day for agricultural pursuits. In lines 279–83 he is described in the same breath as a number of other Olympian pretenders, including Otus and Ephialtes *(fratres)* for whom the politically explosive adjective *coniuratos* has been reserved:

ter sunt conati imponere Peli(o) Ossam
scilicet atque Ossae frondosum involuere Olympum;
ter pater exstructos disiecit fulmine montis

['Three times they tried to place Ossa on Pelion and roll leafy Olympus onto Ossa, three times Jupiter dislodged the pile of mountains with his bolt.']

G. 1.279–83

The birthday of Typhoeus is an unlucky day for farming for reasons both natural and political. The agricultural context of the *Georgics* seems to evoke Typhoeus's roles in nature as an unseemly and inauspicious product of the earth, odious to any serious farmer, and as a producer of harsh winds; this passage fairly closely follows Vergil's pessimistic vision of the arts of civilization[46] and precedes his long description of the destruction that violent winds could wreak on crops in lines 316–21. Thomas opts for a more specifically political reading of this section, where as often in the *Georgics* agriculture and politics are eloquently joined. In his introduction he links the storms of 316–21 to the end of the book, where the prodigies observed after the death of Caesar are recorded: "Natural violence finds its responsion in civil violence at the end of the book (463–514), where Virgil gives a compelling picture of the strife which followed the death of Julius Caesar."[47]

I would extend this reading to suggest that in the passage concerning Jupiter's adversaries directly preceding the storms, Vergil associates the opponents of Caesar with Typhoeus and the other forces of Olympian rebellion. In *Georgics* 1.278–83 Vergil's use of *coniuratos* to describe the Olympian pretenders politicizes and Romanizes the challengers; the term is also employed by Ovid, in both the *Metamorphoses* and the *Fasti,* to refer to the conspiracy against Julius Caesar, and elsewhere in Vergil it refers to foreign armies plotting against either Rome or Aeneas. In addition, at the close of *Georgics* 1, the inclusion of an eruption of Mount Aetna, Typhoeus's Sicilian tomb, among the prodigies of 44 BC evokes Typhoeus's rebellious political associations. The repetition of the verb *volvere* in both *Georgics* passages, governed in each case by the challenger rolling mountains or rolling rocks, strengthens the link between them. Finally, while in *Georgics* 1.281–83 Jupiter and the forces of order have emerged supreme over the forces of chaos *(ter sunt conati, ter pater disiecit),* as in most of Vergil's predecessors, by the end of book 1 Vergil only expresses the *hope* that Octavian/Augustus will also triumph (*hunc saltem everso iuvenem succurrere saeclo / ne prohibete,* 'Don't forbid this youth to salvage our savaged generation,' 1.500–501), and the rumblings of Typhoeus under Aetna are ominous. The inevitability of Olympian triumph, central to earlier versions of the battle, is gone from Vergil's depressing georgic world, in which disruption of the status quo seems inescapable. The rebellion against Jupiter prefigures both the despair of the rebels and the monstrousness of the Roman civil conflicts that are explicitly referred to (and conflated) at the end of the book: Philippi and the assassination of Caesar. Neither victory, of Jupiter or of Caesar, is certain in Vergil's text.

Typhoeus, his fellow mutineers, and the language that follows them about in Latin literature are almost regulars in the *Aeneid,* where political readings of their presence have dominated discussion. Vergil's frequent alignment of Aeneas with Jupiter, and his enemies with Typhoeus and the Giants, has been exhaustively argued by Hardie, who also provides a convenient review of its uses.[48] Among other points of contact we find the fires of Aetna, the final resting place of Typhoeus, on the helmet of Turnus at *Aeneid* 7.785, while Aeneas is strikingly described in his final battle with Turnus in terms usually reserved for Jupiter (15.654, 700, and 922, *fulminat, intonat* and *fulmen*). Hardie's sweeping conclusions have been challenged, however, by O'Hara, whose examples indicate that Typhon and the Giants represent, more often than simple chaos, the 'other,' or the foreign invader, and therefore will often be associated with Aeneas, rather than Turnus, in the second half of the *Aeneid*.[49] They suggest a more complex application of this mythical *topos* to characters with clear ideological import in Vergil's day. Nonetheless, however ambiguous Vergil's employment of the myth may be, he is still in line with the usage of most Greek and Augustan poets: characters associated with Jupiter, whether Aeneas or Turnus, represent a positive order, while those with gigantic associations represent 'the other,' disorder, and unrestrained violence.

Perhaps the Augustan gigantomachy most similar to that of the Emathides appears in Horace's *Odes* 3.4, *Descende caelo.* This ode hosts a cast of characters remarkably similar to those in Ovid's poetic contest. A combination of Horatian autobiography, hymn to the Muses and Jupiter, and encomium to Augustus, the ode is first addressed to Calliope (3.4.2). A long and fantastic autobiographical sketch details Horace's initiation by the Muses into poetry and their relationship with him, which powerfully recalls Hesiod's similar depiction of his early career in *Theogony* 1–34, in the same section where the noteworthy remark about the truth and falsity of the Muses' utterances is made. After the autobiography Horace details the Muses' attentions to Augustus when he finishes his labors. While Horace begins at line 40 with the fairly general *Pierio recreatis antro,* 'you refresh him in the Pierian cave,' in 41–42 he clearly imagines that they participate in Caesar's *imperium* after the civil wars are over: *vos lene consilium et datis et dato / gaudetis,* 'you delight in giving gentle counsel, and delight once it's been given.' We have here a mirror image of Hesiod's depiction of Calliope's attentions to the 'good king' at *Theogony* 79–103, and a very similar alignment of Muses, rulers, and Zeus.[50] A description of the impious challengers to Jupiter's/Augustus's authority fairly erupts onto this peaceful scene, both to caution those who use violence without *consilium* (*consili expers* at 3.4.65, exactly what the Muses give Augustus in line 41), and to predict violence for those who offend the gods. Typhoeus, Mimas, Porphyrion, Rhoetus, and Enceladus are all helpless in the face of the gods' power. Horace and his Muses are thereby set firmly into their role as defenders and counselors of Jupiter and his order, and by extension Augustus and his order, on the Hesiodic model, over the chaotic forces of Typhoeus, the Titans, and other members of the *immanis turba,* including by extension the enemies of Augustus. Only in the *Theogony, Odes* 3.4 and

Metamorphoses 5 do we find the Muses in such close, antagonistic company with the monster, and in such close alliance with Zeus/Jupiter. Lyne calls 3.4 a 'trump' of Pindar *Pythian* 1 and 8, because Horace has found an indirect (and thus less distasteful) way to eulogize Augustus: "the myth substitutes for a direct encomiastic account of the battle" (in his view, of Actium). Encomium is the key word here; with it Lyne identifies gigantomachy as a theme with which each poet offers praise for victory to his patron.[51]

This background of literary appearances in Latin poetry provides us with some ammunition to reconsider the use of gigantomachy in the Augustan *recusatio* from the standpoint of the author's experience of poetic composition for a patron. Propertius's famous *recusatio* in 2.1.19–26 is a classic example of the type. The poet claims he would be happy to document the deeds of Caesar, including Phillipi and Actium, and Maecenas himself, if only he had the sort of talent to compose a gigantomachy: 'But if fate had only granted me the ability to lead bands of heroes into battle, I wouldn't have sung about the Titans, nor about Mount Ossa set on Olympus to make Mount Pelion a highway to heaven . . . I would commemorate the wars and achievements of your Caesar, and you would be my next concern after great Caesar.' Here gigantomachy is explicitly equated with encomium of Caesar and Maecenas, and it is difficult to separate out which is the more distasteful to Propertius. In addition to the graceful *recusatio,* by hyperbolically suggesting that his patrons' accomplishments outshine even Jupiter's over the Giants, the poem is both *recusatio* and a version in miniature of the requested praise poem. The central lines 27–38, which summarize the military exploits of Augustus and Maecenas, end at 40 with the admission that they are too much for the slender breast, *angusto pectore,* of a Callimachean poet. Propertius therefore expresses his unwillingness to undertake the subject of encomium; his protests about his abilities are of course disingenuous, but his preferences about content are clear. In the *recusatio* of 3.9, Propertius's rejected poetic themes are the Seven against Thebes and the Trojan War, explicitly in favor of Callimachean little books (elegies). Yet Propertius relates these themes to encomium of Maecenas, leaving open the possibility of new themes if Maecenas will lead (*te duce* in 47, *da mihi signa,* 58), and again we see gigantomachy (*Iovis arma canam caeloque minantem / Coeum,* 3.9.47–48) and encomium (53–56, from the Parthians to the defeat of Antony) lumped together as a single type of *poesis.* Epic form and encomiastic content are inseparable in these examples.

Gigantomachy is also equally a euphemism for both encomium and epic in Horace *Odes* 2.12. Gigantomachy simply stands in for praise of the *bella Caesaris*, which, he tells Maecenas, should be recounted not in poetry at all but by Maecenas himself in *pedestribus . . . historiis* (2.12.9–10). He argues that gigantomachy is appropriate for other meters, not *mollibus . . . citharae modis* (2.12.3–4). Like Propertius, he protests that his *poesis* isn't up to the task, but again he is clearly being disingenuous.

A final example comes from Ovid's *Tristia* 2.71–72. Here the poet explicitly equates the writing of gigantomachy for the pleasure of Jupiter with the singing of the praises of Augustus in a passage discussed earlier in this chapter for its portrait of gods and kings taking pleasure, as patrons, in the songs of their poets. Jupiter enjoys listening to an account of the gigantomachy just as Augustus would enjoy hearing his own praises: 'And when the battles of the war with the Giants are recalled, I can believe that he is happy to hear his own praises,' followed immediately by *te celebrant alii.* I think Ovid again recalls here both *Descende caelo* and the scene at the opening of the *Theogony,* in which the Muses praise and give pleasure to Zeus and the other gods.

So to paraphrase Hinds referring to epic, gigantomachy is *encomium* of the sternest kind, a hymn to the greatest patron of all, the ruler of the Olympian gods. So it was for Hesiod; and perhaps following upon Hesiod's equation of the good king with Zeus, it became the ultimate model for singing the praises of mortal kings who battled against the forces of evil, variously described and imagined: Pindar's patrons, Vergil's 'ideal Rome' (at least sometimes), and Horace and Ovid's Augustus.

And so the Muses might not in fact have minded this song, either as gigantomachy or as epic, if the Emathides had used it for its traditional purpose, to praise the Olympians. These Augustan examples suggest that the subject of the gods' (successful) battles is certainly one that the Muses, as the entertainers of the Olympians, would approve, not to mention their honored guest, Minerva, who can boast of a few noteworthy *facta* (5.320) of her own. In fact, Minerva's prominent role against Enceladus in these *bella* was represented on Apollo's temple at Delphi, and in the *Ciris* she is the vanquisher of Typhoeus. Most strikingly, the gigantomachy was the subject of the *peplos* woven in Athena's honor for the Panathenaea each year, and her defeat of the giant Asterius in this conflict was thought to be the origin of the smaller Panathenaea.[52] Minerva's egoism about these accomplishments is made evident at the opening of the next episode; a song to honor these achievements would hardly cause her displeasure.

What is *wrong* with the Emathides' song is immediately identified by the narrator in *Metamorphoses* 5.319–20, '*falsoque in honore gigantas / ponit et extenuat magnorum facta deorum*'; the Emathides are rooting for the opponents of the gods and trivializing the Olympian victory. The similarity between the cast of characters found in *Odes* 3.4 and this song is not coincidental, if as I think the song of the Emathides inversely (perhaps perversely is the better word) is modeled upon and comments on Horace's encomiastic practice in that poem. To compare the Emathides' version with other gigantomachies that preceded it in the ancient tradition is on the face of it quite simple: it is incomplete. It treats the challenge of Typhoeus, the flight of the gods to Egypt, and their humiliating transformation into animal forms, but leaves off the concluding Olympian victory. Their failure to complete the gigantomachy with the victory of the Olympians is clearly the Muse's main complaint. This is surely why the Muse closes her description with *hactenus*, 'thus far' (5.332); this is surely why Calliope feels compelled to devote the opening ten lines of her song (5.346–55) to the traditional ending of the Typhonomachy, introducing her version of the rape of Proserpina with a very Ovidian day-in-the-life-of-Dis once Typhoeus has been safely buried beneath Sicily.

Beyond its lack of Olympian finale, however, the Emathides also produce the only full version of the flight of the gods in which Jupiter is transformed with the other Olympians, into the laughable *dux gregis*. This innovation is both an insult to the king of the gods, and a demonstration of their own learned Alexandrianism. In Hesiod's gigantomachy, Zeus's victory is swift; although the horrifying description of Typhoeus is lengthy, the battle is over almost before it has begun (*Theog.* 853–58). Similarly, in Hyginus (*Fabulae* 152.1) Jupiter strikes Typhon with a thunderbolt as soon as the monster issues his challenge. Pindar may have known that the transformation of the gods was a component of this battle (*Prosodia* fr. 81 mentions it), but the full version only appears before Ovid in Nicander *Heteroeumena* (summarized in *Antoninus Liberalis* 28) where neither Athena nor Zeus are among those who flee in panic. In the Emathides' version, Minerva does not figure at all, and they not only claim that Jupiter transformed into a ram but offer learned aetiological proof of it:[53] the transformation explains why the Egyptian god Ammon is represented as a ram in Egyptian iconography. Lucian (*De Sacrificiis* 14) considered the myth an aetiology of Egyptian animal-worship, as did the Greeks in general, from Herodotus forward. But the Emathides' version is unique among literary sources. It is not only an anti-encomium but also a rebellious contribution to aetiological epic, a very Alexandrian project indeed. Their version, an encomium turned on its head to embarrass its recipients, is particularly demeaning.

It is therefore mistaken to evaluate references to gigantomachy even in Roman *recusationes* in isolation from their political significance. When sung in their entirety, usually in contexts with theological intent, gigantomachies function as encomia to Jupiter and, as it happens, Minerva. In Greek and Roman poetry, allusions to gigantomachy add political depth to depictions of other struggles, historical and mythological, by aligning the protagonists, for better or for worse, with the ultimate icons of order (Zeus) and chaos (Typhoeus and the giants). Ultimately, in late Republican and Augustan Rome this tradition is carried forward, with a certain amount of ambiguity in Vergil in particular; in the *Georgics* and the *Aeneid* the giants still represent disorder, but the inevitability or wisdom of Jupiter's ultimate order is no longer taken for granted. While gigantomachy represents poetry to be avoided in the Augustan *recusatio*, it is more than a rejection of a genre or a civic theme; in *Odes* 3.4 and *Tristia* 2 the singing of gigantomachy is explicitly connected with the singing of Augustus's praises by the Muses, in poems expressing distaste for such compositions.

The incomplete gigantomachy of the Emathides, an inversion of the traditional Olympian encomium, is a clear indication of their artistic strategy in the circumstances of their contest with the Muses. It combines defiance of Olympian authority with the employment of one of the most weighty genres of poetry available to them, encomiastic epic. The Emathides pay homage to the stormers of heaven, as we might expect in the song of a group of mortals posed to snatch away from the immortals another of their enclaves, the seat of poetry, Mount Helicon, for humankind. Their opening challenge suggests that the traditional version of the gigantomachy, reiterated by Calliope at the opening of her song, is false, and they offer as proof of their claim that the immortals were transformed into animals at the Nile River, an impeccable Egyptian aetiology. The artistic strategy of the Emathides, therefore, like their challenge, is direct frontal assault: to meet sweet, empty deception with a full and bitter dose of honesty.

What does Ovid think of his Emathides and their truncated gigantomachy? The episode offers one suggestive association of Ovid with his Emathides and their theme. I know of only one other reference to an abbreviated gigantomachy, and it is found in the glib recusatio that opens *Amores* book 2. Ovid rather proudly claims to have been busy composing a successful gigantomachy when his girlfriend locked him out: *ausus eram memini caelestia dicere bella / centimanumque Gyen (et satis oris erat)*, 'I remember I dared once to sing about the wars of the gods and hundred-handed Gyas (and I had the voice for it)' (*Am.* 2.1.11–12). The mountains had been heaped up, Jupiter had seized his weapons, and—*clausit amica fores*, 'My girlfriend slammed her door in my face.' The wars of the gods were out, and love was in: *Ego cum Iove fulmen omisi / excidit ingenio Iuppiter ipse meo*, 'I let Jupiter and his lightning go; Jupiter himself fell out of my thoughts/work' (2.1.17–18). Ovid broke off his poem, he tells us, with an apology to Jupiter (*Iuppiter, ignoscas*, 2.1.19). Barchiesi characterizes the ironic stance of Ovid's narrator as follows: "I was good at them (gigantomachies), but they were quite useless to me in the conquest of a pretty girl." Here, in a far more playful and elegiac context, Ovid produced an abbreviated version of a gigantomachy that, like that of the Emathides, failed (or preferred not) to document the final victory of Jupiter.

So perhaps we are wrong to assume that we, like Ovid's Muses, are meant to dismiss the Emathides because of their anti-Callimachean theme. Within its context and in its particular form, their rebellious gigantomachy would not necessarily have been objectionable to the poet of the *Metamorphoses*. Quite apart from the poetic contest, the Olympian gods repeatedly take a beating in the *Metamorphoses*, depicted as rapists, murderers, capricious tyrants, overly zealous virgins and overly jealous wives. Ovid's exile poems continue his negative take on the Olympians, in which he often associates himself with their enemies.[54]

In the end the Emathides' song provokes reflection upon epic less as a literary genre than as a genre in praise of the powerful. The mortal women cannily deploy epic's authority in the service of their own political allegiances. In this sense the Emathides mirror Ovid's own practice of recasting historical epic as it was defined by the *Aeneid*. In reaction to the appropriation of history (and epic) by powerful authorities, Ovid and the Emathides redeploy epic to offer a different reading of history, still covering basically the same timeline (in the Emathides' case, the gigantomachy, and in Ovid's, the entire history of the universe), but with a different take on the importance of people and events. Ovid is not above omitting important Augustan details from his mini-*Aeneid* in book 14; similarly, the Muses' expectations for a pious gigantomachy are foiled when the Emathides stop short of the final Olympian victory, and the gigantomachy becomes a eulogy of Typhoeus.

As an artistic strategy, however, it is doomed to a short life in Ovid's universe. In a sweeping demonstration of the axiom that victors control the history of events, the Emathides and their version of the gigantomachy perish together, and the Muses, however Callimachean their style, prevail by force. Almost prevail. For Ovid's inclusion of the story of the Emathides, containing at least a shadow of the content of their song, is an act of recuperation and commemoration. At the level of the myth itself, the members of this group of rebellious mortal singers are transformed into magpies, stripped of their talent, and their song, a performance before a hostile audience, vanishes with their poetic ability. Ovid restores the Emathides and the gist of their song to public view, in a subversion of the action and intent of the Muses in the episode to permanently silence them. We cannot help think here of the words of Cassius Severus in response to the burning of the histories of Labienus: "*I* ought to be burnt alive now—for I have those books by heart" (tr. Knox).[55]

Carmina digna dea: The Song of the Muses

Calliope's responding entry in the poetic contest (5.341–661) documents the famous rape of Proserpina by Pluto and the wanderings of her mother, Ceres, in search of her. Her introduction to this theme, however, is unique, and shaped by her immediate performance context. She begins with an invocation of the goddess:

Prima Ceres unco glaebam dimovit aratro
prima dedit fruges, alimentaque mitia terris
prima dedit leges; Cereris sunt omnia munus.
illa canenda mihi est; utinam modo dicere possim
carmina digna dea; certe dea carmine digna est.

[Ceres first turned the fields with the curved plow, first bestowed agriculture and gentle food on the earth, first bestowed laws; everything is a gift from Ceres, and she must be sung by me. I wish I were able to sing a song worthy of the goddess; she is certainly worthy of song.]

Met. 5.341–45

Calliope's hymnic opening establishes a strong contrast between her own piety and the irreverence of the Emathides. She continues with her own bit of mythmaking, creatively linking her subject, the familiar rape of Proserpina by Dis, to the burial of Typhoeus under Aetna by Jupiter, the traditional end of the gigantomachy omitted in the song of the Emathides.[56]

Vasta giganteis ingesta est insula membris
Trinacris et magnis subiectum molibus urget
aetherias ausum sperare Typhoea sedes.

['The great island of Trinacria [Sicily] was piled up on the giant's limbs, and pressed upon him with great force, on Typhoeus, who dared hope for a heavenly home.']

Met. 5.346–48

The effect of Calliope's introduction is the neutralization of the version of the gigantomachy she has just heard.

Most interpretations of the remainder of the song have quite understandably focused upon Calliope's song as art, asking what kind of poetry, or more particularly what genre of poetry, it might represent, and why.[57] I would like to consider here the social and narrative dimensions of her song by way of its significant digression from not only the *Homeric Hymn to Demeter* and *Fasti,* but all versions of the rape: Calliope's attribution of the rape to the sole agency of Venus and Cupid (5.359–79). As I have argued more fully elsewhere,[58] the representation of Venus and Cupid in *Metamorphoses* 5 as both the inspirers of love and as the empress and commander-in-chief of an empire form two sides of a single Ovidian strategy, in the first case making a mockery of Augustan moral legislation, in the second launching a broader assault upon Roman imperial ideology. My focus here is upon the Muses themselves, and how Calliope motivates the rape of Proserpina within the episode. It is the presence of the virginal Minerva in the outer frame, and the regularly victimized nymphs as judges in the inner frame, which shape both Calliope's song of the rape of Proserpina and the narrator's reconstruction of it for Minerva; the pressures of performance and audience are hard at work on the Muse's final artistic product.

Venus and Cupid, who do not appear to have been available motivators of the rape of Proserpina before Calliope's song,[59] are made entirely responsible for Proserpina's demise. Jupiter, the motivator in the *Hymn,*[60] is invisible in book 5 until Ceres' traditional appeal on behalf of her daughter after her wanderings in search of her (5.512 ff.). Pluto, blamed in the *Fasti,*[61] is here merely an unfortunate victim of Venus's ambition. He is caught in the crossfire as he emerges from Tartarus to check for damage caused by the struggling of Typhoeus, with whose burial under Aetna Calliope opened her narrative. As Venus spots the unwitting Pluto she addresses Cupid:

"arma manusque meae, mea, nate, potentia," dixit,
"illa, quibus superas omnes, cape tela, Cupido,
inque dei pectus celeres molire sagittas,
cui triplicis cessit fortuna novissima regni.
tu superos ipsumque Iovem, tu numina ponti
victa domas ipsumque, regit qui numina ponti;
Tartara quid cessant? cur non matrisque tuumque
imperium profers? agitur pars tertia mundi . . .
. . . at tu pro socio, si qua est ea gratia, regno
iunge deam patruo."

['My arms, my hands, my power, my son!' she said, 'Take up the missiles that overwhelm everyone, Cupid, and sink your swift arrows into the heart of the god to whom the last lot for the division of the three-fold universe fell. You tame the gods, and Jupiter himself, and the divinities of the sea and their ruler; why does Tartarus hold back? Why aren't you extending our empire? A third of the world is at stake! . . . On behalf of our joint realm, if it means anything to you, join the goddess to her uncle.']

Met. 5.365–79

In Calliope's song Venus moves beyond her traditional role as the inspirer of love in Latin elegiac poetry to become a rapacious empire-builder, with Cupid as her agent. Political terminology abounds *(matrisque tuumque imperium, pars tertia mundi, pro socio regno)* in concert with a portrait of a fully martial Cupid *(arma, potentia, tela, domas)*.[62] Her plan to inflame Pluto with passion for Proserpina is a premeditated attempt to gain control of the last of the realms denied her, the underworld.[63] Venus reminds Cupid, in expressly imperial language, that he already controls Jupiter, the Olympian gods, and the sea deities and their king (5.370–71), and urges her son to extend their empire to its furthest limit (5.371–72). Her authority over Cupid contrasts with his more typical independence of action in Ovid's elegiac poetry and emphasizes the imperial tone of her commands. In a twist on Cupid's playful assault on Mount Helicon and Ovid's epic project in *Am.* 1.1, where poetic *regna* are at issue,[64] here Cupid's *arma, tela* and *sagittas* have become Venus's literal weapons in a struggle to extend her empire over the 'third realm.' The use of these weapons will inspire a rape, a fitting form of assault in the war for the empire of Love, just as they did against Apollo and Daphne in *Metamorphoses* 1.452–567.

This unusually aggressive and politicized portrait of Venus as empire-builder invites closer consideration of its implications within its narrative context. Like the paranoid tyrant of Greek tragedy, Venus's fear of insurgents shapes the second reason for the rape she is poised to incite. In this case the rebels are any goddesses who choose to remain virgins:

"et tamen in caelo, quae iam patientia nostra est,
spernimur, ac mecum vires minuuntur Amoris.
Pallada nonne vides iaculatricemque Dianam
abscessisse mihi? Cereris quoque filia virgo,
si patiemur, erit: nam spes adfectat easdem."

['Nevertheless we are scorned in heaven (such is our endurance), and your power with mine is shrinking. Can't you see that Pallas and spear-hurling Diana have withdrawn from my camp? Proserpina will join their ranks too if she is not stopped, for she has the same hopes.']

Met. 5.373–77

While in the first half of Venus's speech Pluto and Proserpina are the unwitting victims of the 'empire of Eros,' placing them on a par with the narrators of Roman elegy, in this second half, the true nature of Venus's *imperium* is revealed: compulsory sexuality. The virgin goddesses Minerva and Diana are perceived as dissidents, rebels from her authority. Venus disregards any right to sexual self-determination Proserpina might have[65] in a single-minded pursuit of two goals: the extension of her empire and the suppression of dissidents against it, those who renounce Love. Proserpina apparently has similar aspirations, which Venus is eager to crush. The two halves of her speech recast an old elegiac metaphor regarding the *castra* of Cupid within the framework of imperial ambitions, and thus draw a striking parallel between victims of rape and of expansionist imperial power.

This portrait of Venus takes on special significance when considered within the complex structure of the episode. There are three audiences for the song of Calliope: the Muses themselves; the nymphs, who judge the two songs within the original contest; and Minerva, in the present time of the narrative. Venus's *imperium* is sexuality, and as she herself states, the enemies of her empire are females who choose to remain chaste. Her weapon in this case, through Cupid and the agency of Pluto, is rape. It is therefore significant that all of the several audiences for the original song and its reprise are extra-social or virginal female goddesses or nymphs, who share a particular interest in the success or failure of Venus's designs.[66]

This begins with the Muses themselves, when we recall the peculiar story of Pyreneus at the opening of the episode in which Ovid's Muses count themselves among the self-professed virgin goddesses,[67] and complain bitterly about the violence threatened against them. This rather absurd story of a mortal man aspiring to rape nine goddesses, and committing suicide when he fails, only makes sense in the larger context of the episode in which virginity and its violation are prominent themes.[68] It establishes the virginity of the Muses and links them closely with Minerva, the Muse narrator's addressee, in her role as a sympathetic fellow virgin. Together they are arrayed in the episode against Venus, who singles out Minerva with Proserpina as a rebel against her domain. Diodorus 5.3.4 indicates that Athena and Artemis were raised together with Persephone, and that all three had chosen the same virginity, echoing the same tradition that Venus complains of in her speech. Of course the animosity between Minerva and Venus was proverbial, extending well beyond their sexuality.[69] But appropriately enough, in Calliope's account of the rape of Proserpina it is Minerva's staunch virginity to which Venus objects. Thus the Muse's portrait of Venus as a grasping sexual empire-builder would be one with which the virginal Muses and Minerva, the presiding Olympian judge in the outer frame of the episode, would be inclined to agree.

The judges of the contest, a group of Heliconian nymphs, also have a natural interest in the aspirations of Venus. Although their background is unspecified, in the pages of the *Metamorphoses,* and Greek and Roman mythology generally, most targets of Olympian rape or seduction were nymphs.[70] Their anxiety regarding an expansion of the 'empire of Eros' could certainly be aroused by Calliope's negative portrait of Venus. An additional Ovidian innovation of the traditional account of the rape of Proserpina, however, suggests an even more direct appeal to the sensibilities of the nymphs: the lengthy inclusion in Calliope's song of the actual and metaphoric threats to the chastity of two famous nymphs, Cyane and Arethusa, who align themselves with Proserpina and Ceres during the events of the rape.[71]

Only in *Metamorphoses* 5 does the nymph Cyane boldly step forward to challenge the rape of the maiden Proserpina by Pluto. Although Diodorus Siculus names Cyane as the fountain created by the descent of Pluto with Proserpina into the underworld, no nymph named Cyane gives her name to the fountain in his account (5.4). Cicero also reports in the *Verrines* that a lake was said to have been created by the descent of Pluto, but again no nymph is mentioned (2.4.107). Here in book 5 she insists *roganda non rapienda fuit,* 'she should have been courted, not carted off' (5.415–16). Her opposition not surprisingly provokes the wrath of Pluto, who strikes the pool in which Cyane stands to its depths, and proceeds through it to the underworld (5.420–24). Cyane's grief for the *raptamque deam contemptaque fontis / iura sui,* 'the raped goddess and the scorned laws of her spring' (5.425–26) transforms her into the waters of her own pool. Otis describes the nymph as a "shocked matron," and can therefore provide only the barest explanation of her consequent transformation into a fountain.[72] Segal more sensitively observes that Pluto's blow to the pool in which Cyane stands is characterized by the setting and language of the passage as sexual in nature (*inconsolabile vulnus,* 5.426), and argues that the violation of her pool parallels the rape of Proserpina herself.[73]

Otis is correct, however, to observe that "[Cyane's] disappearance removes one more witness of the rape. Her over-active tongue is quenched."[74] The silencing, deliberate or otherwise, of rape victims is a common *topos* in the *Metamorphoses,* where voices of complaint or protest are cut off as part of their resulting metamorphosis. The list is long, even when it does not include those who are punished for crimes of the tongue, like Echo (book 3) and the Emathides (book 5, whose poetic voices are lost). In book 1, Daphne can only nod her apparent approval of Apollo's appropriation of her foliage (*quoniam coniunx mea non potes esse / arbor eris certe,* 'Since you can't be my wife, then surely you will be my tree,' says Apollo, 1.557–58; *adnuit utque caput* visa est *agitasse cacumen,* 'She nodded and *seemed to* shake the top of her head' says the poet, 1.567, my emphasis). Ovid's treatment of Io's transformation deliberately underscores her inability to speak.[75] Her fate is almost identical to those of both Cyane and Philomela, whose treatment by her persecutor Tereus is the most shocking in the *Metamorphoses,* if not the whole of ancient mythology (6.424 ff.). Philomela and Io are transformed and disfigured by their rapist to avoid detection;[76] and must find innovative ways to communicate their fate. *Grande doloris / ingenium est,* 'Great is the cunning born of grief' (6.574–75); Philomela weaves a tapestry detailing her rape and sends it to her sister (6.574–80), with whom she will carry out a Thyestean vengeance, while Io is reduced to writing the story of her abduction in the sand with her hoof (*littera pro verbis,* 1.649). Similarly, Cyane can only float Proserpina's girdle on the surface of her waters. Her inability to speak despite her desire to do so is described by Ovid:

> . . . ea ni mutata fuisset,
> omnia narrasset; sed et os et lingua volenti
> dicere non aderant, nec, quo loqueretur, habebat.
> signa tamen manifesta dedit notamque parenti . . .
>
> [. . . If she had not been transformed, she would have told everything; but she had no mouth or tongue despite her will to speak, nor anything with which she might speak. Nevertheless she displayed clear signs, a token, to the mother . . .]
>
> *Met.* 5.465–69

This prominence given to the protest, transformation, and testimony of Cyane is one of the most notable digressions of Ovid from the versions of the rape in either his own *Fasti* or the *Hymn*. Its emphatic placement links Cyane and Proserpina to other rape victims of the *Metamorphoses* and keeps the cruelty of the empire of Venus and the theme of violated sexual self-determination in the foreground of the narrative.

The pronounced role of the nymph Arethusa in Calliope's song similarly reflects the native concerns of the nymph judges, and the attempted rape by Alpheus deepens the significance of Venus as motivator of the rape of Proserpina. Arethusa is only mentioned in Diodorus as a spring created by the nymphs of Ortygia to please Artemis (5.3.5–6); in the *Fasti* Ceres is attending her party when Proserpina vanishes (4.423–24). As Segal observes, Ovid's mention of Cyane and Arethusa in the same line (5.409) links them as "victims of violence which is either implicitly or explicitly sexual."[77] Arethusa is the victim of an attempted, and I think actual, rape herself, and bears many resemblances both to Cyane and other victims of divine/male passion in the poem. Recollection of Arethusa's story is delayed to an emphatic position near the end of Calliope's song after the narrative of the rape is complete, and in this location balances the opening story of the Muses' encounter with Pyreneus. Although Arethusa never pledges herself to virginity like Minerva, she claims she was unlike other girls in her aversion to beauty and its effects: *crimenque placere putavi*, 'I thought it was a crime to please' (5.584). Her will is therefore threatened by the attentions of the river Alpheus, just as the Muses were threatened by Pyreneus. Alpheus's pursuit of Arethusa, as Curran has discussed, echoes the terror-in-flight imagery of the rape of Daphne in book 1.[78] The image of the dove torn apart by the hawk, so strikingly employed in the description of Philomela's feelings during her rape by Tereus in book 6.529–30, is reintroduced at 5.605–6: *ut fugere accipitrem penna trepidante columbae, / ut solet accipiter trepidas urgere columbas,* 'as doves flee the hawk on frightened wings, as the hawk is accustomed to press the frightened doves.' Arethusa is protected to no avail by Diana, who surrounds her with a dense cloud that renders the nymph invisible (5.621–25); nevertheless, in her terror Arethusa is transformed into water, *in latices* (5.634–36), as was Cyane. Alpheus changes back into water *ut se mihi misceat,* 'to mix with her' (5.636–38). Hinds ingeniously observes that Arethusa's tale corresponds not only thematically but structurally to Persephone's recollection of the rape to her mother in the *Hymn to Demeter* 406–33, as an inset of the epyllion variety well-known in Hellenistic and Roman poetry, particularly the *Metamorphoses.*[79] Such a correspondence would indicate an even deeper relationship between the experiences of Arethusa and the central victim of the episode, Proserpina.

By devoting so much of the narrative to these related subtales, Calliope keeps before her nymph audience (and the Muse keeps before Minerva, and Ovid keeps before us) a negative interpretation of sexual aggression that relies in turn upon an imagery of empire, specifically Roman empire, established by the imperialistic language of Venus and Cupid at the opening of the episode. The rape of Proserpina is cast as both a sexual and a political act, in which the innocent victim, and even the perpetrator in this case, are pawns in a much larger game played by Venus. Calliope's song expresses the viewpoint of the virginal female to whom the empire of Venus represents repressive authority; her viewpoint is in turn characterized by Venus as revolutionary.

Ovid's, and Calliope's, conflation of sexual and imperial aggression in the Proserpina tale suits both of the narrators, and both of the narrative contexts, of the song. First, as the song of the virginal Calliope to her nymph audience, the Muse arouses her audience's sympathy on behalf of the victims of and protesters against sexual aggression. Second, as the reprise of the unnamed but equally virginal Muse for the virgin goddess Minerva, the song confirms what Minerva already knows full well about the nature of Venus's empire. In Ovid's own context, his presentation of Venus as an unwelcome imperialist aggressor in the realm of sexuality comments negatively both upon sexuality and empire. The irony of portraying the *genetrix* of the straitlaced emperor at the head of her own empire of enforced sexuality is sharp indeed. In the atmosphere of the late Augustan period, Ovid could hardly draw such a portrait without it being read against the moral policies of Augustus, which, in the view of the knights who vocally opposed the strictness of the

Augustan moral legislation, unfairly punished the unmarried and the childless, and 'forced' them into married relationships and offspring. If so, Ovid characterizes the legislation as little more than compulsory (hetero)sexuality, decreed by the emperor who claimed descent from the coercive goddess of (illicit) love herself.

Cedite victae: The Imperial Muses

One final level of interpretation remains. In what seems to be another Ovidian invention, the participants in the poetic contest, the Muses and the Emathides, pledge territories as stakes in the competition (5.311–14): Mount Helicon itself will fall to the Emathides if the Muses lose, while the plains of Emathia will be ceded to the Muses if the Emathides lose.

> . . . vel cedite victae
> fonte Medusaeo et Hyantea Aganippe,
> vel nos Emathiis ad Paeonas usque nivosos
> cedemus campis.

> [' . . . Either defeated you surrender the spring of Pegasus, child of Medusa [the Hippocrene] and Boeotian Aganippe, or we will yield the Emathian fields as far as snowy Paeonia.']
>
> *Met.* 5.311–14

So just as Venus, in her attack on Pluto, had as her goal an expansion of her *regna,* so too the Muses, in their contest with the Emathides, aspire to a larger empire. To Venus, a third of the world is at stake, *agitur pars tertia mundi,* which she will gain at the expense of Proserpina; to the Muses, their entire empire is at stake when the springs of Mount Helicon are wagered. Far more than a spring, the Hippocrene (here atypically distinguished from the Aganippe) metaphorically represents the *fons* of poetry itself. Hinds explores this point in his appreciation of the play of poetic words like *fons, pes* and *ictus* in Ovid's description of the creation of the Hippocrene.[80] That we are to take note of this territorial emphasis is guaranteed by the importance of the spring in the Nicandrian version, to which Ovid clearly alludes and from which he then departs at the opening of the book 5 episode.[81] In addition, the spring plays a pivotal role in the narrative; Minerva is visiting Helicon as a tourist to see it.

So in this episode both the Muses and the Venus they so malign are attempting to either expand or maintain their traditional spheres of authority, here characterized as empires through Ovid's added emphasis upon territory. Venus's weapon, as mentioned above, is rape, induced by Cupid's arrows; the Muses' corresponding weapon is song. In both cases the goddesses deprive their challengers of the possession that epitomizes their rebellion: the virginity of Proserpina, and the rebellious artistry of the Emathides. In the end the Muses will collect far more than they were pledged, and the Emathides will be transformed into chattering magpies in addition to losing their territory. As the Muse narrator herself says, even the Muses can be moved to vengeance: *ibimus in poenas et, qua vocat ira, sequemur,* 'We will proceed to exact punishment, following where our anger leads us' (*Met.* 5.668).

Despite the many episodes detailing the cruelty of the gods in their dealings with mortals in the first third of the *Metamorphoses,* it is nonetheless shocking to find the usually benevolent patrons of poets cast on the side of authoritarian divinity. Ovid has relocated the conventional divine/mortal struggle familiar from the rest of the *Metamorphoses* on the field of poetics, in a dramatization of absolute power confronting art. Although vengeful or cruel Muses are uncommon in ancient poetry (Hesiod's rather tricky Muses, who deride humanity as 'only stomachs' and 'shameful,' and who are as capable of falsehood as they are of truth, are an exception[82]), the Muses of Ovid's world can be dangerous mistresses, as the contest ably demonstrates.

Perhaps this is why tributes to the Muses, so common in ancient poetry generally, are so rare in the poetry of Ovid. In the *Amores* they receive greetings and a farewell, but are otherwise reduced to euphemism, overshadowed by Ovid's more striking poetic motivators, the rascally Cupid in 1.1, and the contentious Tragedy and Elegy in 3.1. The Muses enter the *Ars Amatoria* only when song and letters are recommended to women as tools of seduction. They famously fail to provide a decisive opinion in *Fasti* 5, in a lengthy debate over the etymology of the month of May (5.1–110), where Ovid expresses some anxiety about differing with any of them: *gratia Pieridum nobis aequaliter adsit / nullaque laudetur plusve minusve mihi,* 'may the favor of all the Muses equally be with me, and may none be praised more or less than any other' (5.109–10). They will also close the *Fasti,* at the end of book 6, where they are invoked as the Pierides.[83] And there are but four mentions of the Muses in the *Metamorphoses,* two of which occur in the contest. So the Muses are far less prominent patrons of poetry in Ovid's (largely) pre-exilic collections than in most ancient poetry.

In his exile poems, however, the Muses are depicted often, and almost exclusively negatively, as the cause of Ovid's relegation. The Muses who inspired his offensive poetry are in these poems the offenders, with Calliope singled out as his tormentor: *quem mea Calliope / laeserit, unus ego,* 'I'm the only one whom my Calliope injured' (*Tr.* 2.567–68).[84] Only in *Tristia* 4 does the Muse finally become Ovid's companion in exile, condemned and suffering with him (4.1.19–28, 87–88; 4.9.16, 31–32, 4.10.115–22; 5.1.34). In the *Epistulae Ex Ponto, mea Musa,* with whom his relationship is not so bitter, is often lazy and unwilling. In *Tristia* 5.7.31–36 Ovid's ambivalence is clarified: while he curses the Muses who injured him, but cannot live without them.

It is therefore perhaps less surprising to find a rather obscure tale about despotic Muses punishing bold mortal poets resurrected for a place in the *Metamorphoses.* In a careful manipulation of the literary tradition for such song contests, and the story of the contest itself most likely inherited from Nicander,[85] Ovid transforms Helicon into a setting unsafe for poets, and the Muses into the tyrants of their domain, jealously guarding their prerogatives and silencing those who challenge their version of the truth. Ovid's Calliope, despite her critique of Venus's aggressive empire-building, does not reject the divine/mortal hierarchy that produces the Muses' similar behavior regarding the Emathides and their own sphere of influence. The implications of this hierarchy are further developed in book 6, where the Muses' tale will in turn inspire Minerva to contemplate vengeance against a mortal artistic challenger of her own, the weaver Arachne.

3

The Weaving Contest

Metamorphoses 6

Lend Me Your Ears

If a reader of the *Metamorphoses* were to begin with book 6 of the poem, the undertaking would be stalled by the first word on the page: *praebuerat.* With the pluperfect tense Ovid unmistakably directs us back to an earlier moment in the epic; followed by *dictis Tritonia talibus aures,* 'Minerva *(Tritonia)* (had lent) her ears to words [a story] of this kind,' we are invited to look back and discover just what kind of story the narrator might mean, and why Minerva was listening to it. If we search with particular care, we may notice that the line echoes the introduction to Calliope's song at 5.334–35, where the deferential Muse asks Minerva, *sed forsitan otia non sint / nec nostris* praebere *vacet tibi cantibus* aures?, 'but perhaps you haven't the leisure or the time *to lend* your *ears* to our songs?' The opening line of book 6 is a particularly economical example of the celebrated linking devices with which Ovid unifies his *carmen perpetuum,*[1] in this case turning our gaze backward and insisting that book 6 be read in the context of the preceding episode.

Ovid's directional signals have not, by and large, been heeded by critics. While much has been made of the weaving contest and its eye-catching ekphrases over the years, few scholars other than Harries and Heckel have taken up Ovid's challenge to pursue the relationship between the contests.[2] In one of the most quoted book reviews in Ovidian criticism, Anderson only briefly mines both contests for clues about Ovid's aesthetic principles.[3] Leach's landmark article on ekphrasis in the *Metamorphoses* discusses both contests in some detail but is primarily interested in their demonstration of the differences between "human and divine viewpoints."[4] Lateiner's similarly extensive survey of artists in the *Metamorphoses* does not weigh in on the relationship between the episodes, as he omits the Muses and Emathides from his study.[5] Feeney has more recently argued that the weaving contest best demonstrates the "poles of fixity and flux" in Ovid's *Metamorphoses* (following Barkan's formulation of metamorphosis as a vehicle between the cosmic divisions of the universe), but refers us to Hinds on the poetic contest, whose excellent study focuses entirely upon the song of Calliope in the context of the *Fasti* and the *Homeric Hymn to Demeter*.[6] Scheid and Svenbro note connections between the episodes (e.g., that the Emathides and Arachne both begin their accounts of divine transformation with Jupiter in the form of a bull) but only to demonstrate Ovid's use of weaving as a metaphor for poetic composition; they see "no parallel between the subjects of Calliope and Minerva."[7]

Yet Ovid could hardly make the connection more explicitly. Our interest in an-episode-not-*this*-episode is deepened in the second line of book 6 by yet another pluperfect: *carminaque Aonidum iustamque probaverat iram*, 'and she had approved the songs of the Aonides and their justifiable anger.' *Carmina Aonidum* refers to the verbatim rendition of Calliope's song in her book 5 competition with the mortal Emathides. In chapter 2 I discussed the appeal of this song to Minerva: the story of the rape of Proserpina by Pluto is recounted from the virginal perspective of the victims, shared by the chaste Minerva, and Venus, Minerva's arch enemy, is made fully responsible for it. Moreover, as Barchiesi has recently observed, the traditional conclusion of the rape of Persephone in which Demeter and Triptolemus are largely responsible for the civilizing of Athens through agriculture and the establishment of the Eleusinian mysteries is replaced in Calliope's account by Triptolemus's adventures in Scythia, suggesting for Minerva/Athena an unrivalled *auctoritas* in her namesake city.[8] It follows that Minerva was pleased by Calliope's performance.

The *ira* of the Muses in the second half of the line is striking. As we have seen, angry Muses are a novelty in ancient poetry;[9] although approved by Minerva, their *ira* still requires the qualifying adjective *iustam*. It motivates the divine *poena* imposed by the Muses at the end of the poetic contest when the Emathides refuse to accept the judgment of the nymphs of Helicon against them. The indignation of the Emathides is not surprising; the narrator's ambiguous description of the judgment reveals the judges' potential for bias: *at nymphae vicisse deas Helicona colentes / concordi dixere sono,* 'but the nymphs [inhabiting Helicon] unanimously said that the goddesses [inhabiting Helicon] had won' (5.663–64), where *Helicona colentes* can modify both the nymphs and the Muses. With a flurry of legalistic explication (5.665–68) citing the outrageousness of the Emathides' original challenge, their subsequent insults, and finally the limits of the Muses' own patience, the narrating Muse declares 'we will proceed to exact punishment, following where our anger leads us,' (5.668). The *ira* of the Muses is mollified by the transformation of the Emathides into noisy *picae,* who maintain their capacity to chatter raucously from the trees but lose all poetic ability.[10]

Minerva certainly approves of this example of divine vengeance; she is also angry, we learn, and not a little jealous of the Muses. The goddess privately desires for herself (*tum secum,* 6.3) the same honor she has just bestowed upon the Muses: *laudare parum est, laudemur et ipsae!,* 'Praising is not enough; let me be praised as well!' Minerva wants to satisfy her own *iusta ira* as the Muses had done: *numina nec sperni sine poena nostra sinamus,* 'Let me not allow my divine authority to be flouted any longer without punishment,' she fumes in 6.4.[11] Minerva has in mind the mortal Arachne, who has (to her own misfortune) come to the goddess's attention: she is the famous weaver *quam sibi lanificae non cedere laudibus artis audierat,* 'whom Minerva had heard would not acknowledge her superiority in the wool-working arts' (6.6–7).[12] And so Minerva ponders the Muses' vengeance over the Emathides at the opening of book 6 as she turns her attention to the destruction (*fatis,* 6.5) of her own rival.

The Warp

By comparison with the poetic contest, the narrative of the contest between Minerva and Arachne is simplicity itself. The narrator's voice, so often submerged in the poetic contest, is here only occasionally interrupted by the direct speech of the protagonists; the account therefore has an air of greater accuracy, of being 'unfiltered' by the biases of an interlocutor as in the poetic contest. No landscape description summons up a particular genre or literary tradition; the setting for the contest is only vaguely identified as eastern and urban (in the Lydian town of Hypaepa), and apparently takes place in the presence only of local nymphs and women (6.44–45).

The lack of generic indicators or narrative complexity, however, does not mean that Ovid has lost interest in exploring the context of artistic production. On the contrary, with its focus upon weaving, one of the 'minor' arts and a women's craft to boot, the introduction to the episode is packed with technical details evocative of a world perhaps even less familiar to Ovid's male audience than Mount Helicon. The local nymphs are said to travel often into town to admire Arachne's work (*opus admirabile*, 6.14), but are not only interested in viewing the final product: *nec factas solum vestes, spectare iuvabat / tum quoque, cum fierent: tantus decor adfuit arti*, 'They delighted not only in the finished tapestries, but also in their creation; so great was the loveliness of her art' (6.17–18). Arachne's *ars* includes the preliminary working of the wool, the spinning of thread, weaving,[13] and finally embroidery, or what Barber distinguishes as 'supplementary weft-float' decoration, a kind of supplemental darning with a needle (6.19–23).[14]

Ovid shares the nymphs' delight in the process of artistic creation. As in the poetic contest, the actual ekphrases in the weaving contest are postponed until the 'poietic' groundwork has been set. In book 5, the judges, stakes, and positions of the singers in the bucolic song competition were arranged; here we are treated to a lengthy description of the contestants setting up their looms, hitching up their skirts, and setting to work (6.53–69). Ovid graces his account of these preliminaries with a simile comparing the loom threads' subtle changes in color to the gradual shift from one color to the next in a rainbow (6.63–67), suggesting that the background design of the tapestries was achieved with full-length woof threads, while *illic et lentum filis inmittitur aurum / et vetus in tela deducitur argumentum* (6.68–69) describes the 'picking out' by needlework of the narrative elements in gold thread. Appropriately enough, a golden line at 6.54 describes the weavers stretching their warps 'on twin looms' *(geminas telas)*.[15] The artists are left behind for a time as the tools of the trade take over the narrative: *tela iugo vincta est, stamen secernit harundo*, 'the web is fastened to the beam, and a reed [is used to] separate the threads' (6.55), *inseritur medium radiis subtemen acutis*, 'the woof is woven in between with sharp shuttles' (6.56), *percusso paviunt insecti pectine dentes*, 'as the comb hits [the threads], its notched teeth beat down [the woof threads]' (6.58). This emphasis on the fabrication of the tapestries conforms to Heffernan's concept of the poietic ekphrasis, and confirms the views of Sharrock, that for Ovid all art is a metamorphosis of raw material into finished product (and every metamorphosis itself therefore a kind of art), and of Rosati, on the importance of the weaving metaphor in Ovid's narrative.[16] Most importantly, it heightens the realism of these poetically construed tapestries, and invites readers to compare them as 'real' artworks to tapestries familiar to them from their own world; more on this aspect below.

While the audience for the contest would seem to be the aforementioned Mygdonian women and the local nymphs, they actually have no role in the narrative of the contest either as observers or judges; as Vincent argues, the weavers themselves are each other's only real audience or 'implied reader[s].'[17] No judges are selected, and no stakes are set; in concert with the poem's prevailing view of the Olympians and their deployment of power, Minerva as the presiding divinity is to be contestant, judge, and ultimately enforcer. The simplicity of this arrangement results in a simple set of performance pressures upon the artists as they work: the authority and power of Minerva will shape the course of both tapestries' narratives. Like the Emathides, Arachne will decide upon a narrative that reflects her own performance circumstances; like the Muses, Minerva will directly address her audience and rival (in this case, the same individual), and her rival's artistic perspective.

And so in this episode it is all about the two protagonists. Regarding Minerva, the linkage between books 5 and 6 ensures that the sternly virginal goddess, whose influence on the Muses' narratives was so powerfully felt in book 5, will also dominate the weaving episode in book 6. Her prominence here is appropriate for the poem as a whole, since Ovid will turn his attention in books 6 and 7 to the heroic age of Minerva's city Athens, with the stories of Philomela, Procne, and Theseus. Ovid began his construction of the character of the goddess in book 4 with the story of Medusa, whose rape by Neptune, transformation by Minerva, and finally decapitation by Perseus are all recalled;[18] Medusa's severed head is returned as a souvenir to Minerva, who places it at the center of her shield as an apotropaic device (its effects are best demonstrated upon the Ithacan suitors at the end of the *Odyssey*). This is no obscure tale; virtually every representation of Athena/Minerva *armata* in the Greco-Roman period includes her shield or aegis with the Gorgon Medusa's head at its center. So the Minerva (of book 4) who visits the Muses on Helicon (in book 5) and will take her vengeance upon Arachne (book 6) is a virgin goddess whose severe chastity is commemorated by the head of a raped, hideously transformed, and finally decapitated maiden on her shield. As Ahl observes, Minerva's continuing capacity for violence in book 6 lurks in the dual meanings of *tela* as loom and weapon, a pun that finds full expression when Minerva strikes Arachne with her shuttle.[19] In addition, as I argued in chapter 2, Minerva is endowed by Ovid with a particularly Roman sort of *auctoritas,* portrayed, through a series of allusions in book 5, as a Roman patron-figure with respect to the Muses. There the characterization jarred, as Minerva is not generally associated with the patronage of poetry, and was seen to be a bit of flattery by the Muses; here in book 6, Minerva takes on her more familiar role as the (not very nurturing) patron goddess of weaving.

Arachne, by contrast, has not made an appearance thus far in the *Metamorphoses,* and in fact makes no other appearances outside this poem in ancient literature; her story is known only from *Metamorphoses* 6, although it was apparently in circulation in Greece as early as 600 BC.[20] She is carefully drawn. Headstrong and fiercely independent, Arachne is offended by the idea that her talent is owed to Minerva, *tanta . . . magistra* (either 'such a teacher' or 'such a great teacher,' 6.24) and relies upon her own counsel, *consilii satis est in me mihi* (6.40). Her response to authority in general is dismissive; she denounces her aged advisor (Minerva in disguise) as old and mentally incompetent, and instructs her to advise her daughters or daughters-in-law instead. Motherless herself, Arachne is unmarried, we sense resolutely so. And she is a tough customer: the narrator reports that she alone is not frightened by Minerva's epiphany (*sola est non territa virgo,* 6.45). Her reaction, a blush despite herself *(invita),* is graced with a simile:

sed tamen erubuit, subitusque invita notavit
ora rubor rursusque evanuit, ut solet aer
purpureus fieri, cum primum Aurora movetur,
et breve post tempus candescere solis ab ortu.

['She nevertheless blushed, and a sudden flush marked and then left her unwilling face, just as the air reddens when Dawn first appears but after a short while grows bright with the rising of the sun.']

Met. 6.46–49

The blush sets Arachne among the doomed of the *Metamorphoses,* marking her out for destruction;[21] but its evanescence testifies to her self-control, and rather than acquiesce in the worship of Minerva as the nymphs had done, she instead 'rushes headlong into her destruction' (*in sua fata ruit*, 6.51). She may foolishly think the contest will be fairly judged, or not; either way, she will not let pass the opportunity to demonstrate that she was no pupil of Minerva.

A series of verbal echoes between books 5 and 6 call our attention to several important differences between Arachne and the Emathides that, despite the similarity of their circumstances, distance the weaver and her strategy from her fellow mortal artists, and contribute to the evolving picture of the artist and artistic strategy in the course of the *Metamorphoses*. There is the matter of background. The Emathides' lineage from the wealthy Pieros (*Pellaeis dives in arvis*) and their (prolonged) birth to Paeonian Euippe are described in some detail (5.302–4), and their land-holdings are extensive (*Emathiis ad Paeonas usque nivosos . . . campis*, 5.313–14).[22] Arachne, by contrast, is the daughter of the wool-dyer Idmon of Colophon and an unnamed woman. The fact that she is famous only by virtue of her art is reiterated three times: *non illa loco nec origine gentis / clara, sed arte fuit*, 'she was famous not for her station/ birthplace or the lineage of her family, but for her art,' 6.7–8; *occiderat mater, sed et haec de plebe suoque / aequa viro fuerat*, 'her mother had died, but she too was of humble origin like her husband,' (6.10–11); *orta domo parva parvis habitabat Hypaepis*, 'born to a humble home, she lived in humble Hypaepa,' 6.13. We wonder what Arachne had in mind when she claimed *nihil est quod victa recusem*, 'There is nothing I would refuse [to give up] if I were defeated' (6.25); her only possession seems to be her skill and reputation, which she will in fact lose. Hypaepa locates Arachne in Lydia and the east, renowned for its fabric artisans and products; her humble class background highlights the significance of her artistic achievement.

We sense that some confidence born of noble birth, then, inspires the Emathides to challenge the Muses, traveling through all of Greece to denounce them: *perque tot Haemonias et per tot Achaidas urbes*, 'through many Haemonian, and just as many Achaean cities,' 5.306. This language is echoed in book 6, referring not to Arachne herself, however, but to her widening celebrity. While Arachne remains in her hometown in Lydia, her *nomen memorabile*, her fame, travels throughout the Lydian cities for her: *Lydas tamen illa per urbes / quaesierat studio nomen memorabile*, 'She nevertheless gained a famous name by her work throughout the cities of Lydia' (6.11–12).[23] And while the Emathides are so offended by the untruthfulness of the Muses' poetry that they challenge the Muses' hegemony over poesis (5.308–9), Arachne is simply offended by the idea that her talent should be attributed to the stewardship of

Minerva, as our narrator claims she must have been: she rashly exclaims to no one in particular, *certet . . . mecum,* 'let her compete with me!' (6.25). The narrator uses the same derogatory adjective, *stolida,* to characterize the victory Arachne seeks (*stolidae cupidine palmae,* 6.50) as was used by the narrating Muse to describe the Emathides themselves in book 5 (*stolidarum turba sororum,* 5.305). Yet Arachne does not throw down the gauntlet herself, nor does she have an explicit ideological or aesthetic complaint. Instead, Minerva seeks out Arachne, looking for vengeance and glory after the story of the poetic competition in book 5. Arachne's position as the recipient of the challenge, rather than the challenger, and the particular form Minerva's challenge assumes—in disguise as an old woman—inspire a theme and an artistic strategy for the mortal weaver's tapestry different from that of her fellow-artists in the book 5 poetic contest. Simulation and dissimulation are the central motifs in both weavers' artworks, each producing, as Leach observes, an *argumentum* in both senses of the word: a story and a (didactic) point of view.[24]

The Woof

As I argued in chapter 1, Ovid's deployment of the ekphrasis to include, on the one hand, verbal artworks, and on the other, a detailed elaboration of the conditions of artistic production and performance, results in a powerful affirmation of the objects so depicted as artworks. In book 5 poetic performance was elevated to the status of artwork in his epic poem, a status it had already achieved in bucolic poetry. In book 6 the same will be achieved for the work of women's hands.

In ancient literature, women's woven artifacts occupy a gray area between craft and artform, and between domestic and public life. On the one hand, the expert weaving and/or embroidering of cloth is a domestic skill highly prized in brides. In *Iliad* 3.125–28 Helen depicts in a tapestry the battles being fought on her behalf; her skill in the technology of weaving is praised at the time of her marriage by the (imaginary) epithalamial choir of Theocritus in *Idylls* 18.12–34. In the *Odyssey* Helen gives to Telemachus the largest and most beautiful robe of her own workmanship on the occasion of his visit to Sparta. Although the robe moves from private to public as a gift, it is intended to be given to Telemachus's bride on her wedding day, when it will re-enter its appropriate domestic realm (*Od.* 15.104–10, 123–29). In the same poem

Penelope's famous weaving of the shroud of Laertes is a striking trope of the poem's central theme, the homecoming of Odysseus; the threads of her loom figuratively bind her to the wandering Odysseus, while they less figuratively hold together her marriage household by deferring a new marriage to one of the suitors (e.g., *Od.* 19.138–55, the shroud of Laertes, ~ 2.93–110 = 24.129–46).[25] In none of these accounts does the tapestry itself receive more description than a few adjectives: ὃς κάλλιστος ἔην ποικίλμασιν ἠδὲ μέγιστος (*Od.* 15.107), ἀστὴρ δ' ὣς ἀπέλαμπεν (*Od.* 15.108), ἠελίῳ ἐναλίγκιον ἠὲ σελήνῃ (*Od.* 24.148), λεπτὸν καὶ περίμετρον (*Od.* 19.140) 'most lovely in its embroidery, and the largest,' 'shining like a star,' 'gleaming like the sun or moon,' 'light and very large.' Their value in these accounts lies in their confirmation of female excellence, and of course chastity, not in their status as artworks. Even in Ovid's *Fasti* 3, Minerva oversees women's woolworking generally rather than a guild of professional female weavers or the like.

The turning point for the representation of weavings in the extant literary record is the Hellenistic period, when not only fabrics but other minor arts gain the status of art and thus a place in literary ekphrasis. Theocritus's *Idylls* 15 is of particular relevance for Ovid's episode, as it stands midway between the two traditions of fabric representation and acts as a bridge between them. The poem's narrative moves from a uniquely domestic setting into the public realm,[26] while female fabric-working moves from a scene of domestic fabric manufacture into a public display of fabric art represented in partial ekphrasis. The protagonists are a pair of engaging, gossipy middle-class housewives, Gorgo and Praxinoa, attending a festival of Aphrodite and Adonis in Alexandria at the palace of Ptolemy II. At the opening of the poem, the two women move from a domestic setting at the house of Praxinoa to the public festival, from Praxinoa's maids busy at their spinning to an ekphrasis of an elegant tapestry. At the palace Gorgo's eye is first caught by an embroidered or otherwise figured tapestry in which Adonis appears (τὰ ποικίλα . . . λεπτὰ καὶ ὡς χαρίεντα, 'embroidered cloths fine and graceful,' 78–79).[27] Invoking Athena, the women appreciate the technical workmanship of the weavers and embroiderers (as only women could, we sense).[28] Only then do they remark upon the figures depicted in the tapestries: 'How realistically they stand and turn around; they are alive, not woven!' (82); the image of Adonis is 'wondrous,' θαητὸς (84). Most striking in its similarity to *Metamorphoses* 5 and 6, the idyll combines this conventional ekphrastic description with a performative ekphrasis of a song, as the women turn their attention to a woman's performance of a hymn to Adonis and Aphrodite, which Theocritus reproduces verbatim (100–144). Praxinoa responds, τὸ χρῆμα σοφώτατον ἁ θήλεια, 'That woman is a creature of exceeding wisdom!' (145, tr. Burton), echoing her similar, though gender-neutral, remark about the weavers of the tapestry in 83. As Burton argues, Theocritus emphasizes gender distinctions throughout this *Idyll;* he also highlights, and then breaks down, the conventional barrier between 'art' and (women's) 'craft.'[29]

Ovid takes a page from Theocritus. As in *Idylls* 15, the book 6 weaving contest is set in a 'real' (human, eastern, urban) rather than a mythical world, and the production of the weavings is contextualized within a human, even female space: Ovid's lengthy description of the τέχνη of weaving corresponds to the admiration of Theocritus's protagonists for the palace tapestry's workmanship. Following the more conventional and elaborate epic/epyllion examples of the *Argonautica* and Catullus 64, however, Ovid provides detailed epic ekphrases of both tapestries. By elaborating with obvious admiration the technical process of setting up the looms, as well as the actual process of artistic creation in the competition, that is, by means of what I have called performative ekphrasis, Ovid shifts the emphasis, as he had in the poetic contest, to the artists and the circumstances surrounding the production of art.

ARACHNE'S WEB

Minerva's visit to Arachne disguised as an old woman will provide the mortal weaver with a starting point for the theme of her tapestry. Anderson views the visit as a variant of the motif of the disregarded warning figure;[30] but such figures, which require of the reader a fundamental respect for divinity, are rare in the secular *Metamorphoses.* I agree with Harries that a closer parallel is to be found in stories of divine visits to mortals, in disguise, to test their faith; the mortals' inevitable failure is followed by a theophany and chastisement at the hands of the god.[31] Harries cites as examples such stories from the *Metamorphoses* as Latona asking for water from the Lycian peasants and turning them into frogs when denied (6.317 ff.), and Jupiter visiting the home of Lycaon and transforming him into a wolf (and flooding the entire earth for good measure) when challenged (1.211 ff.). Closer to Arachne's case, Semele experiences a visit from the jealous Juno, disguised as an old woman (3.273 ff.). Juno is better treated, as she assumes the appearance of Semele's beloved nurse, and does not divulge her identity; she leaves revelation to her philandering husband Jupiter, whose fiery sexual epiphany is fatal to Semele but not her son, Dionysus. Perhaps the most relevant of such tales for the weaving contest is the disguise of Jupiter as a bull to rape Europa (*Met.* 2.833–75), which is depicted at the beginning of Arachne's own tapestry.

Arachne's tapestry will pick up and develop the theme of divine dissimulation with an exploration of some of the most famous stories in Greek mythology, the rapes perpetuated by the gods while in disguise. There is a kinship here with the narrative strategy of the Emathides, who detail the disguises donned by the gods to flee Typhoeus. As the Emathides humiliate the gods by recalling the unseemly animal forms they assumed to make their escape, Arachne's tapestry illustrates Ovid's remark in book 2: *non bene conveniunt nec in una sede morantur / maiestas et amor,* 'majesty and love don't go well together, and can't remain long in the same place' (*Met.* 2.846–47); if we replace *amor* with *pavor,* fear, Ovid's *bon mot* could equally describe the flight of the gods in the song of the Emathides.

But Arachne's tapestry represents a more sophisticated approach to her circumstances than had the song of the Emathides. As the challengers in their rivalry with the Muses, the Emathides had adopted the boldest and most authoritative narrative genre suited to praising the gods (epic gigantomachy), turning it on its head to eulogize the gods' opponents. The Muses no doubt assumed at first that the mortal singers would sing the expected hymnic encomium, but were soon disappointed when they eulogized Typhoeus instead. It was the appropriate genre for success in the circumstances (eulogistic gigantomachy), and its subversion required direct and unmistakable changes in the story: an emphasis on the humiliating transformation of the gods into animals, and omission of the concluding victory of the Olympians.

Although Arachne's narrative strategy is as oblique as the Emathides' was direct, her artwork is just as much a parable of her own circumstances in the contest, and designed just as particularly for her rival's eyes, as was the song of the Emathides. But as the nonaggressor in the weaving contest, tricked into the contest by Minerva's disguise, Arachne depicts not violent challengers impelling the gods to transform, but twenty-one free-standing stories of innocent female victims of gods in disguise, related only by the themes of divine dissembling and rape.[32] Just as Minerva *simulat anum* (6.26) to deceive Arachne, the gods on Arachne's tapestry (including Jupiter in nine examples, Neptune in six, Apollo in four, and Bacchus and Saturn in one each) all adopt disguises drawn from the animal, inanimate, human, and mythical realms to lure their victims into a feeling of safety before they are raped; the headlong flights of Daphne and Io demonstrate the response of mortal women to the sudden appearance of gods who fail to disguise themselves.[33] The language of deliberate deception runs throughout the twenty-five-line ekphrasis (compounds of *ludo*, 103, 113–14, 124; *imagine*, 103, 110, 122; *mutatum*, 115, *fallis*, 117; *deceperit*, 125).

Arachne confronts the issue of dissimulation of the gods by representing their treacherous disguises in the rape episodes, all the while conducting a deliberate dissimulation of her own, employing what Ahl has described in detail as the "figured speech" required of the weak both in Roman society and ancient mythology.[34] Arachne's erotic subject matter is doubly useful for her strategy.[35] It neatly disguises her artwork's representation of her own circumstances with Minerva; her treatment of mortal-victims-of-the-gods is displaced from her own dangerous circumstances, in the realm of art and free expression, onto the realm of the erotic, and from the present into mythical time.

More importantly, the erotic themes of the tapestry could hardly be more insulting to Minerva's hypersensitive chastity. The rape stories on Arachne's web are conventional and familiar Greek myths, represented with some regularity in ancient art. Their shock value for Minerva resides in Arachne's unique visual presentation of the events. Many critics have noted the narrator's observation of the tapestry's realism, and seen it as an indication of its conventional Hellenistic qualities.[36] The narrator exclaims in an apostrophe, *verum taurum, freta vera putares*, 'you'd think the bull and the waves were real' (6.104); midway through his description he again attests to its realism: *omnibus his faciemque suam faciemque locorum / reddidit*, 'She gave each of the characters and places their own actual appearance' (6.121–22). But what is realism in visual representations of the erotic? Realism is the defining feature *par excellence* of the pornographic, distinguishing its explicit presentation of sexual acts from the merely titillating. The realism of the tapestry proclaimed by the narrator of the ekphrasis indicates not only its Hellenistic literary heritage, but its graphic sexuality as well.

A close look at the narrator's description of Arachne's representations of the rapes bears out this reading. The first lines of the ekphrasis establish the overall theme of the tapestry: *Maeonis elusam designat imagine tauri / Europam*, 'The Maeonian [Arachne] pictures Europa, tricked by the appearance of a bull' (6.103–4). The attribution of verisimilitude at 6.104 is then quite modestly inserted here: 'you would think the bull and the waves were real.' Europa, still riding atop Jupiter/the bull as she was at the close of Ovid's account in book 2 (2.873–75), links Arachne's tapestry closely to Ovid's own rape narratives; as in book 2, Europa is pictured turning back to her companions and drawing her feet away from the waters below her. But the next victim in the weaving, Asteria, is pictured in the 'hold' of the 'struggling' eagle (*fecit et Asterien aquila luctante teneri*, 6.108), an allusion to a story otherwise unknown. Adams illustrates the sexual semantic range of *luctor* with the perfectly parallel and unambiguous examples from Propertius 2.1.13 and 2.15.5; the image is further sexualized by the more familiar tale of the rape of the beautiful Ganymede by Jupiter in eagle form.[37] Next, Leda lies beneath the swan (*recubare*, 6.109), a preface to the well-known story of the birth of (depending on the version) Helen, Castor, and Pollux from eggs; the compounds of *-cubare* are most commonly used to denote the sexual act. In the most explicit reference to intercourse in the description thus far, the narrator then reports that Arachne 'added how Jupiter disguised as a satyr was filling Antiope with twin offspring' (*addidit ut . . . inplerit gemino Nycteida fetu*, 6.110). Finally, Jupiter 'was Amphitryon [the husband of Alcmena] when he took you, Alcmena' (*cepit*, 6.112). *Capio* is of course a verb of wide range, but its most common meaning of 'take' or 'capture' is not available in this particular story: Jupiter does not run off with Alcmena or remove her from the premises, but simply slips into her bed in the guise of her husband to impregnate her with Hercules.

With the sexually explicit tone of the ekphrasis established, verbs fall out of the narrative, leaving *luserit* to govern several clauses, with its dual senses of 'deceive' and 'have sex with' fully activated:[38] *aureus ut Danaen, Asopida luserit ignis / Mnemosynen pastor, varius Deoida serpens*, 'as gold [Jupiter] tricked/had sex with Danae, as fire Aegina, as a shepherd, Mnemosyne, as a spotted serpent, the daughter of Deo' (6.113–14). As the narrative turns to Neptune, Arachne's depiction of his encounter with an Aeolian girl is ambiguously described: *te quoque mutatum torvo, Neptune, iuvenco / virgine in Aeolia posuit*, 'She set you changed into a grim bull against/upon/into the Aeolian maiden' (6.115–16). The preposition is difficult to interpret; *in* with the ablative after *pono* normally signifies placing an object in or on something else; it certainly does not denote 'accompaniment,' as most translators render this phrase. The mother of the Aloidae herself disappears as Neptune simply 'begets' his sons (*gignis*, 6.117). The rapes of Ceres, Medusa and Melantho are rendered with a conventional euphemism for penetration, *sensit* (6.119, 120), the mention of Medusa recalling Minerva's severe punishment of the victim of this rape in book 4. By the time we reach Apollo there is no need for either victim or verb; our narrator simply describes his disguises for three of the four rapes, and *luserit* for the last (6.122–24). Saturn's partner is similarly unspecified, as he is simply described as begetting *(crearit)* Chiron disguised as a horse (6.126). The narrator seems to recoil from the tapestry's explicitness as he progresses, his lack of verbs and detail giving the reader an impression of a certain discomfort and avoidance. Even Arachne's botanical border is sexually suggestive: *nexilibus flores hederis habet intertextos,* 'It has flowers interwoven with clinging ivy' (6.128), a common sexual metaphor in which flowers denote the female, and ivy the male.[39]

My reading of Arachne's tapestry suggests that Minerva was confronted by a lovely but disturbingly explicit visual catalog of rapes committed by the Olympian gods.[40] In addition to provoking the virgin goddess with its sexual content, however, the tapestry also exposes to view a fundamental contradiction in Minerva's several Olympian roles: as a protector of virgins and a defender of chastity on the one hand, and as a loyal daughter of Jupiter and Olympian on the other.[41] First, Arachne's catalog of rapes by Jupiter culminates with the image of his rape of *Deoida,* Proserpina (6.114). This rather obscure Orphic story of Jupiter's rape of his own daughter as a snake would scandalize any reader, but especially the virgin daughter of Jupiter, particularly following her approval of Calliope's version of the 'marriage' of Proserpina to Pluto, Jupiter's brother, in book 5.[42] Minerva's role as protector of virgins and Proserpina in particular (at *Met.* 5.375–76, Proserpina is, uniquely in the literary tradition, included by Venus with Minerva among the goddesses who rebel against her authority by choosing a chaste way of life) comes into conflict with her role as the lieutenant of Jupiter. The rape of Medusa and its aftermath, recounted by Perseus in book 4 and frequently recalled by the events of book 5, also makes an appearance on Arachne's tapestry (6.119–20). As discussed above, while Arachne depicts Medusa as the victim of Neptune disguised in the form of a bird, in book 4 we learn that Minerva places the blame on Medusa and transforms her into a snaky-haired Gorgon. In a clever bit of her own mythmaking, Arachne proleptically describes Medusa during the rape as 'snaky-haired' (*crinita colubris,* 6.119), in anticipation of the punishment she will receive from Minerva.

And so Arachne's tapestry unveils the great hypocrisy of Minerva's existence: she is a champion of virgins and virginity in an Olympian hierarchy headed up by rapists. Adolescent virgins like Proserpina and

Medusa fall generally under the care of Minerva, and the stories of their rapes by Jupiter and Neptune are at odds with Minerva's promotion of chastity. The explicitness of Arachne's representations strikes a nerve, and Minerva will not forget it.

MINERVA'S WEB

I have left Minerva for last, although her tapestry is described first in book 6; the anger and didacticism of her tapestry seem to me to respond to the developing content and style of her opponent's work.[43] Ovid's Minerva weaves a web dramatically different from Arachne's, both stylistically and ideologically. Leach has discussed the work's hierarchical and authoritarian aesthetic, in contrast to the "cosmic panorama of shifting forms" of Arachne's.[44] As Anderson characterizes it, "the composition of the goddess' work is flawlessly Classical, perfectly centered, balanced, and framed, highly moral and didactic in content."[45]

But the tapestry should not on this account be dismissed as a typical work of Olympian Minerva. In fact, Ovid's description departs significantly from the only other surviving ancient ekphrasis of Minerva's handiwork, the elaborate cloak of Jason in *Argonautica* 1.721–67. The formal symmetry and blunt ideological message of Minerva's tapestry in book 6 have no parallel in Apollonius's description of the cloak, which lacks any apparent ordering principle or manifest didactic purpose. Its paratactic collection of stories,[46] whose location on the cloak are simply marked by ἐν δὲ or καὶ, and the narrator's claim for its realism (1.766–67), suggest that the cloak's design is much more in the spirit of the tapestry of Ovid's Arachne than of his Minerva;[47] it seems to be recalled only by the narrator's parenthetical remark about Arachne's weaving, 'you could tell she was taught by Pallas' (6.23). I suggest that Ovid playfully refers here more to his reader's (Greek) literary education (i.e., 'you could tell if you'd read your *Argonautica*') than to Arachne's apprenticeship, and to an Athena with a rather more laid-back Hellenistic aesthetic instead of a classicizing Roman Minerva.

So Ovid abandons the scant Hellenistic tradition regarding the artistry of Minerva to suit his greater purpose in the episode. As Rosati has argued, the tapestries of Arachne and Minerva in the *Metamorphoses* represent opposing claims to truths, much like the songs in the poetic contest.[48] Arachne's truth is mortal suffering as a consequence of divine dissimulation, her own included by association. Minerva's truth has two elements. One is her version of the origin of Athens, which Tissol identifies as the 'official' version: "Her views of the story are enforceable and will determine the outcome of the plot. Her power allows her to impose her perspective on events."[49] The other is a statement, like Arachne's, on mortal suffering at the hands of the divine, which in her opinion is well deserved.

Minerva's tapestry has two distinct parts corresponding to her two messages, a main central panel and four corner panels. She first depicts the twelve Olympian gods symmetrically enthroned with Jupiter at the center, *sua quemque deorum inscribit facies,* 'and the actual appearance of each marks each of the gods' (6.73–74). In the case of Jupiter, the *facies* is a *regalis imago* of *augusta gravitate,* 'a royal image of august seriousness,' in a phrase gently aligning the king of the gods with Augustus.[50] The gods are located on the *scopulum Mavortis,* the Areopagus, which is thought by most commentators, taken with *in Cecropia arce,* to be a mistaken reference to the Acropolis. But the Areopagus, in keeping with Minerva's stern justice for Medusa in book 4 and for Arachne here in book 6, evokes Athena's important role as its founder and as a champion of divine justice, famously reported in Aeschylus's *Eumenides,* where she casts the deciding vote against the parental claim of Clytemnestra and womankind generally. The Olympians preside in her tapestry over her competition with Neptune for the stewardship of Athens. Ideologically and aesthetically, the centerpiece of Minerva's tapestry shares elements of Calliope's song in the book 5 poetic contest. It is clearly hymnic in its presentation, an encomiastic portrait of the gods similar to Calliope's Olympians; and the symmetrical arrangement of the gods around Jupiter evokes the harmonious conclusion of Calliope's Proserpina/Ceres myth on Olympus.

The central element of the design, and the most striking, is Minerva's representation of herself, receiving a full five lines of the thirteen devoted to the main panel. Ovid's description of Minerva weaving her own image reinforces an impression of the goddess actually arming herself: *sibi dat clipeum, dat acutae cuspidis hastam, / dat galeam capiti,* 'She gives herself a shield, she gives herself a spear with sharpened point, she gives a helmet to her head' (6.78–79). *Defenditur aegide pectus,* 'her chest is protected by the aegis,' recalls once again the Medusa story. The scene of the central panel concludes with *simulat: percussamque sua simulat de cuspide terram / edere cum bacis fetum canentis olivae,* 'She represents the ground struck with her spear producing a shoot of shining olive, with its fruit' (6.80–81).

Although the contestants weave simultaneously, I interpret Minerva's tapestry as a response to lèse-majesté, to the failure or unwillingness not only of Arachne in book 6, but the impudent Emathides in book 5, to praise the Olympians, and particularly herself. As I discussed in chapter two, the Emathides' subversion of the gigantomachy was not simply a humiliation of the gods generally, but of Minerva in particular, whose role in the victory over the giants was the goddess's greatest moment, at least in the view of her namesake city and its arts. Minerva's tapestry of self-praise suggests that she intended more in her opening *laudemur!* than earning the praise of the Muses; she seems also to expect praise from Arachne's tapestry. Arachne's failure to provide it leaves Minerva no choice but to provide it herself.[51]

From both a literary and a religious perspective, Minerva had every reason to expect a tapestry in praise of herself from the hands of an accomplished young weaver. Each year just such a narrative weaving was manufactured for the statue of Athena Polias by the young girls of Athens, assisted by a crew of more experienced women, the *ergastinai,* to be carried in long procession to the goddess on her birthday on the sixth day of the Panathenaia.[52] This *peplos,* an over-skirt worn over a full-length chiton, is depicted in the hands of the Archon Basileus on the east frieze of the Parthenon, folded up, and in the annual festival it may have been carried in the procession by the weavers themselves.[53] Recent opinion suggests that every fourth year a particularly stunning and much larger version was created by professional male craftsmen.[54] In this much larger procession, the Great Panathenaia, this professionally woven tapestry was stretched like a sail on a mast and rode along its route to the Acropolis on a chariot decked out like a ship. Its subject, like the subject of the weavings offered to Athena at the Lesser Panathenaia, of the eastern metopes of the Parthenon,[55] and of the shield of Phidias's famous statue of Athena,[56] was invariably the gigantomachy, with a particular focus upon the role of Athena. This was the very subject turned on its head by the Emathides in *Metamorphoses* 5.

Athena's *peplos* and its gigantomachic theme were familiar to the Romans; ancient literature regularly refers to it.[57] For example, weaving the Titans into Athena's peplos is among the indignities of slavery in Greece imagined by the Trojan women in Euripides' *Hecuba* (466–70): 'will I in the city of Pallas work into the yellow *peplos* of Athena . . . the Titans, whom Zeus the son of Kronos dispatched?' Plautus knows enough about the Panathenaia and Athena's robe to joke about citizens going to Athens every four years to see it.[58] And while narrative weavings do not play much of a role in Roman religious life, to judge from Ovid's *Fasti* garments appear often enough among offerings to the gods to infer that the concept was familiar.[59] In the visual arts, a Roman sculpture of Minerva, for which a date in the first century BC or AD is not unlikely, features the Gorgon and a striking narrative *peplos* in 'ladder' style depicting pairs of warriors fighting.[60] Thomas discusses the unusual prominence given to a *peplos* in the ekphrasis of the images on the temple of Juno at *Aeneid* 1.479–81.[61] In the center of the ekphrasis the Trojan women are bearing a *peplos* to the temple of *non aequae Palladis,* 'an unfavoring Minerva.' This scene of vain entreaty has its origin in *Iliad* 6.289, where 'the *peploi,* the all-embroidered works [ἔργα] of Sidonian women' are offered to mollify Athena by Hecuba and other Trojan women; the offering is similarly rejected, as Troy is already doomed.

The most striking Roman evidence for the *peplos* as an appropriate vehicle for praise is found in *Ciris* 12–34, a poem most likely of late Augustan or early Imperial date,[62] and addressed to a patron, Valerius Messalla. In its opening *recusatio,* the author decides against honoring Messalla with his own slight verses in favor of 'weaving' him (*intexens, si fas est dicere,* 'weaving, so to speak,' acknowledging the metaphor) into a great *peplos, qualis Erectheis olim portatur Athenis, / debita cum castae solvuntur vota Minervae,* 'such as is carried in Erechthean Athens when the vows owed to chaste Minerva are fulfilled' (21–23). The poet's use of the Panathenaic *peplos* as a metaphor for eulogistic poetic composition is evident in his description of its contents:

ergo Palladiae texuntur in ordine pugnae,
magna Giganteis ornantur pepla tropaeis
horrida sanguineo pinguntur proelia cocco.
additur aurata deiectus cuspide Typhon
qui prius Ossaeis consternens aethera saxis
Emathio celsum duplicabat vertice Olympum.

['Therefore the battles of Pallas are woven in order, the great *peploi* are decorated with trophies of the Giants, and terrible battles are depicted in blood red. Typhoeus is added, thrown down by her golden spear, who formerly doubled the height of Olympus with the Emathian peak as he scaled the heavens on the rocks of Ossa.']

Ciris 29–34

This is no doubt a representation (perhaps several times removed) of the contents of a Panathenaic *peplos.* The *Ciris*'s metaphorical tapestry is not only important for an interpretation of the tapestries in book 6, but also provides a bridge to book 5 by recalling the poetic contest. Minerva is depicted in the battle with Typhoeus, in a conflation of the rebellions of the Giants and of Typhoeus; and Emathia is mentioned in the circumlocution for Mount Pelion, a misnomer without parallel. In any case, the Panathenaic peplos, with its account of Minerva's role in the battles against Olympian pretenders, is clearly associated with the composition of encomiastic poetry.

So Ovid's Roman Minerva has every reason to think Arachne might set the record straight with an encomiastic weaving along the lines of the Panathenaic *peplos*, an improvement upon the Emathides' song in book 5. What she receives instead is an erotic exposé of the hypocrisy of her Olympian existence. Her response is an affirmation of her Olympian authority. While the main panel of her tapestry identifies a more appropriate (encomiastic) subject for Arachne, the four corners, the tapestry's most explicitly authoritarian design elements, identify the punishment due for failing to properly honor the gods. In a moment of intrusion clarifying Minerva's intent, the narrator instructs Arachne, and us, how to read them:[63]

ut tamen exemplis intellegat aemula laudis
quod pretium speret pro tam furialibus ausis
quattuor in partes certamina quattuor addit.

['So that her rival for praise might learn by example what price she could expect to pay for her mad audacity, she adds four contests in the four corners.']

Met. 6.83–85

In each vignette mortals undertake dangerous competitions with the gods; in no case (as far as we can tell) are they artistic competitions. The woven admonitions deliver their threat, but also have the effect of removing art and artistic competition from the picture, and reducing the conflict between Minerva and Arachne to its traditional theological components (hubristic mortal, avenging immortal), leaving behind only the reaffirmed power of the gods and the transformed remains of its discontents.

Outcomes

The punishments of the mortals in both episodes of artistic competition indicate the degree to which their artistic offenses are also considered politically subversive. Arachne's tapestry is styled *caelestia crimina,* with *crimina* operating on two levels. On the one hand, Arachne's crime of exposing divine deceptions so explicitly is compounded by an unveiling of the central contradiction of Minerva's existence, as both the loyal daughter and supporter of Jupiter and the protector of virgins. Secondly, in the more natural sense, the rapes she depicts are themselves *crimina* of the gods. As her revelation of the sexual transformations of the gods mirrors the Emathides' depiction of their cowardly transformations in book 5, so too her punishment will mirror theirs.

Minerva's tapestry counters Arachne's demeaning vision of the gods with an image of Olympus that is harmonious, 'august,' and unchanging in power; in this sense it adopts a strategy similar to that of the Muses in book 5. But while Calliope follows and has the opportunity to undo and erase her rival's damage at the outset of her song, the weavers work simultaneously. Furthermore, while the judges pronounce Calliope the winner in book 5, neither Minerva nor Livor (Envy) can find a flaw in Arachne's tapestry; technically, Arachne has won. Minerva must therefore take extra steps. Grieving at her rival's success (*doluit successu,* 6.130), Minerva tears Arachne's tapestry to shreds, an even more effective 'erasure' of her opponent's art than Calliope had managed. At this crucial moment in the narrative, Minerva's severe virginity is recalled with the rather archaic expression *flava virago,* 6.130, 'the blonde virgin,' which I read as a further affirmation of the sexual explicitness of Arachne's tapestry.

This first punishment is followed by what is certainly the most bizarre transformation in the *Metamorphoses,* which is saying quite a bit; it requires careful dissection. In a scene loaded with references to magical practice,[64] Minerva strikes Arachne with her shuttle 'thrice and four times' (*ter quaterque percussit,* 6.133). The same verb is used to describe Minerva striking the ground in Athens to produce the olive tree (6.80), as well as the weaver's comb 'beating down' the woof on the loom (6.58). It is clearly a verb of choice in describing the crafts of Minerva, both spearcraft and loomcraft, which merge in this final scene as the shuttle is put to violent use in the 'unraveling' of Arachne and her art.

I make free use of the pun here because, with the tapestry now destroyed, Arachne herself seems to become weblike. The unfortunate Arachne 'could not endure it' (*non tulit infelix,* 6.134); it is unclear whether the destruction of her web or the blows to her head are more intolerable, but her response suggests the former. Knowing something of knotting and threads, Arachne hangs herself: *laqueoque animosa ligavit / guttura,* 'she bound her courageous neck in a noose,' with the adjective *animosa* connoting the narrator's opinion of the girl and her suicide, both 'proud' and 'fearless.' Again Minerva 'unravels' Arachne's 'weaving' by cutting her down (*levavit,* 'released,' corresponds to and echoes *ligavit,* 'bound' at line end in 6.134), cutting her suicide short, but transforming her into a spider; her action is described as an act of pity (*Pallas miserata,* 6.135).

The illogicality of this sequence shows some evidence of tampering; that Servius's brief précis (on *G.* 4.247) mentions only the final transformation feeds a suspicion that Ovid has embroidered a more straightforward account. For Minerva to pity Arachne at this moment, and then transform her, seems very much out of, and then back into, character. Short of emending the text of 6.135 (and I have no compelling emendation to offer), and despite the fact that sarcasm is rare in the *Metamorphoses* and an interpretation of last resort, I read *miserata* as mildly sarcastic: such, says Ovid, is the nature of divine 'compassion,' to prevent Arachne's suicide only to transform her into a spider. The adjective has led more than one critic to conclude wrongly that being a spider mustn't have been such a terrible fate; but Leach senses the horror in it,[65] and Feeney provides the necessary citations from Pliny, Seneca and others demonstrating that spiders' webs were a topos of vulnerability and abandonment, were in pattern considered utterly repetitive, and were not deemed 'artistic' by Roman sources.[66]

Roman society offers an additional argument against a literal reading of *miserata.* In Roman society, suicide was—long before Ovid's period, and particularly in political circumstances—a noble death and a citizen's right.[67] The examples of Gaius Gracchus[68] and Cato were legendary; Caesar's cynical *bon mot* on the occasion of Cato's death, recorded in Plutarch's *Sayings of Romans,* could have been uttered by Minerva: φθονῶ σοι Κάτων . . . τοῦ θανάτου, καὶ γὰρ σὺ ἐμοὶ τῆς σῆς σωτηρίας ἐφθόνησας, 'I begrudge you your death, Cato, because you have begrudged me my clemency.'[69] Minerva, unlike Caesar, had the wherewithal to stop Arachne's suicide, but she did so only to make the weaver available for a more degrading punishment. In the Augustan period and beyond, suicide was a way of avoiding a more unseemly punishment or death at the hands of the state (witness the case of Gallus in 27 or 26 BC)[70] and in the time of Claudius, Nero, and Domitian, blocking the suicides of political rivals was a way of denying them a noble death (and saving them for imperial execution).[71]

The two aspects of Arachne's punishment, one artistic and one physical, correspond closely to the dual nature of the punishment of the Emathides in book 5. As the Emathides will chatter and only imitate human speech once transformed into *picae,* Arachne will spin as a spider, but no longer be able to produce art. Both punishments are described with the verb *pendere,* 'hanging:' as they are transformed into birds the Emathides hang in the air, *aere pendebant* (5.676), while Arachne's botched suicide by hanging is explicitly commemorated in her transformation into a spider; Minerva cruelly puns *vive quidem, pende tamen,* 'Live, but hang nonetheless.' The description of Arachne's transformation suggests a further cruelty: a return to her humble beginnings, from which she had traveled so far by means of her talent. *Parva* was used twice to characterize Arachne's modest class background at the outset of the episode: *orta domo parva parvis habitabat Hypaepis* (6.13), 'She sprang from a small home and lived in small Hypaepa.' Her transformation is a return to smallness and obscurity: *fitque caput minimum; toto quoque corpore parva est,* 'her head becomes tiny, and her entire body small' (6.142). Worse, particularly in light of *domo parva* in line 13, Arachne as an orb-weaving spider is returned to the domestic setting in which they thrive, alongside those myriad industrious but largely undistinguished women weavers from whom Arachne strove so passionately to distinguish herself.

4

Songs from Hell

Metamorphoses 10

Introduction

The last strictly mythological episode of Ovid's *Metamorphoses* begins in book 10 with Orpheus, the legendary musician and poet of Thrace, and concludes in book 11 with his demise, followed by a brief account of the fortunes and misfortunes of his pupil, King Midas (of golden touch fame). Thereafter, Ovid directs his poem for the remainder of its course into the realm of human history, as promised in the epic's proem (*ad mea perpetuum deducite tempora carmen*, '[Oh gods,] lead a continuous song down to my own times,' *Met.* 1.4), culminating in two more contemporary, Roman metamorphoses, the catasterism of Julius Caesar and the transformation of his adopted son Octavian into Augustus, the first emperor of Rome. Critics for the most part agree that Orpheus acts as a 'hinge' between the mythic and the historical sections of the poem, but they have rarely reached consensus on why any poet, and particularly this poet, would best provide such a transition.

I suggested in my introduction that Ovid anchors the *Metamorphoses* at its one- and two-thirds points with episodes about artists on a collision course with power, in which he reflects upon the challenges and even dangers of artistic production as he knew it. The songs of Orpheus continue Ovid's exploration of the effects of powerful audiences upon artists and their artistic products begun in the episodes of artistic performance in books 5–6. As we might expect, these episodes share some common features. Structurally, a pair of artistic works by a professional artist (in this case, literary) is again presented verbatim in 'performative ekphrasis,'[1] in which the context and audience are carefully sketched, and the artwork is revealed as it emerges in performance. In addition, the performances of Orpheus themselves evoke the earlier contests in several places. In the opening lines of his second song, for example, Orpheus reminds us that (according to Ovid's genealogy) he is the son of Calliope, the singer for the Muses in the book 5 contest, by invoking her as *Musa parens*.[2] He also conspicuously alludes to the themes of both book 5 songs. In his first song in the underworld Orpheus refers not only to the rape of Proserpina by Pluto per se but especially to its *fama*, its celebrity (10.28), which is most notoriously accomplished in Latin by Calliope's song in *Metamorphoses* 5. He also claims at the opening of his second song, as had many a Roman elegiac and lyric poet before him (including Ovid), that he himself had sung a gigantomachy before turning to lighter subjects; this rebellion of the Giants and Typhoeus against the Olympians was the theme of the mortal Emathides in book 5. And we can't help but feel that Orpheus's second song feels and looks familiar; it not only resembles the *Metamorphoses* generally, as many critics have noted, but the tapestry of Arachne in book 6 in particular, with its meandering composition and highly erotic content. Finally, our last glimpse of Orpheus, or rather his severed head, in book 11, singing something inarticulate and sad, *nescio quid flebile* (*Met.* 11.52), unlike the head of Vergil's Orpheus in *Georgics* 4, which is quite eloquent, powerfully recalls the punishments of both the Emathides and Arachne, fated to retain only the mechanics of their former artistry (voice and weaving) without the ability to create coherent art.

So there is much to link the episodes of artistic performance and encourage their joint consideration. There is also much to distinguish them. Ovid's Orpheus finds himself in quite different circumstances from the artists in books 5–6 and therefore employs different strategies. He is not in competition, for example, with an all-powerful opponent; he instead first makes an appeal to the gods of the underworld, what Pagán has aptly dubbed "speaking before superiors,"[3] then composes quite freely to a complacent audience in Thrace; the audience that will be his undoing is unknown to him, and unseen. Perhaps what most differentiates him from his colleagues in books 5 and 6 is his positive relationship with the gods. The Emathides and Arachne are hated and scorned by the gods (and the feeling is mutual), and so assume a defiant anti-authoritarian posture toward them in both their demeanor and their art. Ovid's Orpheus is on the contrary the child of a Muse and Apollo, although he is clearly not immortal. He praises the rulers of the underworld and the Olympians in his songs and is deeply mourned after his death by the divine Dionysus, who punishes his murderers. While Orpheus comes face to face with the awesome gods of the underworld in his first performance and must contend with them, he does not confront them in his song; in fact, the poet does not challenge the authority or power of the gods at any time, even in the midst of his despair over the loss of Eurydice. This is a position unthinkable to the Emathides or Arachne. Ovid's Orpheus therefore faces rather different artistic challenges and is depicted formulating a noticeably different response to them.

Critical reception of the songs of Orpheus has in general been kind neither to Ovid nor Orpheus.[4] And yet Orpheus's first song, for which Ovid has earned much censure, is the only complete success enjoyed by a performing artist in the epic. This initial achievement, in contrast with Orpheus's ultimate failure, invites a consideration of his artistic strategy. I hope to identify below what it is about these songs and settings that produces outcomes so different from the earlier episodes of performance, and from each other. I will argue that Orpheus's *poesis* is based neither on ethical or aesthetic considerations, as we might expect from the legendary super-*vates* of Greek and Roman mythology, but on a canny appraisal of his audience's power, tastes, and expectations; it is, fundamentally, a political strategy. Segal asks, in response to critical dismissals of Orpheus's first song, "May not Orpheus' 'anti-rhetoric' be the trump card of a master player at rhetoric? . . . Do we witness, through their [the gods of the underworld] eyes, a brilliant dramatic performance of myth's greatest, most persuasive poet?"[5] Segal answers his own question in the affirmative but tempers his reply with more questions, as part of a wholesome unwillingness to reduce the complexity of Ovid's Orpheus to either "insipidity" (so Anderson[6]) or dead seriousness (so Primmer[7]). My approach concurs with Pagán, who has recently argued that the song in the underworld "is not restricted or prohibited, rather, it is inflected by the unequal relation of power that exists between speaker and addressee."[8] When the poet is able to clearly define and identify his audience, the result is success; otherwise, the results are unpredictable, to say the least.

Orpheus *vates*

By the time Orpheus arrived in the pages of Ovid's *Metamorphoses* he was a figure so heavily laden with cultural baggage as to be barely able to stand on his own two feet. Gauging the initial expectations of Ovid's Roman audience when faced with the episode is therefore both less and more difficult than for many figures of Ovidian mythology. Almost without exception, Orpheus is viewed by the Greeks and Romans as the greatest singer of the heroic age. References to him taming wild beasts and inanimate objects with song are frequent in Greek drama,[9] while his song in the underworld is less often mentioned but not unknown.[10] Although Orpheus appears in visual media in Italy as early as the fifth century BC,[11] the performances depicted in book 10 may have made an even greater visual impression upon educated Romans who had traveled as tourists in Greece from Polygnotus's painting of Orpheus in the underworld in the Lesche at Delphi,[12] or the sculpture of Orpheus surrounded by the *theatrum Orphei* at the sanctuary of the Muses on Mount Helicon.[13] A fresco from Nero's *Domus Aurea* showing Orpheus with a stag may recall his second song,[14] while a gold ring with Orpheus in Thracian garb with a group of animals dated by Stern to the first century BC certainly does.[15] Jesnick mentions late Republican reliefs of Orpheus and Eurydice from Mantua and Tarentum, and similar tomb murals in Rome and Ostia.[16] Martial describes an Orpheus fountain complete with animal audience in the Subura (*Epigrams* 10.20[19].6 ff.[17]), which sounds remarkably like a statue found outside the Porta Tiburtina dated to the first century BC.[18] This visual tradition is reflected in Vergil's *Eclogues* 3.46, where Orpheus appears on the rustic cup of Damoetas, leading trees with his lyre. These artworks are typical of representations of the musician whose song had transformative powers over both nature and the underworld; the stories told in book 10 would have been as familiar as folktales to Ovid's contemporaries.

The impact of Orpheus's various religious associations on the expectations of Ovid's audience are more difficult to assess, since the cult of Orpheus does not seem to have observed a festival calendar like the Dionysiac or Eleusinian, and the extent of its influence in Rome is unrecoverable. Certain cult evidence, however, is indisputably relevant to Ovid's episode. The regular association of Orpheus with the Eleusinian mysteries of Ceres and Proserpina (Demeter and Persephone) provides another link between Orpheus and the book 5 contests, where Calliope sings of the rape of Proserpina, the foundational event of the mysteries. Diodorus, for example, in addition to affirming Orpheus's legendary ways with animals, trees, and the underworld, refers to his son Musaeus's priesthood at Eleusis (4.25) and to his training in philosophy and the mysteries in Egypt. In his own *Epistulae Ex Ponto* 3.3.41, Ovid refers to Orpheus's induction of Eumolpus, the eponymous ancestor of the Eumolpidae, into the Eleusinian mysteries. West also notes Orpheus's post-classical associations with the Eleusinian mysteries, in for example the *Rhesus* (943, 966), on the Parian marble, and on a papyrus of the first century BC, which attributes to Orpheus the Homeric *Hymn to Demeter.*[19] Even more intriguing for Ovid's episode is the collection of purportedly Orphic poems circulating in the Augustan era; these might provide a fascinating model for Ovid's unique verbatim presentation of two Orphic songs in book 10. Unfortunately, the extant fragments of Orphic song are of only two types, theogonic hymns and ritual prescriptions, and most had been denounced as forgeries long before Ovid's day.[20] While we see traces of this tradition in, for example, Apollonius's representation of Orpheus's cosmic song in *Argonautica* 1.496–511 (an episode with which Ovid was certainly familiar and which might seem the immediate epic model for Ovid's Orphic performances), Ovid distances his poet from the religious and historical tradition and depicts instead a literary Orpheus singing songs neither theogonic nor prescriptive, conforming to a tendency in Roman literature generally to rationalize the figure of Orpheus to the simpler status of a semi-divine poet/hero.[21]

Discussions of Ovid's Orpheus have therefore naturally turned upon Orpheus's other significant Roman literary appearances, particularly in Vergil. In the *Eclogues,* Vergil explicitly compares the magical power of the song of the tightly bound Silenus over the forces of nature with the music of Orpheus (*Ecl.* 6.27–30). Silenus's cosmological opening bears a resemblance to the description of the cosmogonic song of Orpheus in Apollonius's *Argonautica* 1.496–511;[22] but the bulk of his song is a close cousin of Orpheus's erotic song in *Metamorphoses* 10, and for that matter, the *Metamorphoses* as a whole. The narrator acknowledges the breathtaking range of Silenus's composition: *omnia quae Phoebo quondam meditante beatus / audiit Eurotas . . . ille canit,* 'He sang everything lucky Eurotas once heard Apollo rehearsing' (*Ecl.* 6.82–84), an observation that might be made about Ovid's epic; critics have often sought but never decisively determined a unifying thread for its broad smattering of stories from Greek mythology.[23] The song of Silenus thus combines elements of traditional Orphic cosmogony with a free-wheeling display of erotic storytelling that will characterize the second song of Ovid's Orpheus.

More influential for Ovid's episode overall is the account of the Orpheus myth told by Proteus in *Georgics* 4.453–527, published some thirty years before the *Metamorphoses* was underway. The originality of the Ovidian treatment of Orpheus when compared with this Vergilian counterpart is apparent to everyone who has tackled the episode;[24] as Hill remarks, with a certain degree of overstatement, "Everything that Vergil omits, Ovid dwells upon and everything that Vergil concentrates on, Ovid changes or omits."[25] The most striking difference is Vergil's steady focus upon Orpheus's *amor* for Eurydice and its effects on the poet and the inhabitants of the underworld. The anaphora of *te* in 465–66, the pathetic exclamation *immemor heu!* in 491, Eurydice's five-line speech (494–97), the term *furor* in 495, the pathos of the rhetorical questions in 504–5, Orpheus's long mourning (to 520) including the simile of the nightingale (511–15), and his final triple invocation of his wife's name in 525–27, all situate Vergil's episode in the realm of amatory poetry. The naturalistic setting of the episode evokes pastoral, and the pathos, perhaps romance. Thomas suggests that Proteus's song may imitate the style of Gallus, by way of explaining Servius's erroneous claim that the second half of *Georgics* 4 originally contained praises of Gallus that were replaced at the request of Augustus with the Orpheus epyllion.[26] It could hardly be more different from Ovid's treatment, which is so uniquely concerned with the performances and songs of the legendary poet entirely elided in Vergil's episode.

While critics agree on the existence of a relationship between the two texts, they differ on the point of Ovid's different approach. Leach laments, "If he had kept to the model set by Vergil in the *Georgics,* the musical glory of the singer would have transcended the vicissitudes of his emotional life"; for her, Ovid's goal is to "illuminate the human personality and limitations of the artist."[27] Otis says simply, "Ovid's imitation . . . is clearly meant to amuse."[28] Anderson has discussed the passage twice, finding a bold and shrill "exposure of the mythical marvel, Orpheus" in Ovid's text, forming a negative commentary on Vergil's Orpheus, and a demonstration of the vanity of art in the face of nature.[29] Makowski sees parody and humor, following Neumeister.[30] Segal also ponders the problem twice, and decides upon a mixture of seriousness and defiant parody in Ovid's account, resulting in a "more human Orpheus";[31] ultimately he concludes that a Bloomian "anxiety of influence" renders Ovid and his Orpheus timid and silent in the face of their great predecessors.[32] Pagán hears echoes of Gallus, in her case agreeing with Servius's claim that the praises of Gallus were sung by Vergil at the end of the *Georgics.*[33]

Although there is no question that Ovid's Orpheus must in some degree be a response to Vergil's, I think it is a misunderstanding of both the point and the emphases of Ovid's episode to conclude that his departures from Vergil express anxiety or parody.[34] On the contrary, the careful but carefree tone of Ovid's literary allusions to his predecessors indicates a remarkable *absence* of the literary anxiety so characteristic of earlier Augustan poets; the anxiety that specifically emanates from his exilic works is of course of a particularly nonliterary sort. Ovid's departure from the Vergilian model seems instead to be motivated by a desire to engage with the social issues of his own, later location in the Augustan period, and by a conviction that earlier models are inadequate to address those issues. Ovid is not so interested in Orpheus as lover as he is in Orpheus as poet.

So if not in Vergil, where is Ovid's Orpheus to be found? Perhaps the most interesting contemporary Augustan testimony about Orpheus and his *poesis* is offered by Horace in his influential *Ars Poetica.* In lines 333 and following, Horace argues that poetry should not only be enjoyable (for the *iuniores*) but socially useful (for the *seniores*): *omne tulit punctum qui miscuit utile dulci, / lectorem delectando pariterque monendo,* 'He wins every vote [of the citizens] who mixes the useful with the pleasant, equally delighting and instructing the reader' (*Ars Poetica* 343–44). Orpheus is introduced at 391–93 as a legendary *exemplum* of this ideal of poetic usefulness, as a *sacer interpres . . . deorum,* 'a holy interpreter of the gods' (I believe the 'delightfulness' of his poetry went without saying). Horace reports that Orpheus's poetry discouraged men from bloodshed and the eating of meat, *victu foedo,* 'foul sustenance,' whence, Horace argues, the myth that he tamed wild animals arose. Orpheus is grouped with Amphion, who used his lyre to build the city of Thebes, and Homer and Tyrtaeus, who readied men for war. Horace summarizes that the most virtuous poetry and poets 'earned the honor and name of divine' because they 'separated public and private matters, and sacred and profane' *(publica privatis secernere, sacra profanis);* forbade promiscuity and regulated marriage; built communities, and then fortified them with laws. These qualities were in his view characteristic of the poetry of Orpheus.

A further allusion to the songs of Orpheus in Horace's *Odes* 1.12 suggests a final 'useful' quality of Orphic poetry with implications for his songs in *Metamorphoses* 10. Horace anticipates a song of praise he is composing for Augustus. That it is to be an encomium is unmistakable from its opening: *quem virum aut heroa tibia sumis celebrare, Clio . . . quem deum?* 'What man, hero or god are you taking up your pipes to celebrate, Clio?' (1.12.1–3); the answer will eventually be Augustus

(1.12.49 ff.). In circuitous fashion Horace likens his song-to-be to the song of Orpheus, which enchanted streams, the wind, and trees. This Horatian testimony suggests quite a different Orpheus from the Vergilian, a more civic-minded artist whose music served his community, and indirectly (in *Odes* 1.12) his patron or ruler. Such a moral role represents an entirely different angle on Orpheus, one that takes very seriously his combined literary and religious functions, absent from Vergil's episode with its emphasis on Orpheus as a pastoral love poet.

Surprisingly, it is Horace's moral Orpheus that finds a place in the *Metamorphoses,* whose author is well known for his usual resistance to conventional morality. Horace's separation of public and private is represented in the pair of songs in book 10: the first, a public and encomiastic/hymnic *carmen* in the underworld; the second, addressed to a private audience, with a *leviore lyra,* 'in a lighter strain' (10.152), is erotic, but still didactic in tone. In the final analysis, Orpheus's second, private song fails Horace's standard in its adoption of a homoerotic rather than a heterosexual didactic (*concubitu prohibere vago, dare iura maritis,* 'to forbid casual sex, to give laws for marriage,' *Ars Poetica* 398), a view that is shared in the episode by the Ciconian women. In Ovid's poem, the result is the poet's destruction.

The Performances

Orpheus and his songs are presented in two performance contexts in book 10, not counting the spectacular finale in which his severed head floats down the Hebrus singing 'something mournful or other,' *nescio quid flebile.* The pair of performances represent the two major threads of the Orphic myth in antiquity: Orpheus's musical enchantment first of the underworld, and then of the natural world. Pöschl has suggested that these songs represent two poles of an ideal Roman poetic career, the elegiac and the bucolic;[35] Hofmann agrees that they comprise a kind of literary signal.[36] I would argue that allusions in the episode to Ovid's own oeuvre indicate that Ovid was anxious to attribute to his Orpheus not merely two but virtually all of the poetic genres; far from debunking the myth of the legendary singer, he fortifies it. At 10.149–54, Orpheus opens his second song, delivered in a traditional pastoral setting in the countryside, with a classic Augustan *recusatio.* He recalls that he had already sung about the power of Jupiter on many previous occasions (*Iovis est mihi saepe potestas / dicta prius,* 'the power of Jupiter has often been recounted by me before this'), a conventional allusion to the composition of weighty epic. Now he is turning to a *levior lyra,* 'a lighter theme,' namely amatory poetry.[37] Then in his introduction to the Myrrha tale, Orpheus nearly quotes the *Ars Amatoria,* a poem both elegiac and didactic. Ovid introduced that poem with a warning:

> vera canam: coeptis, mater Amoris, ades!
> este procul, vittae tenues, insigne pudoris
> quaeque tegis medios, instita longa, pedes.
> nos venerem tutam concessaque furta canemus.

['I will sing true things; attend my enterprise, mother of Cupid! But remain distant, slender fillets, those symbols of chastity, and you, the long gown that reaches the middle of the foot. I will sing about legal love, and permissible love affairs.']

Ars Am. 1.30–33

Orpheus echoes him: *dira canam: procul hinc natae, procul este parentes,* 'I will sing terrible things; remain distant, daughters, remain distant, fathers' (*Met.* 10.300). So Orpheus is cast in these examples as a poet, like Ovid, of wide range: epic, elegy, bucolic, and didactic poetry. This literary breadth has the effect of underscoring Orpheus's role as the archetypal poet.

The most strikingly original element of Ovid's episode when considered, not only against Vergil's but against any ancient author's, is not so much the version of the myth it presents, which varies wildly in ancient poetry in any case, but Ovid's full reproduction of the performances of the legendary Orpheus: he directly records Orpheus's song in the underworld for twenty-two lines, and his pastoral idyll for almost six hundred. No ancient author had dared this before. The only other detailed treatment of an Orphic song (apart from the notoriously forged Orphic hymns in circulation since the fifth century BC) is the properly respectful description in *Argonautica* book 1.496–511. There Orpheus sings a stately cosmogony (not verbatim), followed by a libation and sacrifice to Zeus, in keeping with the tradition of Orphic theogony and with Orpheus's role as *vates* or priest.

We are understandably uncomfortable with Ovid's stark unveiling of the great Orpheus's talent; we can't bear the idea that Ovid's two songs are his idea of the world's greatest poetry. I think it is highly unlikely that Ovid introduced these songs at such length and in such detail simply to blacken the name of the great Orpheus; nor did he expect us to ignore one song at the expense of the other. Instead we are presented (as in the other artistic episodes) with Ovid's representation of what a poet like Orpheus would have composed under the circumstances. Herein lies the always-lurking Ovidian dark humor; Ovid's Orpheus becomes a *Roman* poet (of course: composing in Latin) sharing Ovid's own mindset and circumstances. We can appreciate the songs somewhat more if we consider the possibility that the importance of Ovid's Orpheus lies in his role as a human rather than a heroic artist, not for the sake of Vergilian parody, but rather to comment on the life of the artist as Ovid perceives it. Segal observes, "Ovid reduces the narrative to more human and more secular dimensions," but in his view, this is part of a portrayal of Orpheus's emotional life and the (basically negative) role his emotions play in his art.[38] I would reformulate Segal's view in this way: Ovid reduces Orpheus to the dimensions of a mortal artist, facing specific, very human social conditions in which he must create. As in books 5–6, the vulnerability of the artist and the circumstances of performance motivate Ovid's construction of Orpheus's songs, and their ekphrastic presentation underscores their fictive status as Ovidian creations, drawing our attention even more keenly to his bold and original enactment of Orphic song.

Orpheus's human dimensions are evident from the very beginning of book 10, where he is introduced not as the great *vates* of legend but as an ordinary husband, using his voice to call upon Hymenaeus to attend his wedding. After the unfortunate death of his wife, Eurydice, he rather sensibly decides, when his weeping above ground proves ineffective, to try his luck in the underworld, *ad umbras.* Within two brief lines Orpheus is standing before Proserpina and Pluto. The long and arduous trip to the underworld that we have come to expect in heroic accounts of this descent is reduced to, it seems, a simple stroll through the Taenaran gate. Cerberus and most of the other fantastic trappings of the traditional underworld journey are deliberately left aside, with only a single line devoted to its inhabitants, *perque leves populos simulacraque functa sepulcro,* '[traveling] through the insubstantial peoples and the buried ghosts' (10.14).[39] Ovid replaces the traditional otherworldly underworld with a familiar human performance context, the throne room of a great monarch and his queen, *Persephonen adiit inamoenaque regna tenentem / umbrarum dominum* (10.15–16). The importance of this context re-echoes throughout his song (10.17–39).

SIC AIT: THE FIRST SONG

Orpheus strikes his lyre and . . . speaks *(sic ait)* in line 17. This prosaic[40] introduction alerts us to the novelty that lies ahead, although nothing really prepares us for the brief and underwhelming song Orpheus delivers, an emotionally slight suasoria marked by even more than Ovid's usual fondness for rhetorical diction and structure.[41] The song (and a song it is, despite *sic ait*) begins with praise of the king and queen, its tone in general agreement with Hyginus's report in *Astronomica* 2.7 that Orpheus's song praised the *deorum progeniem,* the children of the gods. Orpheus appeals to their awesome power over human life (10.17–18): *o positi sub terra numina mundi / in quem reccidimus, quicquid mortale creamur,* 'O gods of the world beneath the earth, the world to which all mortals return . . .' His polite deference is delicately reiterated in 19 with *si licet* ('if it's alright to say so') and in 20, *si vera loqui sinitis* ('if you'll allow me to speak the truth'), echoing the graciousness of the Muse-narrator in the narrative of the poetic contest in book 5: *sed forsitan otia non sint?* she asks Minerva at 5.333.[42] In both episodes courteousness signals sycophancy, and an imbalance in power, as Pagán argues.[43] Midway in the song stands a flattering allusion to the fame of Proserpina and Pluto's so-called marriage, in another allusion to the poetic contest of book 5:

vicit Amor. supera deus hic bene notus in ora est;
an sit et hic, dubito. sed et hic tamen auguror esse,
famaque si veteris non est mentita rapinae
vos quoque iunxit Amor . . .

['Love has overcome me. Up above he is a well-known god; whether he is here or not I'm unsure, but I'd judge that he is, if the story of the ancient rape is not a lie, and Love joined you two also.']

Met. 10.26–29

These lines have the effect both of recalling the gods' great (and almost only) claim to fame in antiquity, and of slyly suggesting that the underworld first is *(supera* vs. *sed et hic tamen),* and then isn't, such a backwater after all. According to Calliope's song in book 5, the underworld was the kingdom that Venus sought to conquer, the last of the Olympian realms still not under her sway, by engineering the rape of Proserpina: 'You have tamed the gods and Jupiter himself, and the defeated gods of the sea and he who rules them; why does Tartarus not yield? . . . a third of the world is at stake!' (*Met.* 5.369–72). With the successful rape of Proserpina, the kingdom has apparently been won.[44] Orpheus's blandishments gather a head of steam at the close of his song, reiterating the sentiments of its opening:

omnia debemur vobis, paulumque morati
serius aut citius sedem properamus ad unam.

tendimus huc omnes, haec est domus ultima, vosque
humani generis longissima regna tenetis.

['We are in every respect owed to you, and after a brief delay on earth we all, sooner or later, hasten to this one resting place. We all head here; this is our final home, and your rule over the human race is the longest of all.']

Met. 10.32–35

In short, Orpheus devotes twelve of his precious twenty-two lines to flattery of his auditors, fourteen if we include his description of the extent of their great realm in lines 29 and 30; in any case, only seven lines refer directly to his wife Eurydice, and only three describe his feelings for her, two of which appear at the rousing conclusion in lines 38–39: *quodsi fata negant veniam pro coniuge, certum est / nolle redire mihi: leto gaudete duorum,* 'But if the fates deny this courtesy to a husband, be assured, I'm not willing to return (above): take pleasure in the death of two!' The pathos of these few lines of devotion have generally been considered the reason for the overwhelmingly sympathetic reaction of the inhabitants of the underworld to his plea. The responses of the citizens precede and seem to influence the response of the king and queen, *nec . . . sustinet oranti nec . . . negare,* 'who can no longer continue (or endure) to deny the suppliant' (10.46–47).

And so Orpheus's most famous song turns out to be hardly a song after all, but instead a self-consciously encomiastic appeal by an obsequious applicant for the mercy of the court, which merely happens to be set in meter.[45] The song is loaded with platitudes and *sententiae,* reiterating traditional Roman sentiments on life as a mere loan from the underworld. But it particularly echoes the last stanza of Horace's *Odes* 2.3:

omnes eodem cogimur, omnium
versatur urna serius ocius
sors exitura et nos in aeternum
  exilium impositura cumbae.

['We are all driven to the same place, the fate of all will be shaken from the urn sooner or later and will set us on Charon's boat in eternal exile.']

Odes 2.3.25–28

Ovid varies *serius ocius* with the synonymic *serius aut citius,* and *eodem* with *in sedem unam;* he also leaves out the urn, since his Orpheus is interested not in the power of Fate (who selects the to-be-dead by shaking lots out of an urn) but rather in the power of the underworld gods to bring about death—a nice allusion, but of a fairly hackneyed *sententia.*

However tempted we may be to agree with Anderson when he calls the first song of Orpheus "inept," it is nonetheless a mischaracterization. On the contrary, the song produces exactly its desired effect: the underworld's inhabitants are unanimously moved to release Eurydice. Orpheus made the right call about his audience's preferences, whatever we may think of the song aesthetically: his is the only successful artistic performance by a mortal in the *Metamorphoses*.[46]

By incorporating the story of Orpheus in the underworld into the *Metamorphoses*, Ovid created for himself the opportunity of a lifetime: to imagine and present the ancient world's most famous poetic achievement—the triumph of art over death—in his own terms. Why then does he not take it? Because this, Ovid argues, is the sort of song that is demanded by and effective in the real world. The inhabitants of the underworld are no doubt in caricature, the not-very-discerning rulers and denizens of an Olympian backwater. We suspect that a number of Romans lurk behind the portrait, the sort who held poetry readings in their homes with throngs of clients in attendance; the garbled recitations of Homer at the dinner-party of Petronius's Trimalchio, created some sixty years later, come to mind. Orpheus's genius, in Ovid's text, is not so much his poetic ability (although the second song will testify to that) as his rhetorical savvy. He knows exactly what his audience wants: for the gods, praise and recognition (especially for the insecure Pluto, who got the short end of the stick when Olympian kingdoms were being distributed); and for the crowd, romance, brevity (at all costs!), and a pathetic, emotional conclusion. Ovid demonstrates with the pleading of Orpheus what constitutes safe and successful poetry in the presence of the powerful. His vision of the interaction of poetry and power could hardly be more bleak.

As it happens, this song is not the only one performed in the underworld in Augustan poetry, so we have some grounds for comparison. The other appears in Horace's *Odes* 2.13, and I would argue that Ovid had it very much in mind as he conceived Orpheus's underworld song as a performance. As I noted above, Ovid seems already indebted to Horace's second book of *Odes* for the *sententia* of Orpheus regarding the inevitability of death. But unlike the serious 2.3, *Odes* 2.13 begins as one of Horace's truly funny odes, cursing a tree that almost fell on him; it is one I would expect Ovid particularly enjoyed. As he considers his nearly fatal encounter with the tree, Horace anticipates an afterlife of residence in the *sedes discriptas piorum,* the 'apportioned realm of the virtuous,' where we find none other than Sappho and Alcaeus enchanting the underworld with song. Sappho sings of her beloved girls, accompanied by the Aeolian lyre, while Alcaeus's song, described as *plenius*, 'more full,' sings of the evils of sailing, of exile, and of war. Love and war are the complementary themes of Horace's imaginary dead poets' society, and the ode might have ended nicely with this image of their chthonic jam session. But Horace continues into an additional stanza, with an emphasis on audience and reception that I think Ovid found inspirational:

Utrumque sacro digna silentio
mirantur umbrae dicere; sed magis
pugnas et exactos tyrannos
densum umeris bibit aure vulgus.

['The shades are in wonder that each poet speaks things worthy of their reverent silence; but a more dense crowd, packed shoulder to shoulder, drinks in the songs of battle and overthrown tyrants.']

Odes 2.13. 29–32

As Garrison observes in his commentary on the ode, popular taste runs to poetry of war and revolution, even in the underworld.[47] I think Horace's mass audience gave Ovid the idea of casting the underworld as an Orphic audience, a people with its rulers (Ovid calls them the *leves populos* in line 14). Yet in his underworld (mostly likely, as in Ovid's own world) popular taste runs to praise, clever rhetoric, and pathos rather than to the lyrics of Alcaeus.

AUCTOR AMOREM TRANSFERRE: THE SECOND SONG

This line of analysis can be taken a step further, to view Orpheus's second, less successful, performance above ground as a continuation of Ovid's commentary on the dangers of performance, and in particular, on the difficulty of controlling an audience or the effect of one's art upon them. Orpheus's second song is introduced by an announcement of his new role, as an instructor of pederastic love: *ille etiam Thracum populis fuit auctor amorem / in teneros transferre mares*, 'He was the originator, for the people of Thrace, of transferring their affections to still-young males' (10.83–84). I noted above the pointed allusion in lines 300–303 to *Ars Amatoria* 1.30–33, also a didactic poem on illicit love. Orpheus's second song is, however, stylistically more consonant with the rest of the *Metamorphoses* than with the *Ars*, with its loosely connected sequence of amatory myths, as Nagle has observed.[48] Makowski's careful delineation of homoerotic elements in this song is particularly important because this well-known Hellenistic tradition about Orpheus (in Phanocles) is entirely suppressed in *Georgics* 4: Vergil's Orpheus is interested in *nulla Venus,* while Ovid's rejects only *femineam Venerem* (no sex vs. sex with women). Makowski concludes that Orpheus's effeminacy and disregard for Eurydice, in comparison with Vergil's Orpheus, underscore Ovid's rejection of the Vergilian model in the creation of a new, misogynistic, and basically negative Orpheus.[49]

But again the great innovation is not Orpheus's homoeroticism or pederasty, which have a long history, but Ovid's careful presentation of the performance context for the didactic song, and of the song itself in its entirety. This time the model is not the throne room or the law court, but the theater; the term *theatrum* is applied to Orpheus's natural audience (11.22), and when Orpheus is destroyed in book 11 he is likened in a simile to a stag torn apart in the amphitheater, the *structo theatro* (25–28). This image recalls Horace's complaints to Augustus in *Epistles* 2.1, discussed in my introduction, about the theatrical tastes of the Roman audience, who prefer spectacles to poetry readings.

The setting for the song is also pastoral, although, as Hinds points out, missing some key ingredients; his reading of Orpheus's attraction of his traditional enraptured audience of birds, stones, and particularly trees, presented in a lengthy catalogue (10.90–142), as an aetiology of the *locus amoenus* topos, is surely correct.[50] Ahl observes a further distinction from the traditional pastoral setting, that Ovid's Orpheus does not in fact draw the standard Orphic audience of uncomprehending nature, but instead an assembly of very comprehending ex-human beings, now trees, many of whose transformations are detailed in Ovid's poem.[51] Transformed characters in the *Metamorphoses* frequently retain their human cognition beneath their new exteriors; Daphne seems to nod to Apollo as a laurel, and Io is still so human that she takes fright at her own moo, and dislikes the grass she must now eat. The narrative in book 10 is unambiguous on this point. The catalog explicitly refers to the once-human state of several of the trees present for the song: the poplar trees were once the sisters of Phaethon; the virgin laurel tree was recently Daphne; the pool-loving lotus was once Lotus; and Attis had been transformed into a pine tree. The list is crowned by the lengthy digression (thirty-five lines) on the transformation of Cyparissus, beloved of Apollo, into a cypress tree, in grief over the death of a tame stag. The overwhelming impression of Ovid's catalog is of the silenced, transformed characters of the *Metamorphoses* arriving at an open-air summer concert. It is as safe, and as captive, an audience as a poet could imagine.

Such is the docile group that Orpheus will instruct in the ideology of pederasty. He combines the praise of boys and of loving boys (Ganymede with Jupiter, Hyacinthus with Apollo, and Adonis with Venus) with a denunciation of the evils (not all sexual) of various women (the Cerastae, the Propoetides, and Myrrha); these are clustered around the centerpiece of the song, Pygmalion's creation and Venus's animation of the artist's perfect, nameless ivory woman. Orpheus opens this story with an invocation of the Muse, also his mother, which in combination with the hymnic overtones of *ab Iove* situates Orpheus's song in the realm of serious, and I think specifically didactic, poetry; *ab Iove* also occurs in Ovid's *Fasti* 5.111, where it introduces the calends of May with a discourse on the birth of Jupiter. The invocation is followed by a classic elegiac *recusatio* (*Met.* 10.150–51), mentioned above as a demonstration of Orpheus's generic athleticism, which declares the traditional shift from military praise poetry to amatory poetry: *cecini plectro graviore Gigantas / sparsaque Phlegraeis victricia fulmina campis,* 'I have sung in a more serious tone the Giants and victorious thunderbolts of Jupiter scattered on the Phlegrean fields.' In this instance, the shift is from Jupiter's successes in the gigantomachy (another nod to the poetic contest in book 5, where the story forms the theme of the mortal opponents of the Muses) to his sexual success with Ganymede.

It is erotic didacticism, framed at open and close by stories of both homosexual and heterosexual pederasty, rather than personal misogyny, that motivates the themes of Orpheus's song. The love of Venus for Adonis, and of Hippomenes for Atalanta, are obviously heterosexual and turn out badly, but by no particular fault of the females involved. The Cerastae are female monsters, but their crime is not sexual and does not have to do with their gender; they practice human sacrifice and are punished for it. The Propoetides are called *obscenae,* but the adjective is surely proleptic, since their crime is not sexual or gender-related but a *Metamorphoses* commonplace: denying the divinity of a god, in this case Venus, who forces them to become prostitutes, then finally stone. Myrrha's tale is the longest in the book, and brings us back finally to Orpheus's announced *inconcessis ignibus,* disallowed passions. The story has been identified as an example of Orpheus's misogyny, since Myrrha is overcome by an unnatural lust for her father, for which Cupid refuses to take the blame. But the treatment is far from misogynistic: Orpheus accords her thirty-five lines of desperate, suasoria-style soliloquy, and devotes another sixty to her suicide attempt; her passion is only consummated because of the interference of her old nurse seeking to save her life. Orpheus condemns the passion, but not the girl. The only unambiguous misogynist in the episode is Pygmalion, who is disgusted by the prostitution of the Propoetides; but we have just seen that Venus was the cause of this. Orpheus's audience is not a particularly misogynistic crowd, either. Cyparissus transforms for love of a wounded stag; Daphne and Lotus, to escape male pursuers; the Heliades, in grief for their brother Phaethon; only Attis suffers his fate at the instigation of a female, the goddess Cybele.

So neither the song nor its audience has a consistently misogynistic bent; the only theme that seems to structure the song is the love of young boys, by members of both sexes, recalling Ovid's description of Orpheus as the inventor of romancing youths, *amorem / in teneros transferre mares* (*Met.* 10.83–84).[52] I think Ovid has cast Orpheus's leafy *theatrum* as yet another Roman audience, here actually called *turba,* in 106 and 144, replacing the *vulgus* of Horace's ode, both synonyms for 'the masses' in Roman political parlance. But in this case, it is the perfect audience: silent and appreciative. And as in the underworld, Orpheus knows what his audience wants (just as the author of the *Ars* or the *Metamorphoses* knew from experience). Illicit love between the gods (even Venus) and mortals, males and females with boys, racy stories about sculptors having sex with their sculptures (in the original Pygmalion, he is not a sculptor, and has sex with a statue of Venus), sex between fathers and daughters, the seduction of virgins (by both men and boys); this is a list of subjects begging for censorship, but sure to draw a crowd, in almost any society. We sympathize when Ovid complains to Augustus in *Tristia* 2 that he has been unfairly singled out for the *Ars:* isn't all of ancient culture filled with stories about illicit sex, from Homer to Sappho, from Catullus to elegy, from the games Augustus himself had paid for, to the mimes he so enjoyed? Murder, adultery, incest, rape are the stuff of entertainment: why is Ovid alone punished?

Outcomes

But as Ovid will do in his own career, Orpheus tragically miscalculates the nature, or rather the extent, of his audience. There is no doubt that the grove of trees and the other nonhuman auditors are attracted and held by Orpheus's song, much like the audience for Ovid's popular *Ars.* But there are others, listening, whom Orpheus fails to notice. His plea for daughters and fathers to stay away has not been answered, just as Ovid's tongue-in-cheek plea to respectable women in the *Ars* to stay away from that work was ignored: daughters (or rather, daughters-in-law) are lurking nearby. Orpheus's audience abruptly changes at the outset of book 11, when the *nurus Ciconum,* the daughters-in-law of the Cicones, spot Orpheus, their *contemptor,* their mocker, and tear both him and his audience 'limb from limb' (*Met.* 11.50, *membra iacent diversa locis*). Ovid had explained in book 10 that many women grieved over Orpheus's decision to reject the love of women (*multae doluere repulsae,* 10.82). But 'no fury like a woman scorned' is hardly a sufficient explanation for such an elaborate and vicious attack, even if the females in question were crazed maenads. I suggest that although the Ciconian women are not physically present in the audience for Orpheus's second song, the song itself expresses his teachings, his ideology of pederasty and of illicit sexuality in general; all of this scorns their wifely status, which is foregrounded by Ovid with the term *nurus* (11.3). They form, in essence, an audience before and after the fact. Other sources for the myth of the death of Orpheus, particularly Phanocles, with whose account the Vatican Mythographers and Hyginus largely concur, attribute the rage of the Ciconian women to his teaching of homosexual practices among the Thracians: either because the women are scorned by Orpheus himself, as Ovid says, or because he drew their husbands away—the verb in line 84, *transferre,* suggests the latter very decisively. Thus their anger and their attack is in essence an audience response to Orpheus's didactic song.

At first, Orpheus's song is more powerful than the violence of the women, and it magically repulses their weapons in midair. Ultimately, however, Orpheus is drowned out by their loud flutes, drums, and Bacchic howls, to the point, Ovid slyly comments, where they now cannot hear him (*non exauditi . . . vatis,* 11.19): he is already effectively silenced. Nor, we presume, can his audience hear him over the din, for they begin to drift away, absolutely powerless (and unmotivated, once the entertainment is over) to help their poet. This 'silencing' of Orpheus is referred to again at line 40, when for the first time, Ovid says, Orpheus 'speaks in vain,' *inrita dicentem voce,* to beg for his life, *nec quicquam voce moventem,* 'moving them not at all with his voice.' Orpheus did not count on this new hostile, silencing, and unhearing 'audience' for his second song; or perhaps he considered himself safe in the midst of his quiet, appreciative listeners. In any case, he pays for his miscalculation with his life.

The drowning out of Orpheus's song by the Ciconian women leads back one last time to Horace's *Epistles* 2.1, discussed in my introduction, and its allusions to the theater. Horace describes the difficult atmosphere for poetic performance in Rome: 'But what voices have been strong enough to drown out the noise with which our theaters echo?' (2.1.200–201). The noise, of course, comes from the Roman theater crowd, greater in number, but lesser in *virtus* and *honos*, uneducated, stupid, and ready for a fight if the knights argue with them (2.183–85), as they call out *inter carmina* for the bears or the boxers to be brought in. Horace's words for the noise are *sonum* (201) and *strepitu* (203); Ovid adds *ingens clamor* (11.15–16) and *ululatus* (11.17), gathering Horace's terminology into a single neat phrase, *obstrepuere sono* (11.18). Horace urges Augustus to take care for those poets who prefer to entrust themselves to a solitary reader rather than to brave this crowd (2.214–18) if he wishes to fill his new Palatine Library with books; Ovid and his Orpheus would surely agree.

Orpheus's third and final performance takes place in book 11, when his severed head, floating down the Hebrus, mumbles a few indistinct words. For this performance, of course, we and Ovid are the only audience. Many critics note that it is precisely in his death throes that Proteus's Orpheus in *Georgics* 4 finally takes voice and is most moving and pathetic, crying out his wife's name with his dying breath. By contrast, Ovid's Orpheus falls mute, his final words veiled by the poet: *flebile nescio quid queritur lyra, flebile lingua / murmurat exanimis, respondent flebile ripae*, 'his lyre complained sadly, his expired tongue sang something sad, and the river banks echoed his sadness' (11.52–53). Some have seen this as a rationalizing correction to Vergil's talking head. But Ovid's head, like Vergil's, (irrationally) speaks; it just cannot be understood. Others see it as vicious parody of the pathos of the Vergilian original: Segal proposes that the singing head may have been "too much even for his fanciful world."[53] But if Philomela's severed tongue could flap about and seek the feet of its mistress in *Metamorphoses* 6; if, as the veins and entrails of Marsyas quiver in the open air once his skin was flailed away, he could cry out *quid me mihi detrahis*, 'Why are you tearing me from myself?' surely it is not too much for Orpheus's tongue to utter a few more words in conclusion. Ovid's Orpheus is certainly not shy; he is in fact the first Orpheus in ancient literature to speak to his audience in his own voice. Yet here his actual words cannot be determined. And surely it is significant that after his death and reunion with Eurydice in the underworld's *arva piorum*, the fields of the devout (11.61–66), he is again silent; he and his wife walk together, and are free to look back at one another without penalty, but do not speak.

While Vergil's Orpheus finds his voice, tragically, in his final moments, Ovid's Orpheus, like the other transformed artists (and most of the transformed characters) of the *Metamorphoses,* irrevocably loses the ability to communicate. Arachne will weave, but as a spider, not as an artist; the Emathides will imitate human voices as magpies but not sing; Orpheus's head will murmur something sad, but is ultimately inarticulate. This is a peaceful, but certainly not a happy, ending. We are consoled by no Elysian fields, such as Vergil describes in *Aeneid* 6.637 and following, where in the abodes of the blessed Thracian Orpheus is depicted cheerfully accompanying singers and dancers with his lyre. *That* would be 'too much' for Ovid's fanciful, but in so many details realistic, world.

I'd like to take one final step, out of the *Metamorphoses* and into the world of Ovid himself. In *Tristia* 1.7 the poet famously likens his fate in exile to the fate of the transformed characters of the *Metamorphoses:*

> . . . sed carmina maior imago
> sunt mea, quae mando qualiacumque legas
> carmina mutatas hominum dicentia formas,
> infelix domini quod fuga rupit opus.

['My poem, which I ask you to read no matter what its quality, the poem telling the changed forms of human beings, the work which the flight of its unlucky master interrupted, this is a greater image of me.']

Tr. 1.7.11–14

He compares it with the image of the poet on a ring worn by the addressee. This passage is an open invitation to cross the biographical barricades modern literary critics are trained never to breach; we cannot, and must not, resist pursuing Ovid's allusion to his own work.

One Ovidian exile poem catches my attention as particularly Orphic. *Tristia* 3.3, a long poem of eighty-eight lines, is addressed to Ovid's wife, perhaps in 9–10 AD, when they are still on good terms and before he begins to chastise her in, for example, *Epistulae Ex Ponto* 3.1. The poet's mind is wracked by disease and beset with worries, but his foremost thought is of her: *te loquor absentem, te vox mea nominat unam; / nulla venit sine te nox mihi, nulla dies,* 'You I speak to though absent, my voice names you alone; no night comes without you, and no day' (*Tr.* 3.3.17–18). With this address Ovid vividly echoes Vergil's Proteus at *Georgics* 4.465–66, addressing Eurydice in his Orpheus episode:[54] *Te dulcis coniunx, te solo in litore secum / te veniente die, te decedente canebat,* 'You [Eurydice] he sang of, sweet wife, you he sang of on the lonely shore, you at sunrise, you at sunset, too.' The anaphora of *te* appears at the opening and at the primary caesura of the third foot in the first hexameter line of each passage *(te vox / te sol);* while Vergil repeats the pattern of the first hexameter in the second, in Ovid's pentameter *te* is placed at the more emphatic central caesura, with a neat rhyme between *te vox* and *te nox* indicating Ovid's approval of Vergil's *veniente* and *decedente.*

Perhaps we've been looking in the wrong places for echoes of Vergil's Orpheus; perhaps he has gone into exile in the person, specifically the body parts, of Publius Ovidius Naso. Ovid continues in *Tristia* 3.3.21–24, 'If my tongue should fail and were cleaving to my palate [*suppressa lingua palato*], barely able to be recalled by a bit of wine, and someone announced that my *domina* had come, I would rise again,' recalling the *frigida lingua* calling out Eurydice's name in *Georgics* 4.525. He fears a death in exile in Tomis, in terms reminiscent of the heroic warrior's fear of dying at sea, but with a particularly Orphic twist: *sed sine funeribus caput hoc, sine honore sepulcri / indeploratum barbara terra teget!,* 'but without a funeral or honor of a tomb, this head will lie unwept in a barbarian land!' (*Tr.* 3.3.45–46). Although the synecdochic use of *caput* for the whole person or someone's life is allowed in Latin, especially in ritual formulations, in the context of other allusions to the story of Orpheus and Eurydice, this seems a striking recollection of the severed head of Orpheus.

Ovid draws his poem to a close with another lingual reference: his dry tongue allows no further dictation. *Accipe supremo dictum mihi forsitan ore, / quod, tibi qui mittit, non habet ipse, 'vale'* (*Tr.* 3.3.87–88), 'Take what may be my last word, a word which does not hold true for its sender: "Fare-well!"' We are reminded that one of the most striking differences between Ovid's and Vergil's Eurydices are their final words. Vergil's addresses her husband at length: 'What is this great furor that has destroyed miserable me, and you too, Orpheus? So the cruel fates call me back again, and sleep settles over my swimming eyes. So now, farewell; surrounded by a vast night I am carried off, stretching out my weak hands to you, no longer yours!' (*G.* 4.494–98). Ovid's Eurydice, like his Orpheus, is in her final moments more circumspect; unlike Vergil's she, like Ovid in exile, speaks only one word as she falls back into the underworld: 'Fare-well!' (*Vale!, Met.* 10.62). In *Tristia* 3.3 Ovid gives her one last nod, traveling a full circle of allusion from his own Orpheus, backward to Vergil's, and forward to his own sad fate in exile.

5

Ovid Anticipates Exile

Encountering Ovid's stories in the *Metamorphoses* about artists, art, and creativity can be a disheartening experience, issuing as they do from the stylus of one of the most free-spirited and innovative poets of the Augustan age. The dreadful fate of the weaver Philomela, the flaying of the flute-player Marsyas, the demise of Icarus on his father Daedalus's wings: all cast shadows on the epic's typically bright surface. Even Pygmalion's sculptural 'success' in book 10 is disfigured by the narcissistic misogyny and the hint of sexual perversion that motivates his creation of the ideal woman. We can't help but wonder how such a successful and seemingly autonomous artist as Ovid could embrace such a dismal view of the artistic experience.

The same pessimism pervades the episodes of artistic performance discussed in this book, particularly evident in their universally bleak conclusions. These episodes are more contemplative than the poem's other mentions of art and artists, as they explore the dynamics of artistic failure. I have argued in this book that Ovid's innovative 'performative' ekphrases wrap the artworks (which include performed poetry) in their performative or creative contexts, compelling the reader's attention toward the artists at work. Each artist faces a powerful, often divine, audience with a particular set of expectations or desires for the emerging artwork; in each episode the artists adopt a unique strategy to either meet or confound those expectations. The audiences are characterized in one or both of two ways, both of which strike me as very Augustan: by their position of authority, which they are keen to maintain; and/or by their morality, which they are keen to enforce. Ovid depicts the often-violent intersection of power and artistic expression in detailed descriptions of the circumstances leading up to performance, and of the artworks that are their result. He reveals in these longer episodes how and why these artists he seems to admire, despite their various shortcomings, so often meet with failure.

Ovid's artists adopt strategies to contend with the challenges of performance, depending upon the diverse circumstances in which the artists find themselves and to a certain degree upon their own inclinations. The Emathides' condemnation of the aesthetics and ethics of the Muses' poesis, and their challenge to the Muses' hegemony over poetic discourse, is aggressive and direct, and so is their song. The Muses naturally expect praise of the gods from the lips of mortal singers. But while the Emathides oblige them *generically* by singing of the battle between the Olympians and the giants, they boldly subvert the genre *politically* by using it to praise the earth-born insurgents. By keeping the Muse in control of the narrative of the contest, Ovid leaves as an open question what or how the Emathides 'really' sang on that day. Their strategy of confrontation (both physical and literary), however, is clearly identified as a failure; the Emathides neither win the contest nor survive it as artists, and their song is condemned to obscurity.

Apparently it is not only the Emathides who must contend with powerful and influential auditors, however: the song of Calliope is also tailored with an eye to both her original (nymph) and her current (Olympian) audiences. For Minerva, the Muses 'erase' their opponents' humiliation of the gods; and they win over both the virgin goddess and the contest's judges with lengthy sympathetic accounts of the sufferings of accosted nymphs. Their affirmation of their audience's views is a success. With this episode Ovid issues his first lesson: direct confrontation of authority is a losing strategy, and the survival of art and artists relies upon their ability (or willingness) to suit the taste and point of view of their powerful audiences.

And so in book 6 Arachne does not seek out Minerva for a competition, but must be tricked by the disguised goddess into challenging her to a weaving contest. She weaves a parable of her own circumstances: gods in disguise and their victims become the central subject of her tapestry. In what is certainly the most brilliant ekphrasis in Ovid's *Metamorphoses,* Arachne does not dramatically change the (relatively) familiar subjects of her artwork, the gods in pursuit of mortal lovers. Her subversiveness is more subtle: the tapestry is an obscene representation of the rapes *in flagrante,* by a *pornographos* intending to shock the chaste Minerva with its realism. Furthermore, she fails to provide Minerva with the praise she expects; the goddess will have to supply it herself on her own tapestry. Ovid places the poem's narrator in firm control of the episode, and this sympathetic eyewitness provides all-important testimony to the impeccable loveliness of Arachne's tapestry and the injustice of the destruction of both her artistic powers and her artwork. The commemoration of this friendly narrator (and I think we can safely say of Ovid himself, in whose poem the tapestry is preserved) is the only mitigation of Minerva's autocratic destruction of her rival's tapestry. The explicit acknowledgment of the aesthetic superiority of Arachne's tapestry drives home Ovid's second lesson: even great artists, employing subtle tactics in a critique of authority, can and will fail in the face of an all-powerful and disapproving audience.

With the significant figure of Orpheus in book 10 we finally encounter an artist whose artwork is successful, who, far from being punished, is rewarded by the gods for his artistic efforts. Ovid's artists finally seem to be getting the idea that art's effects on powerful audiences must be carefully calculated. His savvy Orpheus's first audience is daunting: Pluto and Proserpina (in a nod to book 5), and the shadowy, insensate inhabitants of their chthonic court. That the artwork created under these circumstances is barely worth saving should not come as a surprise, considered in the framework of the other performance episodes; Orpheus has learned Ovid's lessons well. In order to achieve his goal of regaining Eurydice from death, Orpheus sets aside the poetic skill he will display so vividly later in book 10, and delivers to his royal audience exactly what he determines (accurately) they want to hear: a concise (twenty-three lines), encomiastic and rousingly pathetic entreaty. The aesthetic cost of success for an artist in the face of power is high indeed: and so Orpheus's address to the court of the underworld is reproduced verbatim. Such is Ovid's third lesson.

We are not, however, to be left with the impression that Orpheus has lost his famous talent; the point of the underworld episode would be lost if he were not quickly redeemed as an artist. Out among the rocks and trees who compose his new audience, Orpheus freely sings a wandering and highly entertaining composition about love affairs licit and illicit, hetero- and homosexual, divine and mortal, incestuous and pederastic. The ancient myth about the enchanting effect of Orpheus's song upon extra-human nature becomes in Ovid's poem a fantasy of the perfect audience, self-selected and uncritical; his song is in any case well-suited to many of the assembled trees who were themselves once participants in such love affairs. The singer has unfortunately made a fatal miscalculation. Beyond his apparent audience is a latent one, the Ciconian women, whose husbands Orpheus is said to have led away from love of women to the love of young boys; not only divine audiences possess power over life and death in Ovid's poem. This is Ovid's last lesson: beware the hidden audience. Like his predecessors in the contests and in contrast to Vergil's Orpheus, Ovid's loses his ability to communicate at all; his head, floating downstream, murmurs but cannot be understood, and he remains silent in the underworld when reunited with Eurydice.

The lessons I have drawn from these episodes have a natural home in the late Augustan period, as I have described it in my introduction, and the career of Ovid. As I discussed there, in *Tristia* 2 Ovid distinguishes a 'before' and 'after' of a sort, distancing himself from the poetry of his foolish youth, hoping to convince Augustus that he is a changed poet. He expresses regret for his previously *lasciva Musa: paenitet ingenii iudiciique mei* (2.316), 'I regret my talent and my judgment.' *Iudicium* is usually translated 'taste,' but I think 'judgment' captures it better, in the sense of the lessons of the performance episodes: the young Ovid, feeling invulnerable and cocky from his public success with the *Amores*, made the wrong call about how far he could go, specifically in the *Ars Amatoria.*

I argued above that Ovid connects the rather different fate of Orpheus to his own, in literary rather than thematic terms; through a twisting set of allusions, the Ovid of the exile poems echoes his own Orpheus. In addition, I think we can add that Orpheus's final destruction at the hands of an invisible audience evokes several details of the poet's offenses as outlined by Ovid in *Tristia* 2. First, Ovid reminds Augustus that he explicitly excluded married women from the readership of the *Ars Amatoria* (*Tr.* 2.245–52, re: *Ars Am.* 1.31–34, *este procul, vittae tenues* etc.), yet he is charged with teaching them adultery (2.212). The poet is being punished for moral corruption of an audience he claims he didn't address, a latent audience. In addition, regarding the audience of the emperor himself, Ovid complains that the poem is too trivial to attract his attention (i.e., the poem is not for him), but its most scandalous sections have been read to the prince by one of Ovid's enemies (2.77–80, 219–44): Augustus is another unintended audience that gets him into trouble.

But it is the especially strong resemblance of the punishments of the Emathides and Arachne to the artistic purgatory of Ovid's exile that requires a few words to assess the relevance of the episodes to the poet's life. The Emathides are not completely silenced by the Muses, but lose their poetic ability, condemned to raucously imitate human speech as magpies. Arachne is condemned to weave, without art, as a spider. And

Ovid is relegated to Tomis at the command of the emperor. I have argued that long before Ovid's relegation, the literary world of Rome had changed, and that Ovid found himself in isolation, with few worthy poetic peers and none as daring at innovation and interrogation of the Augustan world. With relegation his books are removed from the public libraries (*Tr.* 2.212), a form of silencing, however ineffective it may have been, and he is condemned to merely complain, and beg, without (in his opinion) his old skills. Ovid ceaselessly laments (in the epilogue to the third book of *Tristia,* the opening of *Tristia* 4, and regularly throughout the *Epistulae Ex Ponto*) that the evils of exile have ruined his talent, both for poetry and for speaking. Ovid and his artists are allowed to live on, as cautionary *exempla* of artistic endeavor that dared too much, but are kept, one way or another, from practicing their art.

In *Tristia* 1.1, Ovid famously compares himself to the transformed characters of the *Metamorphoses,* and tells a friend in *Tristia* 1.7 that the *Metamorphoses* are a *maior imago,* a greater likeness, of Ovid than the likeness of the poet on his ring. Certainly we cannot think that he is comparing himself to the winners in the *Metamorphoses;* and who of the transformed losers are more like the relegated Ovid than the Emathides and Arachne? I conclude that these similarities were not accidental. The horror of the artistic disempowerment suffered by his fictional artists must have been within Ovid's, and the Augustan, imaginative range.

If deliberate, these resemblances would seem to require that the episodes of artistic competition were revised in exile, with the hindsight provided by Ovid's own career-ending experience. Although this may be true, it cannot be conclusively demonstrated, and is not in my view at all necessary. Despite Ovid's protest that the 'lightning bolt' of Augustus that sent him into exile had descended from a clear blue sky (e.g., *Tr.* 1.3.7 ff.), the decline in artistic freedom in the late Augustan period that I posit in my introduction must have begun gradually, perhaps with the death of Maecenas and the last of the great Augustan poets in 8 BC. I have to agree with Jasper Griffin that "the question of compulsion, and of loss of freedom, was vividly present in men's minds in the generation of Caesar. Augustus and the poets his contemporaries will not have been less mindful of it."[1] While we should avoid anachronism in our judgment of Augustus's record on free speech, it is also unreasonable to insist that just a few years prior to Ovid's relegation, the poet and his contemporaries could not even imagine the emperor taking steps to suppress artistic freedom if it challenged his authority. By demoting the Emathides from poets to prattlers, Arachne from weaver extraordinaire to spider, and Orpheus from poet to a murmuring floating head, Ovid vividly expresses an anxiety over an artistic fate-worse-than-death that must have reflected, to some degree, the atmosphere surrounding artistic production at the turn of the millennium, and that in his own case proved well-founded.

But Ovid, even at his most despairing, maintained a remarkably optimistic belief in the power of his own poetry to survive anything and everything. Part of Ovid's purpose, perhaps a large part, in creating the episodes of artistic performance in the *Metamorphoses* was surely commemorative, to preserve, in the form most appropriate to epic poesis, these artists and their artworks; the epic testifies to the power of poetry to rescue artists and their art for a posterity less autocratic or narrow-minded than their own. Ovid makes us painfully aware of the vulnerability of these particular arts (the oral poem, the tapestry): the oral poems are entirely at the mercy of the narrator, who in the poetic contest is the vengeful victorious Muse, while the tapestry of Arachne is torn apart by Minerva before our eyes. Yet, as the poem's *sphragis,* written after Ovid's relegation, explicitly demonstrates (*Met.* 15.871–79), Ovid is openly optimistic about the chances of the survival of his *Metamorphoses,* despite its removal from the public libraries in Rome. We sense that he intended his artists to live on through the survival of his *Metamorphoses,* which he never questions. Why not?

At the close of the *Metamorphoses* Ovid claims that his completed work will survive not only fire, iron, and gnawing time, but (first in the sequence), the *ira Iovis,* the wrath of Jupiter, his metaphor of preference in the exile poems to refer to the heavy hand of Augustus against him. Michael Putnam has thoughtfully observed that while both the *Aeneid* and *Metamorphoses* begin and end with *ira,* "Ovid's poem is victorious . . . in a sense over the *Aeneid* itself, by controlling the emotion Vergil makes finally paramount, and over the anger of Jupiter-Augustus with its power to alter a human life but not to surpass or suppress the enduring product of its imagination."[2] The very presence of the *Metamorphoses* in our modern hands is proof that Ovid's optimism was not misplaced. But what gave him such hope, in the face of the vulnerability of art he portrays so vividly in the *Metamorphoses?* The key, I believe, lies in the penultimate line, and final sentence, of the *sphragis: ore legar populi* (*Met.* 15.878). The expression, following a description of his inevitable death as a mortal, refers literally to the collection of the last breath or words of the deceased by the lips of a survivor: 'I [my soul, my words] will be gathered up by the lips of the people.' It is a simple step for a poet to extend this to indicate the gathering of the poet's final verses; with this shift from breath to poetry, a second meaning of *lego*, 'to read,' is activated. The phrase then becomes 'I will be read by the lips of people (wherever on the conquered earth the power of Rome extends).' *Legar* is an unusual form, in the first person; only Ovid had used it before in this sense (probably in the subjunctive rather than the future), to close *Amores* book 1, in a poem replete with optimism about the survival of written works: *atque a sollicito multus amante legar!* 'And may I be much read by the anxious lover!' He will frequently use it in the exile poetry. In *Tristia* 3.7.51–52 it expresses the same sentiment as the *sphragis* of the *Metamorphoses: dumque suis victrix septem de montibus orbem / prospiciet domitum Martia Roma, legar,* 'and as long as the Rome of Mars looks out on the conquered world from its seven hills, I will be read.' Ovid claims that his wife's fame will continue as long as he is read (*Tr.* 5.14.5): *dumque legar, mecum pariter tua fama legetur,* 'as long as I am read, your fame will also be read of with mine,' as will Cotta's (*Pont.* 3.2.27–30): *meriti . . . gratia vestri . . . superabit tempora vitae, si tamen a memori posteritate legar,* 'My gratitude for your help . . . will exceed my lifetime, if I am read by a mindful posterity.'

Ovid's confidence, I believe, is based upon a technological development recent in Ovid's own lifetime, namely the widening distribution of bookrolls to satisfy the taste for literature in the expanding Roman empire.[3] Against Farrell's argument that the *Metamorphoses* as a performed work is claimed by Ovid to be less vulnerable than, say, the tapestry of Arachne, I think Ovid relies upon the poem's published form, portable far from the prying eyes of the emperor and his readers, to provide longevity to it and his own reputation.[4] No one could have better appreciated the power inherent in separating a poem from the voice and body of its author than the exile in Tomis; exile forces him to adopt the genre designed for negotiating distance between writer and reader, the epistle. The performed song of Ovid's Emathides is scarcely recoverable after the editing of the contest's victors; the song of Ovid's Orpheus, unlike Vergil's, is silenced to an incomprehensible muttering by the violence of the unfavoring mob. After Ovid's exile, it is likely that his own poetry (and certainly the *Ars Amatoria*) only survived in private collections as bookrolls; his exilic works certainly only reached Rome, and posterity, as bookrolls crossing the Mediterranean. Some years before, in the poem with which I opened this book, Horace neatly drew the distinction between performed poems and the poetry book when he entreated Augustus to support those who prefer to write books (*Epist.* 2.1.214–18). On two occasions Horace takes note of a thriving international book trade that he argues could extend the life of a well-known poet.[5] By the time of Martial, booksellers and multiple copies of books of poetry are casually discussed, as a fact of life. Ovid, situated squarely between them, is unafraid in the final lines of the *Metamorphoses* even as his own books are removed from public collections at Rome, for they remain nonetheless in private collections, what Gibson calls "perhaps a more dangerous [i.e., to Augustus] form of reception."[6] Perhaps the power of publication helped him keep writing, despite terrible discouragement, in exile. And perhaps the experience of exile in remote Tomis, where despite the cultural and geographical distance his work and the work of other Latin poets is familiar, convinced him of the power of the written word to transcend time, fire, and the displeasure of the emperor.

Notes

Introduction

1. Barchiesi's joint discussion of these poems, particularly Ovid's construction of Augustus as a rather incompetent reader of poetry, demonstrates that Ovid was quite conscious of his predecessor (Barchiesi, *Speaking Volumes*, 79–103; e.g., *Tr.* 2.337–38 "puts in a nutshell the complex of problems dealt with in the closing of *Ep.* 2.1" (87).

2. Feeney, "*Una cum scriptore meo*," 173. The terms of his description of Horace's literary isolation "as a living classic" (176) in 12 BC are similar to my own of Ovid's less privileged isolation roughly twenty years later.

3. For a full discussion of the role of the *recitatio* in the early empire, as well as thorough bibliography, see Markus, "Performing the Book," 138–79.

4. McNeill marks the beginning of this period in 20 BC; see his discussion of Horace and Ovid in the changed circumstances in "Horace," 131–38.

5. Feeney, "*Una cum scriptore*," 182.

6. W. R. Johnson, *Darkness Visible*, 13. On Ovid he observes, "[This] ironic view of the impermanence of the Augustan formulation could not be precisely formulated until long after Vergil was dead, until Ovid imagined it thoroughly because he had had the unfortunate advantage of living under the completed settlement and had begun to guess what price had been paid for it and would continue to be paid" (137).

7. Wheeler, *A Discourse of Wonders;* Raeburn, *Ovid*.

8. Hardie, *Ovid's Poetics of Illusion*, 177 ff.

9. Hinds, "Generalizing about Ovid," 4.

10. The most recent and thoroughgoing of such responses is the tour-de-force defense of Ovid by Hardie, "Ovid and Early Imperial Literature."

11. Ahl, *Metaformations*.

12. To mention only a few of the most important in this area: Curran, "Rape and Rape Victims in the *Metamorphoses*"; Joplin, "The Voice of the Shuttle Is

Ours"; Janan, "The Book of Good Love?"; Sharrock, "Womanufacture"; Richlin, "Reading Ovid's Rapes"; Segal, "Ovid's Metamorphic Bodies"; Keith, "Versions of Epic Masculinity in Ovid's *Metamorphoses*"; for overview and bibliography see Sharrock, "Gender and Sexuality."

13. A debate often chaired by Galinsky; see *Ovid's* Metamorphoses, chapter 5 (for a pro-, or at least not anti-Augustan reading), which responds primarily to Otis, *Ovid as an Epic Poet;* Segal, "Myth and Philosophy in the *Metamorphoses*"; Curran, "Transformation and Anti-Augustanism"; and Holleman, "Ovid and Politics."

14. An excellent example of the benefits of this approach is Oliensis, "The Power of Image-Makers."

15. Ahl, in "The Rider and the Horse," was one of the first critics to consider Augustan poets together with their "silver age" counterparts.

16. Feeney, *"Si licet et fas est"*; Kennedy, "'Augustan' and 'Anti-Augustan'"; and Hardie, "Augustan Poets and the Mutability of Rome."

17. Sluiter and Rosen, *Free Speech in Classical Antiquity,* especially chapters 15–18: Chrissanthos, "Freedom of Speech and the Roman Republican Army"; Pagán, "Speaking before Superiors"; McHugh, "Historiography and Freedom of Speech"; and Braund, *"Libertas* or *Licentia?* Freedom and Criticism in Roman Satire."

18. This brief tour is of course not exhaustive; on the major issues see the survey by Hinds ("Generalizing about Ovid," n.1), and for recent bibliography see Myers, "The Metamorphosis of a Poet."

19. Galinsky considers the *Metamorphoses* "as Augustan as any literary work of the long and changing period," yet must have recourse to the popularity of pantomime after 22 BC to account for what he calls Ovid's "avoidance of moral problems" in favor of crowd-pleasers like humor and spectacle; Galinsky is grappling, as we all do, with Ovid's range, "from the deeply moving to the hilariously grotesque, with every imaginable shading and tone in between" (*Augustan Culture,* 266). Edmunds, in *Intertextuality and the Reading of Roman Poetry,* similarly argues that Ovid is not anti-Augustan but "countercultural" in his "taste, lifestyle and worldview" (58). But many such "personal" choices became political choices in the Augustan period; the distinction between the cultural and the political is most notoriously blurred in the figure of Maecenas, both patron of the arts and trusted confidant of Augustus. One might also point to the often ideological nature of Augustan art and architecture, as well as the invasion of the world of Roman private behavior by the civic with the *Leges Juliae* of 18 BC.

20. On the genre of the *Heroides* see Knox, *Ovid* Heroides, 14–18, and Lindheim, *Mail and Female,* especially chapter 1. On the authenticity of the double letters, see Kenney, *Ovid* Heroides *XVI–XXI,* 20–26.

21. In the excellent formulation of Barchiesi, *The Poet and the Prince,* "The *Fasti* emerges as the literary heir . . . of two traditions, one of which is closely

associated with the prince and his celebration, while the other (almost on principle) ignores the prince and his achievements. . . . Elegy had cultivated its own autonomous vision of the world by the very fact of having delegated to its opposite number, lofty poetry, the interests of Augustan discourse" (66). See Carole Newlands's sensitive study, *Playing with Time.* On Augustus's temporal interests, see Barchiesi, *The Poet and the Prince,* esp. 69–73.

22. As Richard Tarrant observes, "The *Metamorphoses* most clearly embodies Ovid's global outlook, subsuming all major forms of Greek and Latin literature into a unique and transforming synthesis" ("Ovid and Ancient Literary History," 19).

23. The standard discussions from earlier in the twentieth century are Heinze's 1919 "Ovids elegische Erzählung," and Otis, "Ovid and the Augustans." See bibliography and discussion in Hinds, *Metamorphosis of Persephone,* 99–114.

24. Williams, *Change and Decline,* 52–101.

25. Kenney, "Ovid," 436.

26. For an excellent discussion of the levels of revision of the *Fasti* see Green's introduction, "Textual and Temporal in *Fasti* I: Exile, Revision and the Reader," to *Ovid* Fasti *I,* 15–25.

27. Fantham's discussion of the *Metamorphoses,* in which she depicts a poem marked by the sorts of evasive strategies we might expect in unsettled conditions, is regrettably brief (Fantham, *Roman Literary Culture from Cicero to Apuleius,* 116, 119–20). While Syme provides a useful description of the later principate as the *locus historicus* for Ovid's exile works, he is rarely interested in the unprosopographical *Metamorphoses* (Syme, *Roman Revolution,* 487 ff., and *History in Ovid,* 205–29).

28. Ahl, *Metaformations,* 52.

29. Tarrant, "Ovid and Ancient Literary History," 13, assigns the tragedy to Ovid's first period of composition, but all that can be said for certain is that it predated *Am.* 2.18 and 3.15 (i.e., probably the revised edition of the *Amores*), as well as *Tr.* 2.

30. Williams, *Change and Decline,* 153–92.

31. Williams, *Change and Decline,* 70 ff., identifies "the mark of times of stress" beginning with the *Ars Amatoria.* Otis's view ("Ovid and the Augustans") that Ovid began to produce what the emperor wanted is revised in *Ovid as an Epic Poet,* 323 ff.

32. The phrase is from Hinds, "Generalizing," 29. Studies of the *Fasti* have benefited from the poem's partial location within the timeframe of Ovid's exile, which invites a discourse of distance from the "high" Augustan period and its freedom of expression. Barchiesi implicitly, and once explicitly, acknowledges that the *Metamorphoses* arises in a period very different from the early principate; considering the prayers for Octavian/Augustus that close the *Metamorphoses* and the *Georgics* he writes, "the prayer from the *Georgics* is at least forty

years earlier than the conclusion of the *Metamorphoses*, and it is confusing to speak of an 'Augustan Age'" (Barchiesi, *The Poet and the Prince*, 211). For discussions benefiting from this approach see Fantham, *Ovid Fasti Book IV*; Feeney, "*Si licet et fas est*"; Hinds, "*Arma* in Ovid's *Fasti* Part 2"; and Wallace-Hadrill, "Time for Augustus."

33. Harries, "Causation and the Authority of the Poet," 164–85, esp. 166 and 171.

34. See Barchiesi, *The Poet and the Prince*, esp. chapter 2, "Syntagmatic Tensions," on Harries, and 53–62 on gods (Venus and Mars); on unreliable Augustan narrators, see Newlands, *Playing with Time*, passim.

35. Ahl, *Metaformations*, 86.

36. For an excellent review of the data regarding "the changing circumstances of literature during the final years of Augustus' rule" see Knox, "The Poet and the Second Prince."

37. Fantham, *Roman Literary Culture*, 111, 124–25, on *Controversiae* 10 *praef.* 3–8. Karl Galinsky provides a valuable assessment of the *Metamorphoses* in light of Lucan, Valerius Flaccus, Silius Italicus, and Statius, but I think mischaracterizes the late Augustan period ("Was Ovid a Silver Latin Poet?"). See also *Augustan Culture*, 227.

38. Suetonius *Divus Augustus* 51; Galinsky, *Augustan Culture*, 212–17.

39. For a balanced discussion of the "intellectual opposition" to Augustus, and the politicization of the genre of historiography, see Raaflaub and Samons, "Opposition to Augustus," 436–47.

40. Galinsky, *Augustan Culture*, 79. Syme, *Roman Revolution*, 487 ff.; Syme, *History in Ovid*, 205–29.

41. Syme, *History in Ovid*, 205.

42. Fantham, *Roman Literary Culture*, 114, 126.

43. See Knox, "The Poet and the Second Prince," 4. This argument is attractive, as it tidily maintains the division noted above between good Augustus and bad Tiberius. It is unfortunate that, in the absence of Dio and Tacitus's records for the year 8, it must primarily rest on deductions from the later reign of Tiberius.

44. Feeney, "*Si licet et fas est*," 7, on Galinsky, *Augustan Culture*, 256.

45. Seneca, *Controversiae* 10 *praef.* 5–7, and the discussion in Knox, "The Poet and the Second Prince," 6.

46. Tacitus, *Annales* 1.72.2–3, and Knox, "The Poet and the Second Prince," 6–7.

47. Fantham, *Roman Literary Culture*, 125.

48. For the impact of Gallus on Ovid's imagination, see Pagán, "Speaking before Superiors," 378–84.

49. Fantham, *Roman Literary Culture*, 126.

50. The mention of the defeat of the Sugambri, 4.6.77, dated by Cassius Dio to 16 BC (54.20.6).

51. For his sensitive appreciation of Horace's later work see Putnam, *Artifices of Eternity,* and *Horace's* Carmen Saeculare.

52. Syme, *History in Ovid,* 172. See also McNeill, *Horace,* 131–38.

53. On Ponticus's name and descendants, see Syme, *History in Ovid,* 98 n.2. He is addressed in Propertius 1.7 and 1.9. Propertius dedicated 1.4 to Bassus; Suits argues persuasively that Ovid's and Propertius's iambist Bassus are one and the same ("The Iambic Character of Propertius 1.4").

54. See Duret, "Dans l'ombre des plus grands," on "la génération d'Ovide," and on lists of poets, Tarrant, "Ovid and Ancient Literary History," 15–17.

55. Unmentioned by Ovid, but quoted by him (*Tr.* 4.10.6 = [Tibullus] 3.5.18). There are nearly as many theories about the date and identity of Lygdamus as there are scholars interested in the question; see Butrica, "Lygdamus, Nephew of Messalla?" on a likely identification, and the discussion by Navarro Antolín (*Lygdamus,* 3–20).

56. Syme, *History in Ovid,* 123–25; against Syme, most recently see Jeffreys, "The Date of Messalla's Death." Messalla's only public role after 11 BC was *curator aquarum,* a post of uncertain importance.

57. Knox, "The Poet and the Second Prince," 3–5.

58. Syme, *History in Ovid,* 107–8.

59. See Tarrant, "Ovid and Ancient Literary History," 15 ff., where he calls the list in *Pont.* 4.16 "Ovid's characteristic literary-historical gesture." They are: Domitius Marsus, Rabirius, Pompeius Macer, Albinovanus Pedo, Carus, Cassius Severus, Clutorius (?) Priscus and another Priscus, Numa, Iulius Montanus, Sabinus, Largus, Camerinus, Tuscus, Marius, Trinacrius, Lupus, Tuticanus, Rufus, Turranius, C. Maecenas Melissus, L. Varius Rufus, Sempronius Gracchus, Proculus, Passer, Grattius, Fontanus, and Capella. Tarrant is less kind than Bramble to the cast of characters: "Is Ovid pretending to be impressed by this throng of nonentities?" (31). See the comments of Bramble, "Minor Figures," which includes the *Appendix Vergiliana,* 467–75.

60. Unknown are the second Priscus, Numa, Camerinus, Tuscus, Marius, Trinacrius, Lupus, Turranius, Proculus, Passer, Fontanus, and Capella. Possible or limited identifications have been offered for several others. The first Priscus may be Clutorius, executed for anticipating the death of Drusus in a poem of 21 AD. A Iulius Montanus is called *tolerabilis poeta* in Seneca the Younger *Epistulae* 122.11. Sabinus may be the poet of *Am.* 2.18.15–16 who composed responses to the *Heroides,* but if so is deceased by the late Augustan period. Largus is thought by some to be identified with Valerius Largus, the accuser of Gallus. Rufus is perhaps Titius Rufus of Horace *Epistles* 1.3.9.

61. Seneca the Younger, *Epistulae* 122.15; the fragment appears in Seneca the Elder *Suasoriae* 1.15.

62. Bramble, "Minor Figures," 483, records a *Heracleid* by Carus.

63. Conte, *Latin Literature,* 430.

64. Ibid.

65. Fantham, *Roman Literary Culture,* 122.

66. And, as Hardie observes (*Ovid's Poetics of Illusion,* 303–6), reflected in *Tr.* 5.3.47 ff. (of an unspecified group of poets celebrating a festival of Bacchus), *Pont.* 2.10 (of his literary friendship with Macer), and *Pont.* 3.4.67 ff. *(sunt mihi vobiscum communia sacra, poetae).*

67. Galinsky, *Augustan Culture,* 265–66.

68. I am indebted to Elaine Fantham for recalling this final sense of *tempora,* as used in the title of Cicero's *De temporibus meis* and at *Tr.* 1.9.6, to refer to the fortunes and misfortunes of one's own life.

Chapter 1. Ovid's Artists

1. Art and artists were much less common in Greek drama, but used to great effect. The ekphrasis of the reliefs on the temple of Apollo at Delphi at the opening of Euripides' *Ion,* for example, may have provided a model for descriptions of works of art in Hellenistic pastoral and its Roman descendants; similarly the tapestries from around the world depicted at the play's close may have influenced Theocritus's urban *Id.* 15 and Catullus 64. Zeitlin characterizes dramatic ekphrastic discourse as 'hyperviewing,' a particularly powerful wedding of language and image in the visual context of the theater, which "renders thematic the act of viewing" ("The Artful Eye," 138–45). Zeitlin defines ekphrasis by the identification of its viewers as enchanted spectators, while Goldhill's viewers are critics; ekphrasis is "the moment of looking as interpreting, reading. Seeing meaning" (Goldhill, "The Naive and Knowing Eye," 204).

2. The following examples are not exhaustive, but comprise the most striking instances of plastic arts: Hephaestus's shield of Achilles, *Il.* 18.468–617, and of Heracles in the Hesiodic *Shield of Herakles* 139–317; Daedalus's doors to the Temple of Apollo, *Aen.* 6.14–33; Vulcan's shield of Aeneas, *Aen.* 8.407–53 (manufacture) and 8.626–731 (the shield itself). Works by lesser or unknown craftsmen include Athena's armor, *Il.* 5.738–44, and Agamemnon's, *Il.*11.15–28; Heracles' terrifying sword belt in the underworld, *Od.* 11.609–14, including an apostrophe to the artist; the realistic pin of a hound and a captured fawn, *Od.* 19.226–31, which is decisive if Odysseus is to gain the trust of Penelope when disguised as a beggar; the painted panels on the temple of Juno at *Aen.* 1.441–93 (see Putnam, *Virgil's Epic Design,* chapter 1 and n.2); and, briefly, the armor of Turnus at *Aen.* 7.183–92. Interestingly, the decoration of the sword belt of Pallas, so pivotal for the *Aeneid*'s conclusion, is only obliquely described in 10.496–99.

3. Demodocus, *Od.* 8.62–82, 266–366; the Sirens, *Od.* 12.155–200, *Argon.* 4.891–921; Orpheus, *Argon.* 1.496–511, 1.569–72, and 2.703–10, *G.* 4.453–527, *Aen.* 6.645–47; Iopas, *Aen.* 1.740–46. Outside of epic, there are the bucolic songs of Theocritus and Vergil, but without the heroic element.

4. Helen, *Il.* 3.125–29, *Od.* 15.107–8; Penelope, *Od.* 2.89–110, 19.138–55, 24.125–50; Minerva, *Argon.* 1.721–67; Catullus 64.47–266.

5. Homer's references to the elaborate fabric woven by Helen, which "was loveliest in design and the largest and shone like a star" (*Od.* 15.107–8), and by Penelope, of which he says only that "it shone like the sun or the moon," are tantalizingly brief. All translations of Homer are by Richmond Lattimore: *The Iliad of Homer* (Chicago: University of Chicago Press, 1951) and *The Odyssey of Homer* (New York: Harper & Row, 1967).

6. *Deus et . . . melior natura,* 1.21; *quisquis fuit ille deorum,* 1.32; *mundi fabricator,* 1.57; *opifex rerum, mundi melioris origo,* 1.79. See Solodow, *World of Ovid's* Metamorphoses, 214–15, on these terms; Leach, *The Rhetoric of Space,* 448, argues I think unconvincingly that *opifex* carries negative connotations.

7. As Wheeler has argued *("Imago Mundi").* He notes the vocabulary of artistic materials (105) and follows Feeney's "tantalizingly brief footnote" that the creation reads like an ekphrasis to demonstrate that it is largely modeled upon the ekphrasis of the shield of Achilles in *Il.* 18.483 ff. (*Gods in Epic,* 189 n.4). Lateiner, "Mythic and Non-Mythic Artists," 11–12 and n.51, also notes the vocabulary of artistic creation in the passage, which he argues "sets a moral baseline" for the poem.

8. Primarily through the lens of Arachne's tapestry; Barkan, *Gods Made Flesh,* chapter 1 and p. 3.

9. Cf. Farrell, "Dialogue of Genres in Ovid's 'Lovesong of Polyphemus,'" and Tissol, "Polyphemus and His Audiences," who demonstrates that the passage evokes first Theocritus's nonviolent, then Homer's violent, version of Polyphemus's biography.

10. See Hardie's meditation on metamorphosis, art and viewing ("Perseus' Statue Gallery," in Hardie, *Ovid's Poetics of Illusion,* 178–86). He observes, "Ovid elides fully the gap between ecphrastic image and narrative reality by producing a 'work of art' that *is* the event that it depicts" (179). Even Andromeda looks like a *marmoreum opus* to Perseus the metamorphic sculptor. Lines 5.177 ff. are filled with art-speak: *signum de marmore; ora loqui credas,* an expression often used of realistic art in the *Metamorphoses; armata imago; simulacra;* and the incredible transformation of Phineus into *mansura monimenta per aevum,* a *sponsi imago* for Andromeda to keep in her father's home to recall his *facies obnoxia*!

11. For reasons which will become obvious; see below, chapter 2.

12. Von Albrecht remarks on the significance of the placement of the Arachne episode ("L'Episode d'Arachné," 267), Heckel notes the positioning of the Arachne and Orpheus episodes ("A Genius on Genius," 233), while Farrell appreciates the significance of the placement of all four episodes ("The Ovidian *Corpus,*" 136). See now Habinek's similar conclusions about the relationship of the episodes (*World of Roman Song,* 58–59).

The bibliography on the poem's structure has been reviewed by Barchiesi ("Endgames"), who blames the lack of rigid boundaries in the poem for the lack of critical consensus on its structure. He comments, "There is a profound lack of agreement on the details of Ovid's plan, and on our chances (even on the legitimacy) of reconstructing it" (182), noting the disruption of the poem's chronology "by advances and backtrackings." Wheeler has persuasively distinguished between the implied author and narrator of the poem, the former the author of the book divisions and the latter oblivious of them; in his model, the placement of these episodes would be significant for the author rather than the narrator (*Discourse of Wonders,* 87–93). Feeney undertakes an evaluation of the consideration given to book organization by Latin poets generally *("Mea Tempora").*

13. The poem has largely escaped attempts to impose a restraining orderliness. Otis concluded that the poem must in some sense be a symmetrical whole (*Ovid as an Epic Poet,* chapter 3, "The Plan of Ovid's Epic," esp. 84–85); unfortunately, his categories must become more and more vague to contain Ovid's rambunctious material, and ultimately the content of the episodes and the poet's own emphases become distorted by his classifying lens. Crabbe, in "Structure and Content," reintroduces the relevance of the book divisions, which Wilkinson had abandoned (*Ovid Recalled,* 149). In her proposal for an organization balancing books 1, 8, and 15, Crabbe reminds us (with Galinsky, *Ovid's* Metamorphoses, 80 ff.) that "a *perpetuum carmen* need not be *unum*" (2276). Holzberg has also argued for the pentad division *("Ter quinque volumina* as *carmen perpetuum").* Tissol persuasively argues, "The historical vision of the *Metamorphoses* remains deeply fractured, stubbornly resistant to schematizing, and intentionally incoherent" ("House of Fame," 314).

14. The relationship of the structure of the *Metamorphoses* to universal histories of the day was proposed by Ludwig *(Struktur und Einheit der Metamorphosen Ovids),* but his twelve-part arrangement ignores book divisions, which are clearly significant in both of the passages under discussion here. Nepos's *Chronica* included both mythological and historical material and covered *omne aevum* (so Catullus C. 1.6). Livy's history shows marked division into pentads; the first book is set off as differing in its credibility, with a new preface at the beginning of book 6. On the relationship between the pentad in Livy's *Ab Urbe Condita* and poetry books in the Augustan period, especially the *Aeneid,* see Vasaly, "Structure of Livy's First Pentad." On echoes between the *Metamorphoses* and the *Annales* see the bibliography in Hofmann, "Ovid's *Metamorphoses,*" 224–25 and n.10. It is worth observing the importance of the placement of the song of Orpheus in *Argon.* 1.496–511; see Nelis, "Demodocus and the Song of Orpheus," 153–70, esp. 166.

15. Some rapes successful (Io, Europa, Callisto, Clymene, Semele), some not (Daphne, Syrinx). The consequences are often disruption and grief among mortals (like Phaethon's anxiety over his father's identity, which culminates in the cosmic conflagration in book 2, and the exile of Cadmus from Phoenicia to find his sister Europa in book 3) without the usual mitigating result of heroic progeny, as in, for example, Hesiod's catalogue of women at *Theog.* 970 ff.

16. The *communis opinio* regarding the broad themes of the poem's three pentads, succinctly characterized by Barchiesi, "Endgames," 182 (the gods, the heroes, and the Romans), does not account, for example, for the 'dominant' heroes before book 6.421, particularly Cadmus and Perseus in books 4–5, or for the importance of Dionysus in book 11.

17. It might also be part of Ovid's framing that the first pentad opens with the *opifex mundi* and ends with the poetic contest; the second pentad opens with the weaving contest and closes with Orpheus; the third pentad opens with the death of Orpheus and ends with Augustus, arguably the *opifex* of a new golden age.

18. Lateiner, "Mythic and Non-Mythic Artists," 12, includes Deucalion and Pyrrha, Midas, Narcissus, Niobe, and Polyphemus, each of whom he claims "in his or her own way is an artist."

19. Vincent distinguishes between Minerva and Arachne respectively as 'artist' and mere 'artisan,' and ultimately concludes, "Arachne's paratactic style recalls the compositional principles of pre-literate (or transitional) oral cultures" ("Between Ovid and Barthes," 379).

20. Leach, "Ekphrasis and the Theme of Artistic Failure"; for a sophisticated gendered reading of the passage see Janan, "'There beneath the Roman Ruin.'"

21. *Utile opus manuum vario sermone levemus . . . quod tempora longa videri non sinat,* 'Let's lighten our work with various stories . . . something to make the hours seem shorter' (*Met.* 4.39–41).

22. Echoing the charge of the Emathides that the Muses' songs deceive with 'empty sweetness' (*vana dulcedine, Met.* 5.308); see chapter 2 below.

23. Heckel considers the Emathides in "the class of amateurs and would-be artists" ("Genius on Genius," 232), which case I will argue against below in chapter 2. In the cases of Orpheus and Minerva, Apollonius paraphrases Orpheus's songs at several points (see below) and provides an ekphrasis of Jason's cloak, woven by Minerva, at 1.721–67.

24. The term is indebted to Goldhill's sophisticated reading of several Hellenistic ekphrastic epigrams and Theocritus *Id.* 15, which resemble Ovid's episodes in their reworking of traditional ekphrasis; he refers to *Id.* 15 as "representing the performance of ecphrases" ("Naive and Knowing Eye," 216). Goldhill observes a remarkable reflexivity in the Hellenistic epigrams: "these ecphrastic epigrams represent not merely a work of art but also *the poet as seeing subject*" (205). Ovid occasionally barges into his ekphrases with the second-person singular (see, e.g., *Met.* 6.104, *verum taurum, freta vera putares*) but as Wheeler warns in his close analysis of the narrative levels of the poetic contest (*Discourse of Wonders,* 81 ff.), who is addressing whom can be a dicey question.

25. The description of the lofty home of the gods in book 1.168 ff., and the watery home of Peneus in 568 ff.; the description of the doors of the Palace of the Sun in book 2.1 ff.; the depiction of the House of Sleep in book 11.592 ff.; the

depiction and personification of Rumor at 12.39 ff.; and the cup given to Aeneas at 13.681 ff. have all been identified by one critic or another as ekphrases.

26. I defer the controversial consideration of the poetic works as ekphrases to its proper place later in this chapter.

27. Putnam, *Virgil's Epic Design*, ix.

28. This distinction is reminiscent of Hollander's categories of ekphrasis, the iconic and the poietic ("Poetics of *Ekphrasis*"). The iconic is a straightforward translation from one medium to the other (is there such an ekphrasis in ancient literature?), while the poietic emphasizes process rather than product. All of the ekphrases here would certainly qualify as poietic, although on the change of media see below. Wheeler observes that Ovid's opening creation and the shield of Achilles are shown in the process of creation ("*Imago Mundi*," 106), but does not discuss the numerous other examples in the *Metamorphoses* apart from Arachne, and only mentions the shield of Aeneas in passing (116–17).

29. Putnam reads Daedalus's panels as a "spiritual autobiography" of the artist, culminating in the unraveling of his own labyrinth, and an inability to picture the fall of his son Icarus (*Virgil's Epic Design*, 75 ff.). He argues that the ekphrasis "serves as a paradigm of the Virgilian career" and of the structure of the *Aeneid* itself (82).

30. Similar to the ekphrastic "discourse of viewing" described by Goldhill for Hellenistic poetry: "the mass of epigrams . . . create and police the position of the Hellenistic viewing subject by promoting and projecting a way of viewing the monuments, literature, events, of the past and present" ("Naive and Knowing Eye," 206).

31. Similar to what Hardie describes in the Perseus episode (*Ovid's Poetics of Illusion*, 178–86). See below, chapter 2, on the deliberate suppression of the song of the Emathides.

32. See Genette, "Frontiers of Narrative." The artwork's status as art is typically less important than its status as a visual object, so much so that many ekphrases, particularly in the Hellenistic and Roman periods, are not of artworks at all. Ovid's definition of these artworks as art through ekphrasis participates in a kind of aesthetic economy that decides what is and is not art, often the subject of the work of Pierre Bourdieu (e.g. "The Historical Genesis of a Pure Aesthetic").

33. Lessing might have used this quality of Homer's shield scene to excuse the poet for representing "bodies," which are in his schema more appropriately a subject of painting than of poetry (*Laocoön*, chapter 16); instead he discusses *inter alia* the assembly of Juno's chariot by Hebe in *Il.* 5.722 ff., and the history of the scepter of Agamemnon, *Il.* 2.101 ff. For a clarifying discussion of the history of critical views of ekphrasis with full bibliography, see Fowler, "Narrate and Describe."

34. It is noteworthy that Thetis's visit was immediately preceded by a brief exchange between Zeus and Hera, in which Zeus wryly observes that Hera had managed to rouse Achilles to war (only with the death of his best friend), and

Hera responds that no one else would do any less to accomplish their goal, mortal or divine. Zeus addresses her by the traditional epithet βοῶπις; Hephaestus echoes him with his own epithet for his mother, κυνῶπις, thereby linking the ekphrastic scene to the injustices of the main narrative.

35. See notes and bibliography in Scully, "Refining Fire."

36. Ibid., 106–8.

37. Discussed by Ahl, *Metaformations,* 228 ff.

38. Leach, "Ekphrasis." See also Bartholomé, *Ovid und die antike Kunst.* Note that the image of Orpheus singing his first song in the underworld was a very common visual image in antiquity.

39. Hardie, *Ovid's Poetics of Illusion,* 174.

40. Vincent, "Between Ovid and Barthes," 361–62 and n.3.

41. Heffernan, *Museum of Words,* 192 n.6; see his excellent reading of Arachne's tapestry in Dante's *Purgatorio* canto 12 (51–53).

42. Krieger, *Ekphrasis,* 266. So too Rohde, *Der Griechische Roman.* I prefer a more fluid definition, closer to Mack Smith, *Literary Realism,* which would include any deliberate representation of one artist's work within another's, such as the painting-within-a-painting tradition. He observes that ekphrastic pairs are often presented in realist novels as a way of contrasting "a variety of aesthetic models by which worlds are constructed" (20); this surely has relevance for all three pairs of Ovid's ekphrases.

43. Genette, "Frontiers of Narrative," 134. I am indebted here to the insights of Fowler, "Narrate and Describe."

44. As Knox observes concerning Orpheus's song in the *Argonautica* (*Ovid's* Metamorphoses, 12).

45. And perhaps the *Fasti.* In *Fasti* 4 the Muses are summoned, as the granddaughters of the Dea Magna, to explain her rituals; Erato's lengthier responses (4.197–214, 222–44, 249–348) could be considered songs or poems in pentameters. Similarly, *Fasti* 5 opens with an argument over the origin of the name of May (Maius) between Polyhymnia, Urania, and Calliope (5.11–52, 57–78, 81–106).

46. His confidence is characterized in Quintilian's slur (*Institutio oratoria* 10.88.1): *nimium amator ingenii sui,* 'too enamored of his own talent.'

47. Ovid is likely to have had in mind traditions about legendary or fantastic song contests, such as the probably Hellenistic tradition of a contest between Homer and Hesiod, and real song contests conducted in honor of the Heliconian Muses in Boeotia (on both, see Lamberton, *Hesiod,* 4–11, and "Plutarch, Hesiod and the Mouseia,"491–97). There are several other brief allusions in epic to singers and performances, such as Orpheus's songs about Artemis (*Argon.* 1.569–72) and Apollo (*Argon.* 2.703–13), Iopas in Dido's court in Carthage (*Aen.* 1.740–46), who sings a cosmogony, and Orpheus himself, playing the lyre (and presumably singing) in the underworld (*Aen.* 6.645–47). On the indirect speech of Orpheus's song in the *Argonautica* as a means for Apollonius to maintain control of the narrative, see Hunter, Argonautica *of Apollonius,* 148 ff.

48. Segal, *Orpheus,* 8. It is puzzling to find no mention of this song of Orpheus in Albis, *Poet and Audience,* despite the author's argument that such scenes of performance are part of the poet's strategy "to compensate for the lack of actual social context by recreating it, in an artificial way, within the poetry itself" (5).

49. An aspect that did not escape Vergil; in *Aen.* 1, though encouraged by the distant commemoration of his city, Aeneas responds to the depiction of the war on Juno's temple in Carthage with grief (*constitit et lacrimans,* 1.459).

50. Ovid's ekphrases are not disobedient in this sense; although the tapestries of Minerva and Arachne, and the songs of the Emathides, Muses, and Orpheus are complex, they do not exceed what can be visualized or heard (Laird, "Sounding Out Ecphrasis," 19).

51. See Clausen, *Commentary on Virgil* Eclogues, xv–xx.

52. See Tissol, "Polyphemus and His Audiences," who identifies a combination of Homeric and Theocritean elements in the passage.

53. Segal, *Landscape in Ovid's* Metamorphoses. For a further discussion of the violence in Ovid's other Arcadian settings in the *Metamorphoses* see Segal, "Ovid's Arcadia."

Chapter 2. The Poetic Contest

1. As Wheeler has discussed in detail, the more narrators and narrative levels are multiplied, the less authoritative becomes any single interpretive point of view (*Discourse of Wonders,* 81–84). This becomes particularly important in an evaluation of the narrating Muse's reliability as a narrator. See also Leach, "Ekphrasis," 114–15. Barchiesi identifies the problems created by privileging a single narrator in the episode by playfully contemplating the motives and desires of each of the narrators and audiences ("Narrative Technique,"180–99, esp. 187–95 on the Arethusa subtale).

2. Although she is never mentioned in the account of his battles, our episode begins, *Hactenus aurigenae comitem Tritonia fratri / se dedit,* 'Thus far had Tritonian Minerva accompanied her brother Perseus, born of the golden shower' (5.250–52).

3. Hinds, *Metamorphosis of Persephone,* 3–24. The central role of the Muses and the mountain in the episode, Hinds observes, invites the reader to conclude that the poet is taking this opportunity "to contemplate more obtrusively than elsewhere the nature of his own craft." That craft is construed by Hinds in the context of an ongoing debate current in Roman literary circles of the Augustan period over the relative aesthetic merits of the epic and elegiac genres, a debate born in the Hellenistic period and best known from the literary theorizing of Callimachus. The bibliography on Callimachus and Roman poetry is vast; I refer the reader to the controversial *Callimachus and His Critics* by Alan Cameron for the broader issues and bibliography to that date. On Ovid, see Hinds,

Metamorphosis of Persephone, 19, on the Callimachean aesthetic lurking behind *deducite* at *Metamorphoses* 1.4, and 129–30 on the Callimachean and Roman rejection of the (epic) gigantomachic theme.

4. See Hinds, *Metamorphosis of Persephone,* chapter 2, and more recently, "Landscape with Figures," for a discussion of the ramifications of the similar bucolic setting in Sicily of the rape of Proserpina.

5. Segal's foundational *Landscape in Ovid's Metamorphoses* exhaustively treats the subject of landscapes generally, and the *locus amoenus* in particular (4–30); his brief discussion of the ambivalence of Ovid's landscapes in this episode (53–57) provides the framework for this discussion.

6. For an extended reading of Horace's deployment of the poetic retreat in these poems see Putnam, *Horace's* Carmen Saeculare, chapter 2.

7. In Propertius as in Ovid it is nearly impossible to distinguish between the *locus amoenus* as poetic and erotic setting, e.g. 1.20, on Hylas.

8. Specified in *Ecl.* 5.8, *montibus in nostris.*

9. Especially the amoebaean poems (Theocritus *Id.* 5–6, 8–9, and Vergil *Ecl.* 3, 7, 8).

10. Within the reprise of the earlier contest no description appears, apart from the seats taken by the nymph judges: *factaque de vivo pressere sedilia saxo* (5.317). The Muse does say that the Emathides came to them, *stolidarum turba sororum . . . huc venit* (5.305–7), so it is a safe assumption that the setting for the poetic contest was basically the same as that of Mount Helicon itself.

11. The Muses describe themselves as having *virgineas mentes* later in the passage (5.274). This virginal characterization is very unusual, particularly in a poem in which the various children of the Muses make an appearance; the significance of the Muses as virgins is discussed below. On the 'virginal associations' of bodies of fresh water, often threatened in Ovid's poetry, see Segal, *Landscape in Ovid's Metamorphoses,* 24–33.

12. All but the woods receive a subchapter in Segal, *Landscape in Ovid's Metamorphoses.*

13. E.g., *Ecl.* 7 begins *forte sub arguta consederat ilice Daphnis.* We can compare the rather fuller description of the setting in *Id.* 5.31–34, 45–49, or 9.15–16.

14. Said by Pausanias to have dedicated the first sanctuary to the nine Muses in Thespia (29.3).

15. Tibullus's rustic Priapus so names the Muses in 1.4, but so too, to no apparent end, does the interlocutor in the homoerotic elegy to Marathus, 1.9. A case could easily be made that Propertius uses the patronymic purposefully in the fragmentary poem for Augustus, 2.10. His new subject requires 'new dances on Helicon' and a 'Haemonian [i.e., Thessalian, not Boeotian] steed' (2.10.1–2); he then invokes the Pierides to call for a 'great voice' (*magni . . . oris,* 2.10.12), but to take up a military, not a rural, theme. Horace's only use of the patronymic in *Odes* 4.8.20, of the Muses of Ennius, is a similar context. In the *Fasti* Ovid invokes the Pierides to reveal the rites of Pan (2.269); the patronymic

is used of the Muses in their discussions of Cybele (4.222) and the name of the fifth month in book 5 (5.109); and the Muses who close the *Fasti* with praises of Marcia are invoked as the Pierides, where Clio is specifically named. They are the Muses of non-elegiac poets in *Am.* 1.1.6. and of love poets in *Ars Am.* 3.58.

16. Also true of the legendary contest of Homer and Hesiod (in Evelyn-White, *Hesiod, the Homeric Hymns and Homerica,* 566–97), a text of Hadrianic date but probably conceived in the Hellenistic period, according to Lamberton, as a form of advertisement for the Hellenistic festival of the Heliconian Muses (*Hesiod,* 4–11, and "Plutarch, Hesiod and the Mouseia," 491–97).

17. Coleman, *Vergil,* 226.

18. See below for a fuller discussion of this transition and its significance.

19. As argued by Tissol, "House of Fame," 315.

20. As Segal observes, "Ovid sometimes seems to relish pointing up the deliberate contradictions between the traditional Arcadian-pastoral setting (as handled by Theocritus and Vergil) and his own more violent tales" (*Landscape in Ovid's Metamorphoses,* 77).

21. Hinds, "Landscape with Figures," 130.

22. For a full discussion of Vergil's transformation of standard bucolic settings see Boyle, *Chaonian Dove,* 15–19.

23. On Ovid's transformation of the pastoral landscape, see Segal, *Landscape in Ovid's Metamorphoses,* 74 ff.

24. Hinds, *Metamorphosis of Persephone,* 25–35, and "Landscape with Figures," where he provides an excellent discussion of the literary self-consciousness of Ovid's landscape descriptions generally.

25. Segal, *Landscape in Ovid's Metamorphoses,* 53–57.

26. Otis, *Ovid as an Epic Poet,* 146 ff. remarks upon Ovid's deft connection of the poetic contest with the weaving contest in book 6 through the figure of Minerva, but does not discuss her audience role in book 5. Galinsky mentions the poetological importance of the contrast between Perseus's battlefield and the contest on Helicon but unfortunately does not specify how it might be relevant ("Review"). See Keith's valuable survey of the many allusions to the *Odyssey* and *Aeneid* nestled within the Perseus saga ("Sources and Genres," 240–45).

27. This has been the most popular question posed about the episode: the most influential discussions include Heinze, "Ovids elegische Erzählung," Hinds, *Metamorphosis of Persephone,* and Knox, *Ovid's* Metamorphoses.

28. Hinds, *Metamorphosis of Persephone,* 6–16, discusses this inclusion of Pegasus and argues persuasively that it might indicate reliance upon Aratus's *Phaenomena,* of which Ovid composed a translation in his youth. He identifies a linguistic allusion (Ovid's *pedis ictibus* [5.264] appear in Germanicus's translation of Aratus, 220), and argues that Uranie (5.260 ff.) suggests an astronomical connection. Finally, Aratus's account of the constellation Andromeda directly preceded that of the Horse (Pegasus), just as the Perseus/Andromeda saga precedes Ovid's reference to the Hippocrene.

29. *Fasti* 3.833, as part of the praises of Minerva sung on her birthday; the goddess has so many talents, the narrator says, *certe dea carminis illa est*, 'surely she is the goddess of song.'

30. Hinds, *Metamorphosis of Persephone*, 141 n.62.

31. Similar sentiments are addressed to Augustus by Ovid, *Tr.* 2.219–20: *scilicet imperii princeps statione relicta / imparibus legeres carmina facta modis?*, 'Are you, the leader of our empire, to leave his post to read poems written in elegiac meter?'

32. Pyreneus is identified as an ally of the Thracians who had taken possession of Daulis and Phocis, which traditionally controlled Delphi and the coveted routes into northern Greece. The detail is therefore geographically plausible. Strangely, the Muses respond to a comment about their idyllic lives on Mount Helicon with a complaint about an event at some distance from their home.

33. See Bömer's commentary ad loc., where he is also troubled by the wing-sprouting of the Muses, also nowhere else attested *(P. Ovidius Naso: IV–V).*

34. On the implications of the virginal overtones of the song of Calliope and the contest in general, see below and my earlier discussion (Johnson, "Constructions of Venus").

35. E.g., *Theog.* 11–21, 36–52.

36. A full discussion of the effect of both Minerva and the nymphs as auditors of the Muse's reprise of the songs presented in the contest is discussed below.

37. It is actually Typhoeus who storms Olympus in the lines that follow. Such conflation of the challengers of Jupiter, common enough in Roman sources, reflects the freedom of poets to make creative use of the gigantomachy tradition. In *Aen.* 9.716, for example, Vergil portrays the wicked Typhoeus buried at Jupiter's command under Ischia in the Bay of Naples rather than Aetna in Sicily, thereby placing him among the Latins ranged against Aeneas; Aetna covers the less threatening Enceladus instead. In *Odes* 3.4 Horace tosses every conceivable rebel into a single pot to maximize the threat to Jupiter/Caesar.

38. Hofmann, "Ovid's *Metamorphoses.*"

39. Hinds, *Metamorphosis of Persephone*, 128–33. Yet the Emathides' version of the gigantomachy, with its omission of battle descriptions in favor of the transformations of the gods, makes it peculiarly akin to Ovid's (unepic) practice in the *Fasti* as described by Hinds, "*Arma* in Ovid's *Fasti.*"

40. Rosati rejects the imposition of a "rigid oppositional scheme" in evaluating these artworks ("Narrative Techniques," 293). Anderson briefly raises some of these problems in his rather severe review of Hinds's *Metamorphosis of Persephone* and more recently in his edition and commentary (*Ovid's* Metamorphoses, *Books 1–5*). I don't share his view that programmatic or generic questions are "an entirely artificial problem," of no interest to Ovid. But several key interpretive problems raised at different narrative levels of the episode are left unresolved if we have recourse only to programmatic considerations. There is the obvious methodological problem of associating Ovid with any of his narrators,

Muse or otherwise, much less one appearing in a deeply embedded Hellenistic-style narrative.

41. Almost simultaneously, Barchiesi, "Narrative Technique," 192–93, and Rosati, "Narrative Techniques," 299–301. Similar questions about reliability are raised in *Fasti* 5, where the Muses (Calliope, Polyhymnia, and Urania) offer competing versions of the name of the month of May; see the discussions of Newlands in *Playing with Time* and "Ovid's Narrator in the *Fasti*," and of Myers in *Ovid's Causes.*

42. In addition, one might heed Statius's inclusion of the Emathides as rebellious literary markers in *Silvae* 2.4.19 among the *doctae aves,* 'the learned birds'; see the excellent discussion of Dietrich, "Dead Parrots Society," 99–103.

43. Feeney observes that gigantomachy in ancient literature and art paradigmatically represented "brutish revolt against the order of divine power" (*Gods in Epic,* 119).

44. In the Pythian odes, Pindar regularly identifies his victorious patrons, particularly those in Sicily whose own Mount Aetna was Typhoeus's traditional burial ground, with Zeus as victor over the Giants or Typhoeus. Zeitlin calls Typhon a "master sign" of disorder in his appearance on the shield of the Argive Hippomedon in Aeschylus's *Seven against Thebes* (*Under the Sign of the Shield,* 83–98).

45. Feeney, *Gods in Epic,* 118–19.

46. As described by Ross in *Vergil's Elements,* 74–83.

47. Thomas, *Virgil:* Georgics *Vol. I,* 18.

48. Hardie, *Virgil's* Aeneid.

49. O'Hara, "They Might Be Giants." Some of O'Hara's examples are not convincingly gigantic to my eye: I would not agree, for example, that every use of *ingens* or every mention of men as big as mountains necessarily evokes the battle of Jupiter and the giants. But there remain many convincing examples that suggest a greater degree of ambiguity in Vergil's message than Hardie's argument allows. E.g., book 10.565–70, where Aeneas is likened in a simile to the anti-Olympian Aegaeon, one of the 100-Handeds, unambiguously depicted fighting *against* Jupiter; Aegaeon is everywhere else depicted on the side of the gods, as in *Il.* 1.401–6 and *Theog.* 617 ff., where the 100-Handeds are the allies of Zeus against the Titans, and are called Zeus's φύλακες πιστοί in Hades. Also, Turnus is clearly cast *against* two gigantic opponents, the Trojans Pandarus and Bitias, in *Aen.* 9.706 ff., where he, rather than the Trojans, receives the *fulmen* to fight with, and Typhoeus's defeat is mentioned in the simile describing Bitias's final collapse.

50. The patent identification of Jupiter and Augustus on-the-job is reminiscent of Ovid's identification of the two monarchs in *Met.* 1, leaving aside Ovid's sense of humor.

51. Lyne, *Horace,* 54–55.

52. See Scheid and Svenbro, *Craft of Zeus,* 18 ff., and chapter 3 below, on the importance of Athena's peplos in Roman thought about Minerva.

53. Similar to other interrogated narrators in Ovid's poems, including, for example, the Muses themselves in *Fasti* 5.1–110, where they are referred to, interestingly, as the Pierides (5.109).

54. He repeatedly likens his own punishment by Augustus, for example, to Jupiter's violence against his enemies, functioning both as complements to the nearly divine Augustus and as a disquieting recollection of his absolute power. I count over twenty examples (*Tr.* 1.1.72 and 81–82, 1.3.11, 2.33 ff., 2.143–44, 2.179–80, 3.4.6, 3.5.7, 4.3.69–70, 4.5.5–6, 4.8.46, 5.2.53; *Pont.* 1.2.125–26, 1.7.45–46, 2.2.115–16, 3.2.9–10, 3.6.17–18). See *Tr.* 5.3.29–30, a prayer to Dionysus, where Ovid likens himself to Capaneus of the *Seven against Thebes,* who taunts Zeus and carries a Prometheus-like figure on his shield, a naked man carrying a torch.

55. Seneca, *Controversiae* 10 *praef.* 8; Knox, "The Poet and the Second Prince," 6.

56. Calliope here borrows a page from Ovid, who similarly devised an otherwise unattested myth to link the rape of Callisto by Jupiter to Phaethon's fiery ride between *Met.* 1 and 2. In Ovid's humorous recreation of life at this early stage in human history, these bastard children of the gods and their rape victims belong to the same playgroups. Callisto bears a son, Epaphus, to Jupiter, who torments Phaethon with doubts about his descent from Sol. The resulting visit to his father ends in disaster when Phaethon insists on test-driving his father's car (the chariot of the Sun).

57. Heinze, "Ovids elegische Erzählung"; Hinds, *Metamorphosis of Persephone.*

58. Johnson, "Constructions of Venus."

59. Kannicht, *Euripides,* 342–33, concludes that Aphrodite's appearance in the Euripides ode (*Helena* 1346 ff.) as an independent comforter of Demeter at the time of the rape (she was not sent by Zeus but is introduced by a separate verb, ἔλαβε, 1347) indicates her involvement in the rape of Persephone together with Zeus for which she here makes amends. He cites Pausanias's description of the throne of Apollo at Amyclae (3.19.4) as possible evidence for a very early representation of Aphrodite in this role. It seems clear from Pausanias, however, that grouped as she is with Artemis and Athena leading Hyakinthos to heaven, Aphrodite represents one of Persephone's companions. Kannicht mentions an Italian hydra of the fourth century with the goddess in this role, and Eros alone is involved in the rape on a fifty-century skyphos from Eleusis.

60. In the *Hymn,* the responsibility lies entirely with Zeus, who (presumably as her father) is actively involved in her seduction by Pluto. He is said to have given Persephone to Hades (3, 79–80), to have willed Gaia's creation of the narcissus to seduce Persephone (8–9), and in general to have approved the proceedings (30, 414–15). Helios confirms it, telling Demeter that no other immortal is to blame but Zeus (77–78).

61. Pluto here carries off Proserpina with a speed matched only by Jupiter's rape of Io in *Met.* 1 (*hanc videt et visam patruus velociter aufert,* 'her uncle swiftly

sees and swipes her,' 4.445). When Sol is consulted by Ceres in the *Fasti* he claims that Proserpina has been married to the brother of Jove (*nupta Iovis fratri,* 4.584). Although Jupiter seems to style it a legal marriage (*vincla tori,* 4.602), he takes no responsibility for its planning and execution; Jupiter maintains the same pretense in the *Metamorphoses,* where he calls Pluto a worthy *gener* and styles the seizure romance, not rape (5.525–26). This claim is disputed by the nymph Cyane (*Met.* 5.415–16).

62. See Cahoon, "Bed as Battlefield," for an extensive discussion of the common use of military metaphors for the pursuit of love by the *amator* of the *Amores:* e.g., in *Am.* 1 alone, see 2 (advisability of 'surrender' to Cupid), 6 (elusion of the doorkeeper as a military foray), 7 (the violent lover, ironically, as a general in triumph over a 'worthy' opponent), 11 (all lovers marching beneath the same standards), and 15 (poetic vs. military vocation). The *Met.* 5 passage is distinguished by its shift from metaphoric to literal imperial authority. As reflected in my translation, *domas* is an animal tamer's word often transposed in regular Latin literary usage to military contexts.

63. The irony of Venus's world empire is strengthened by her own reference to the tripartite division of the world, in which Jupiter, Neptune, and Pluto each had to settle for only a third. For the tradition see *Il.* 15.187–93 and Apollodorus *Bibliotheca* 1.2.1.

64. See 1.1.13–15: *sunt tibi magna, puer, nimiumque potentia regna: / cur opus adfectas ambitiose nouum? / an, quod ubique, tuum est? tua sunt Heliconia tempe?* 'Your kingdom is great, boy, and far too powerful: why are you so ambitious for a new venture? or does everything everywhere belong to you, even the grove of Helicon?'

65. Not as anachronistic as it might sound; Cyane protests *non potes invitae Cereris gener esse; roganda / non rapienda fuit,* 'you can't be Ceres' son-in-law without her permission; she should have been courted, not carted off' (*Met.* 5.415–16). Ceres insists, preempting the argument of Jupiter (*sed si modo nomina rebus / addere vera placet, non hoc iniuria factum / verum amor est,* 'If you are willing to give things their proper names, this isn't injury; in fact it's love,' 5.524–26), 'your daughter deserves better than a thief for a husband' (*neque enim praedone marito / filia digna tua est,* 5.521–22).

66. Leach, "Ekphrasis," 102–42, observes the community of sentiment among the audience (nymphs) and the inclusion of Cyane and Arethusa's stories in the song, but does not elaborate; to Zissos the nymphs are partial to "glamorization of their own kind" ("Rape of Proserpina," 98). Segal, *Landscape in Ovid's Metamorphoses,* sees irony (in virgins talking about rape) where I see deliberate manipulation of a traditional story around the figure of Venus to reflect the concerns of the virginal audiences (on both the frame and inset narrative levels, the contest and the recitation) and Ovid's Augustan audience (in the real-world production of the poem in the city of Rome).

67. For the purposes of this episode only. See e.g. *Met.* 10.148, where Orpheus invokes *Musa parens,* presumably Calliope; Apollodorus *Bibliotheca* 1.3.2–4 reports that at least Calliope, Clio, Euterpe, Thalia, and Melpomene bore children.

68. *Pace* Leach, "Ekphrasis," 113, for whom Pyreneus seeks not violence but "poetic inspiration" and "longs for the society of the Muses." As a crude mortal, however, he must fail, and perishes: "such a man must fall on his face." This, of course, from the viewpoint of the Muses. I agree with her note (n. 23) that the passage is vital to the portrait of the Muses here, but as virgins, I think, not distant custodians of poetry. Viarre, *l'Image et la pensée,* 385, records Pyreneus's response among "plusieurs rêves de vol correspondent aux désirs volupteux."

69. Ovid recalls the shame of both Pallas and Juno at Paris's preference for Venus in the famous judgment that began the Trojan War (*Ars Am.* 1.625–26). During the war itself Athena and the other gods have a good chuckle over Diomedes' wounding of Aphrodite, permitted by Athena (*Il.* 5.416–30), and Venus will remember this wound twice in the *Metamorphoses,* by punishing the companions of Diomedes when she gets the chance (14.494 ff.) and during a recollection of her pain and humiliation when she learns of the plot against Julius Caesar (15.769). The duties of Venus and Minerva are of course diametrically opposed throughout antiquity, as described in *Am.* 1.1, where their realms are provided as *exempla* of incompatibility (*arma* vs. *fasces,* 1.1.7–8). As Stephens points out ("Cupid and Venus"), Arachne's tapestry in book 6, depicting as it does the power of Venus and Cupid over the Olympians, seems designed to particularly anger Minerva; this is the premise of chapter 3 below.

70. Those in the *Metamorphoses* who are specifically referred to as *nymphae* of one sort or another are Daphne, Syrinx, and Io in book 1; Callisto and Ocyrhoë in book 2; Liriope and various (willing) nymphs with Jupiter in book 3; Leucothoë in book 4; Lotis and Hesperia in book 9; Galatea and Scylla in book 13; and Pomona (willingly) in book 14. Callisto appears in *Fasti* 2 as well, where Juturna and her sister Lara/Lala join the list.

71. The following discussion is drawn from my article "Constructions of Venus." An argument along similar lines but without the linkage to Venus appears in Zissos, "Rape of Proserpina."

72. Otis, *Ovid as an Epic Poet,* 56–57.

73. Segal, *Landscape in Ovid's Metamorphoses,* 54. Curran, "Rape and Rape Victims," 222, argues that Arethusa is characterizing Cyane's 'violation' at 5.492. I think that *terra . . . patuitque invita rapinae,* 'the unwilling earth opened to the rape,' must literally refer to the rape of Proserpina, not Cyane. Arethusa is begging Ceres not to punish Sicily, as it unwillingly endured the rape. Nonetheless Curran's interpretation at least suggests that the language is ambiguous here.

74. Otis, *Ovid as an Epic Poet,* 57.

75. E.g. *conatoque queri mugitus edidit ore / pertimuitque sonos propriaque exterrita voce est,* 'Trying to complain she mooed, and was startled by the sound and terrified by her own voice,' 1.637–38; *littera pro verbis . . . duxit,* 'Instead of speaking she wrote,' 1.649; *ad mea verba remugis!,* 'You moo your reply to my words!,' 1.657; *metuitque loqui, ne more iuvencae / mugiat, et timide verba intermissa retemptat,* 'She feared to speak, lest she moo like a cow, and timidly tries her unused voice again,' 1.745–46.

76. Io: *coniugis adventum praesenserat inque nitentem / Inachidos vultus mutaverat ille iuvencam,* 'He had sensed the approach of his wife and had changed the face of the daughter of Inachus into a shining cow,' 1.610–11; Philomela: *ille indignantem et nomen patris usque vocantem / luctantemque loqui conprensam forcipe linguam / abstulit ense fero,* 'As she indignantly and repeatedly called out the name of her father, he grasped her tongue struggling to speak with a forceps and cut it out with a sword,' 6.555–57.

77. Segal, *Landscape in Ovid's* Metamorphoses, 55.

78. Curran, "Rape and Rape Victims," 234–35.

79. Hinds, *Metamorphosis of Persephone,* 90–92, 157 n.46.

80. Ibid., 3–24.

81. See Johnson and Malamud, "Ovid's *Musomachia.*" In Antoninus Liberalis's synopsis of an account in Nicander *Heteroeumena* book 4 (*Met.* 9.8–10), the Hippocrene is created as a *result* of the contest; Mount Helicon swells with such pleasure at the sound of the Muses' song that Pegasus must arrest its growth with a kick that opens the spring.

82. *Theog.* 26–28. The mythographic tradition preserves tales about two other poetic challengers of the Muses, Thamyris and the Sirens, that underscore Ovid's departure from the theological emphases of the tradition. Thamyris competed with the Muses in song for their collective hand in marriage; the Muses could collect whatever they wished of his if they triumphed. Thamyris is blinded for his presumption, and in most accounts loses his musical ability like the Emathides. The subject of his song is irrelevant to ancient authors in the face of his hubristic challenge. Accounts of the challenge of the Muses by the Sirens also omit any mention of their theme. Pausanias (9.34.3) reports that they challenged the Muses to a singing contest at the suggestion of Hera and lost. As punishment the Muses plucked out their wings, which they fashioned into crowns for themselves. In no version do they lose their famous ability to sing, although now their talent is employed only to the harm of mankind, as in the *Odyssey* (12.39, 165 ff.) and the *Argonautica* (4.891 ff.).

83. On the distinction between the Muses and the Pierides in Ovid's poetry, see the discussion earlier in this chapter, pages 33–34.

84. *Quod eram Musas, ut crimina nostra, perosus,* 'because I hated the Muses like/as my own crimes,' *Tr.* 1.7.21; echoed by *cur modo damnatas repeto, mea crimina, Musas?,* 'why do I seek out my already-condemned Muses, my crimes?' 2.3; *Musaque quam movit motam quoque leniet iram,* 'The Muse who provoked

anger will also quiet it,' 2.21; *(ego) quem sua perdiderit Musa;* 'I whom my own Muse destroyed,' 2.496; *nec vos, Pierides . . . tulistis opem;* 'Nor have you, Pierides, helped me,' 3.2.3–4; *nisi me mea Musa fugasset,* 'If my Muse hadn't sent me into exile,' *Pont.* 3.5.21.

85. Nicander of Colophon (second century BC) is the only known pre-Augustan source for the story, and his version survives only in a brief summary of the second-third century AD, chapter 9 of Antoninus Liberalis's *Metamorphoseon Sunagoge* (Papathomopoulos, *Antoninus Liberalis*), which cites chapter 4 of Nicander as his source. For a discussion of the relationship between Ovid and Nicander see Bethe, "Ovid und Nikander"; Lafaye, *Les Métamorphoses d'Ovide;* Gow and Scholfield, *Nicander.* The location of the stories of Typhon, Ascalabos, and the Emathides together in both book 4 of the *Heteroeumena* and book 5 of the *Metamorphoses* argues strongly for Ovid's use of Nicander. Vatican Mythographer I also recounts the story of the contest (no. 86), but seems to have as its source pseudo-Lactantius *Narrationes fabularum Ovidianarum.* For a discussion of Ovid's digressions from Nicander, see Hinds, *Metamorphosis of Persephone,* 54–55.

Chapter 3. The Weaving Contest

1. Although this type of linking device is rare; the pluperfect is otherwise so used only at the beginning of book 3, where the second half of Jupiter's rape of Europa is recounted, *deus . . . se confessus erat,* 'The god had owned up to who he was' (3.2), and book 14, of Glaucus's swim to Circe's island, *liquerat Euboicus tumidarum cultor aquarum,* 'The Euboean inhabitant of the swelling waters had left behind . . .' (line 4, repeated in line 5).

2. Harries, "The Spinner and the Poet." Heckel notes that the cruelty of Minerva in book 6 is foreshadowed by her admiration of the punishment of the Emathides in book 5 ("Genius on Genius," 239–40).

3. Concluding that the Muses and Arachne "affirmed his own artistic breadth" (Anderson, Review, 356–58).

4. Leach, "Ekphrasis"; see also Leach, *Rhetoric of Space,* 442 ff.

5. Lateiner, "Mythic and Non-Mythic Artists."

6. Feeney, *Gods in Epic,* 190; Barkan, *Gods Made Flesh,* 66; Hinds, *Metamorphosis of Persephone.* The weaving contest poses a particular problem for Hinds's generic interpretation of the poetic contest. He ultimately argues that the Muses represent an Alexandrian aesthetic of lean, elegant poetry, as learned *(doctae)* and ultimately Ovidian poets. According to this model, Arachne is undeniably the 'Alexandrian' artist, while Minerva's tapestry reflects epic values. The trouble is that Arachne is depicted as foolish *(stolida)* like the epinician Emathides, and her mortal status and final transformation mirror their own. Hofmann, "Ovid's *Metamorphoses,*" 223–41, anticipates some of Hinds's conclusions but is hampered by an overly zealous identification of 'Alexandrian' buzzwords.

7. Scheid and Svenbro, *Craft of Zeus*, 131 ff.

8. Barchiesi, "Narrative Technique," 193.

9. See pages 72–73 above for a discussion of their infrequent appearances in this mood.

10. On the non- or even anti-poetic sense of *facundia* as applied to the transformed Emathides by the narrating Muse in 5.677 see my article "Ovid and Poetic *Facundia*."

11. Echoing, ironically, her enemy Venus's similar complaint at 5.373–74: *et tamen in caelo . . . spernimur.*

12. Arachne's crime shifts somewhat in the course of the episode; in 6.24–25, in response to Ovid's editorial *scires a Pallade doctam*, Arachne indignantly denies it, and is 'offended by the idea of such a teacher,' *tantaque offensa magistra*, while here it is her unwillingness to acknowledge her superiority.

13. Presumably; the actual weaving, omitted from the list, is understood in *factas vestes* (6.17).

14. Barber, "Peplos of Athena," 111; her chapter provides an excellent reconsideration of the details of the decorative weaving process. Harries, "The Spinner and the Poet," 66, argues that this passage is drawn from "the weaving of the Fates" in Catullus 64.311–17, but only *digitis* in 6.20 recalls the language of Catullus, who shows no particular interest in the artistic aspect of the work (and ends with the grotesque image of the wool stuck to the lips of the old women); finally, the Fates are not weaving but only spinning threads (of destiny).

15. Arachne is a double of Minerva much as the Emathides were doubles of the Muses in book 5; on the 'twinning' of characters in the poetic contest see Johnson and Malamud, "Ovid's *Musomachia*."

16. Heffernan, *Museum of Words;* Sharrock, "Representing Metamorphosis"; Rosati, "Form in Motion," esp. 248–53.

17. Vincent, "Between Ovid and Barthes," 367.

18. Discussed in full in chapter 2, pages 48–49.

19. Ahl, *Metaformations*, 226. Harries's argument that Minerva's advantage over Arachne is her "wider experience" ("The Spinner and the Poet," 66) has no support from the text; Minerva's violence wins out over all aesthetic considerations.

20. The story may have been represented on a Corinthian aryballos of that date: Weinberg and Weinberg, "Arachne of Lydia."

21. As observed elsewhere in the poem by Rhorer, "Red and White."

22. Harries, "The Spinner and the Poet," 66, suggests a programmatic literary indication in the contrast between the *dives* Emathides and Arachne *orta domo parva*.

23. My translation of the verb *quaero* as "obtain" (i.e., = compound form *acquiro*), is somewhat idiosyncratic but supported by Bömer (*P. Ovidius Naso: VI–VII*, 14) with several parallels in Ovid and by the lines that follow; the nymphs must come to Arachne's town to see her work (6.14–16, quoted above). I would

add the precisely parallel use of the phrase in Propertius 3.2.25: *ingenio quaesitum nomen*, 'the fame I have earned by my talent.'

24. Leach, "Ekphrasis," 116.

25. Here including the detail that she displayed it to the suitors after washing it, and it shone like the sun or the moon; as Scheid and Svenbro argue (*Craft of Zeus*, chapter 3), she is structurally if not in fact weaving a nuptial blanket like the one in Catullus 64.

26. Literally, as Burton points out (*Theocritus's Urban Mimes*, 118); the Adonia is usually a private women's festival, here made public.

27. I concur with Dover (*Theocritus*, 206) and Burton (*Theocritus's Urban Mimes*, 98) that Adonis appears on the tapestry itself. Burton notes that the phrase is Homeric in origin (103). See Thomas, "Callimachus, the Victoria Berenices, and Roman Poetry," for the proposition that the epyllion of Heracles and Molorchus by Callimachus may have been an ekphrasis of a woven garment.

28. My parenthetical remark is justified by the comment of Gorgo at the end of the poem.

29. Burton, *Theocritus's Urban Mimes*, 41 ff.

30. Anderson, *Ovid's* Metamorphoses, *Books 6–10*, 155.

31. Harries, "The Spinner and the Poet," 65.

32. Barkan's formulation, that the gods in her tapestry are transformed by *amor* for mortal women, requires an overly optimistic reading of the meaning of metamorphosis in Ovid's text. He argues: "Arachne's transformations . . . take on a life of their own, not as the expression of outraged mortal victims but as glories of love, magic, and divine beauty" (*Gods Made Flesh*, 4). I see no evidence for this in Ovid's text, apart from Arachne's aesthetic triumph in the contest. If Ovid were such a fan of flux, I would expect fewer portrayals of the suffering it often produces in the poem, particularly in such episodes of divine rape. Barkan's argument culminates in the view that Arachne as a spider earns "an eternal life as an artist"; see below and Feeney, *Gods in Epic*, 193 n.24, for Roman ideas about spiders. Arachne's emphasis on divine deception and the subversiveness of her tapestry is briefly discussed by Heckel, "Genius on Genius," 247–48.

33. In the case of Daphne, she flees at the sight of Apollo, and he fails to rape her; in the case of Io, the rape is consummated, but Juno has her revenge on both Jupiter and Io.

34. Ahl, "Art of Safe Criticism."

35. The linkage of Arachne's plight with the plight of the raped in her tapestry also serves an important narrative purpose for the poem overall, providing a connection between the many victims of the gods' power in the poem.

36. See e.g., Harries, "The Spinner and the Poet," 68–69, where he demonstrates the relationship of the "appeal to verisimilitude" here with those in the ekphrases of Vergil and Apollonius, and compares the use of 'poietic' verbs in each.

37. Adams, *Latin Sexual Vocabulary*, 157–58.

38. See ibid., 161–63, esp. the example of Catullus 61.204–5: *ludite ut lubet, et brevi / liberos date.*

39. Just one example, again from Catullus 61: the bride as flower, 184–88, husband as ivy, and intertwining as sexual embrace, 102–5.

40. It is no wonder that the tapestry is characterized in the plural by *caelestia crimina* (6.131). While Barkan claims that Arachne's tapestry as a whole "was not a favorite among artists either in antiquity or in later times" (*Gods Made Flesh,* 5), it does seem to have had a noteworthy afterlife, as a source for Jacopo Caraglio's *Loves of the Gods,* itself modeled on (and designed to make less offensive) the anonymous pornographic poses of *I Modi* by Marcantonio Raimondi (prints from the drawings of Giulio Romano), which landed its producers in prison. Bull discusses the influence of the *Met.* 6 series of rapes on the *Loves* and the volumes and painting schemes derived in turn from the printed text (*Mirror of the Gods,* 155 ff.). The foundational discussion of the relationship of these texts to one another and to *Met.* 6 is Talvacchia, *Taking Positions,* chapter 7.

41. Leach does not believe the tapestry of Arachne expresses a moral point of view on the rapes of the gods ("Ekphrasis," 115–18). But following as it does the song of the Emathides and several books filled with stories of the gods' rapes of mortal women and nymphs, this reading seems overly cautious.

42. See Bömer, *P. Ovidius Naso: VI–VII,* 40, for the bibliography and sources of this tale; the offspring of the union was Dionysus Zagreus, the chthonic Dionysus.

43. Barkan, *Gods Made Flesh,* 3, prefers to read Arachne's as a response.

44. Leach, "Ekphrasis," 117.

45. Anderson, *Ovid's* Metamorphoses, *Books 6–10,* 160.

46. The Cyclops at work, the founding of Thebes, Venus with the shield of Mars, the battle between the Teleboaeans and the Taphians, Pelops in a chariot race, Apollo shooting Tityos, and Phrixus and the ram.

47. The two also share a common element: the sons of Antiope (6.111), Zethus and Amphion, conceived on Arachne's tapestry, are at work in Apollonius on the city of Thebes (1.736–41).

48. Rosati, "Narrative Techniques," 294–96.

49. Tissol, "House of Fame," 313.

50. Anderson, *Ovid's* Metamorphoses, *Books 6–10,* 161.

51. As observed by Heckel, "Genius on Genius," 244–45, where he briefly discusses "Pallas' self-centered craving for admiration." One immediately thinks of Cicero's infamous poem on his struggle with Catiline, *De consulatu suo,* about which Conte remarks, "Of Cicero's works this was the one most ridiculed, already by his contemporaries and then by the literary critics of the first century AD, not only because of its small poetic value but also because of the tiresome praises the author heaps on himself" (*Latin Literature,* 201).

52. As Vincent observes ("Between Ovid and Barthes," 361–86), the mythical

contest would antedate the construction of the historical Parthenon, so Ovid establishes Minerva's tapestry as the model for the Parthenon sculptures!

53. See Barber, "Peplos of Athena," 113 and fig. 72.

54. Barber citing Mansfield ("Peplos of Athena," passim; Mansfield, "Robe of Athena"). For the Panathenaia generally see Ridgway, "Images of Athena."

55. The corresponding narrative on the Parthenon's western gable was the story Minerva represents on the central panel of her tapestry, her victory over Poseidon for patronage of the city, as noted by Anderson, *Ovid's* Metamorphoses, *Books 6–10*, 161.

56. Pliny *Naturalis historia* 36.5.4.

57. See Zeitlin, "The Artful Eye," 154 and n.45, for references and bibliography.

58. Barber, "Peplos of Athena," 114; Plautus, *Mercator* 66–68.

59. See Scheid and Svenbro, *Craft of Zeus*, who in their thoroughgoing discussion of weaving in Rome cite one example from the third century BC (185 nn.3–5). There is little other evidence for such *peplophoria*, and Scheid and Svenbro conclude it was an emergency measure.

60. Barber, "Peplos of Athena," 115; Fullerton, *Archaistic Style of Roman Statuary*, 50–53, discusses the dating.

61. Thomas, "Virgil's Ecphrastic Centerpieces."

62. So suggests Pierini, "Due Note sul Mito di Scilla," but not according to the poem's Cambridge editor, Lyne, whose commentary is invaluable for understanding what we have of the poem (*Ciris*, 48–56). I see nothing in the poem to argue against a date in the late Augustan period, from which we have regrettably few examples for comparison outside the works of Ovid (see chapter 1 above).

63. Ably discussed in detail by Harries, "The Spinner and the Poet," 71–73.

64. See Tupet, "La Magie dans la métamorphosis d'Arachné."

65. Leach, "Ekphrasis," 118: "a compulsive weaver whose work is always liable to sudden destruction."

66. Feeney, *Gods in Epic*, 193 n.24; he calls Arachne's fate "sickening."

67. *Liberum mortis arbitrium* (the time of Claudius), Tacitus *Annales* 11.3.1.

68. Reported in Appian *Bella Civilia* 1.3.26.

69. *Moralia* 3.206.13.

70. See Raaflaub and Samons, "Opposition to Augustus," 423–25.

71. See Tacitus *Annales* 11.3 (Claudius), 15.60 (Nero, where the right to consider one's form of death seems the norm, but denied by Nero), and 16.33, Suetonius *Life of Domitian* 8.4 and 11.3 (Domitian).

Chapter 4. Songs from Hell

1. See chapter 1 above.

2. Following one of multiple traditions (Hyginus *Fabulae* 14 and Apollodorus 1.3.2 concur with Ovid) about his birth.

3. Pagán, "Speaking before Superiors."

4. Most focus on the aesthetics and structure of the second song and compare it with Vergil's Orphic passages (see below). Even a positive assessment of Orpheus's second song, like Nagle's ("Two Miniature *Carmina Perpetua*"), for whom the second song is a 'miniature' of the larger poem, Orpheus's song in the underworld is typically ignored or elided. The welcome exception has been Pagán, who undertakes a close rhetorical study of the first song, and with whose chastisement of Anderson's double dismissal of it I agree ("Speaking before Superiors," 371, referring to Anderson, "Orpheus of Virgil and Ovid," and *Ovid's* Metamorphoses, *Books 6–10*, 475–76).

5. Segal, *Orpheus*, 82–83, a study surprisingly overlooked by Pagán.

6. Anderson, "Orpheus of Virgil and Ovid," 42.

7. Primmer, "Lied des Orpheus."

8. Pagán, "Speaking before Superiors," 370.

9. Aeschylus *Agamemnon*, 1629–30; Euripides *Rhesus*, 944–46; *Medea*, 543; *Iphigenia in Aulis*, 1211; *Bacchae*, 561–64; *Cyclopes*, 646.

10. Euripides *Alcestis*, 357, with scholiast. For further examples see Sansone, "Orpheus and Eurydice."

11. I was alerted to Panyagua's catalogues by Jesnick, *Image of Orpheus*, who documents numerous non-mosaic representations in her introductory chapter. By way of example: Orpheus with his lyre, surrounded by Thracian horsemen or satyrs, on an Apulian red-figure crater from Egnazia, Latium, 430–20 BC; see Panyagua, "Figure de Orfeo," 189, and his "Catálogo I,"114, no. 65; the Maenads poised to attack Orpheus, on a column crater from Naples, 450 BC (Panyagua, "Catálogo I," 111, no. 57); and a series of fourth-century Apulian funerary vases depicting Orpheus in the underworld (Jesnick, *Image of Orpheus*, 11), in one example with Eurydice (Panyagua, "Catálogo I," 122–27, nos. 77–85).

12. Pausanias, 10.30.6.

13. Pausanias, 9.30.4, where he also expresses the opinion that Orpheus was the son of one of the daughters of Pieros (the father of the Emathides of book 5).

14. Reinach, *Répetoire des Peintures*, 122, fig. 11.

15. Stern, "Débuts de l'Iconographie," 162, fig. 16. He dates it rather too closely for Jesnick's comfort to 47–46 BC.

16. Jesnick, *Image of Orpheus*, 12. Tarentum: Panyagua, "Figure de Orfeo," 217 and n.228; Panyagua, "Catálogo de Representaciones de Orfeo III," 444–45, no. 162. Mantua: Panyagua, "Figure de Orfeo," 216–17, fig. 11; Panyagua, "Catálogo de Representaciones de Orfeo III," 445, no. 163. Murals: Panyagua, "Catálogo de Representaciones de Orfeo III," 457–58, 462–63, nos. 184, 191–92.

17. So numbered in the edition of Shackleton-Bailey, *Martial*, 342.

18. Panyagua, "Figure de Orfeo," 213; Panyagua, "Catálogo de Representaciones de Orfeo III," 437–38, no. 148.

19. West, *Orphic Poems*, 24; Kern, *Orphicorum Fragmenta*, fr. 49.

20. West, *Orphic Poems,* 26 ff., observes that almost any book of sacred rituals could have been ascribed to Orpheus, if the list in the *Suda* is any indication, but apart from a few formulaic phrases like *esto procul* in Orpheus's second song, there are few if any evocations of this part of the tradition.

21. The term *vates,* used of Orpheus on four occasions in the episode, had largely lost its religious meaning. Cicero indicates that Orpheus did not receive worship as Achilles did (*De natura deorum* 3.45.12); at *Tusculanae disputationes* 1.98.9, Orpheus is 'just' a great poet alongside Musaeus, Homer, and Hesiod, a list that, with some variations, regularly appears in Roman authors, including Ovid (*Am.* 3.9.14). He observes at *De natura deorum* 1.107.11 that even if the *carmen Orphicum* is a forgery, what Orpheus represents is more important.

22. As observed by Clausen, *Commentary on Virgil* Eclogues, 176.

23. To Clausen, *Commentary on Virgil* Eclogues, 176–77, Callimachean poetry; to Skutsch, *Aus Vergils Frühzeit,* 28–49, a catalog of the poetry of Gallus; to Otis, *Virgil,* 137–43, the fall of man from the Saturnian golden age.

24. And they have been numerous. The most helpful for this chapter have been Anderson, "Orpheus of Virgil and Ovid" and "Artist's Limits"; Hill, "From Orpheus to Ass's Ears"; Knox, *Ovid's* Metamorphoses, 48–62; Leach, "Ekphrasis"; Makowski, "Bisexual Orpheus"; Neumeister, "Orpheus und Eurydike"; Pagán, "Speaking before Superiors"; Segal, "Ovid's Orpheus" (also found in Segal, *Orpheus,* chapter 3) and "Virgil and Ovid on Orpheus: A Second Look," chapter 4 in *Orpheus;* and R. Alden Smith, *Poetic Illusion and Poetic Embrace,* chapter 3.

25. Hill, "From Orpheus to Ass's Ears," 125.

26. Thomas, *Virgil:* Georgics *Vol. 1,* 15–16; *Virgil:* Georgics *Vol. 2,* 225–26 (4.453–257 n.).

27. Leach, "Ekphrasis," 119.

28. Otis, *Ovid as an Epic Poet,* 184.

29. Anderson, "Orpheus of Virgil and Ovid," 48; "Artist's Limits," 2: "Here is the paradigmatic moment when art demonstrates its power over death, its claim to be eternal . . . the triumph of Orpheus and art is brief and abortive."

30. Makowski, "Bisexual Orpheus"; Neumeister, "Orpheus und Eurydike."

31. Segal, "Ovid's Orpheus," 483.

32. Segal, "Virgil and Ovid," chapter 4 in *Orpheus,* 93–94.

33. Pagán, "Speaking before Superiors," 378–86. She cites the parallel between *omnia vincit amor* (*Ecl.* 10.69) to *vicit Amor* (*Met.*10.26). I find this less persuasive in the light of the other prominent appearances of *amor* with *vincere* in the active voice in Ovid (*Heroides* 9.26, *Am.* 3.11b.2, 3.2.46) and others (e.g. *Aen.* 6.823, Tibullus 1.4.40). Pagán does an excellent job of describing relationships between poets and the powerful in the time of Gallus. Her interesting conclusions are unfortunately, as she herself acknowledges, "a tantalizing scenario within our reach but which eludes our grasp" (384).

34. For an anti-anxiety reading of Ovid's 'little *Aeneid*' see Hinds, *Allusion and Intertext*, 104–7.

35. Pöschl, "Katalog der Bäume." Each generic type is presented with some humor: Orpheus the elegiac lover complains on a threshold (but of the underworld), while Orpheus the pastoral poet attracts a host of leafy admirers (but who were for the most part originally human beings).

36. Hofmann, "Ovid's *Metamorphoses*."

37. On the genre(s) of the Orpheus episode see Knox, *Ovid's* Metamorphoses, 48–64.

38. Segal, *Orpheus*, 91.

39. See Segal, "Ovid's Orpheus," 58–62, for a comparison of Orpheus's descent in Vergil and Ovid.

40. Never used of song in either Vergil or Ovid; only used of divine speech for Venus, as she begins her tale of Atalanta in book 10, of Neptune addressing the winds in *Aen.* book 1, and of Jupiter speaking to Hercules on Olympus in *Aen.* book 10. There is a hint of ritualized speech in the uses by the wife of the Flamen Dialis in *Fasti* 6 and by Iris removing Dido's lock in *Aen.* 4, but they are as close as previous usage comes to song. It is unfortunate that in his discussion of the contrast of verbs of singing and speaking that Habinek's *World of Roman Song* does not address the use of this verb in *Met.* 10.

41. The rhetorical structure of the song is discussed by Gugel, "Orpheus' Gang in die Unterwelt," and Anderson, *Ovid's* Metamorphoses, *Books 6–10*, ad loc. The fullest treatment is presented by Pagán, "Speaking before Superiors," 374–78, who observes an emphasis on issues of free speech in Orpheus's language.

42. See my discussion in chapter 2, pages 49–51.

43. Pagán, "Speaking before Superiors," 375, connecting the appearance of *si licet* with Feeney's discussion of *si licet et fas est* at *Fasti* 1.25 (Feeney, *Si licet et fas est*, 12–19).

44. Echoing the sentiments of Ovid's announcement in *Am.* 1.8.42: *at Venus Aeneae regnat in urbe sui*, 'But Venus now reigns in the city of her Aeneas.'

45. Pöschl, "Katalog der Bäume," has argued that Orpheus's song in the underworld is structured as an ironic *paraklausithyron*, the elegiac lament of a locked-out lover before the door of his beloved, in which the role of the *janitor* is played by Persephone and Pluto. But I see few similarities apart from the figure of the singer who seeks a favor from his addressee, a quality shared by a variety of Latin poetic forms.

46. One might claim success for Orpheus's own Pygmalion, who apparently lives happily ever after with his ivory girl. Significantly, however, Pygmalion's statue is created for (very) private consumption; there is no audience or patron (apart from the readers of the *Metamorphoses*) to shape his 'womanufacture,' as Sharrock has dubbed it, either to pass judgment or to determine its success or its failure. See Elsner's discussion of the episode (chapter 5 in *Roman Eyes*), in

which he argues that "Ovid dramatizes this transgression [of realist art] by making his Pygmalion an artist" (124).

47. Garrison, *Horace,* 278.

48. Nagle, "Two Miniature *Carmina Perpetua,*" 111–12.

49. Makowski, "Bisexual Orpheus," 27.

50. Hinds, "Landscape with Figures," 127–28.

51. Ahl, *Metaformations,* 214: "The audience of wild beasts and birds that Orpheus addresses is in the midst of a grove of people metamorphosed into trees (10.143–54). By the end of his story, Myrrha will herself have joined the dendroid crowd."

52. Critics have been overly influenced by the phrase *omnemque refugerat Orpheus / femineam venerem* (79–80) and the success of Pygmalion. I disagree with Coleman, "Structure and Intention," that misogyny dictates the course of the narrative.

53. Segal, *Orpheus,* 68.

54. As observed by Hardie, *Ovid's Poetics of Illusion,* 288.

Chapter 5. Ovid Anticipates Exile

1. Griffin, "Augustus and the Poets," 191.

2. Putnam, *Virgil's* Aeneid, 217.

3. For a good general discussion of the dissemination of literature and books in a variety of Roman periods see Fantham, *Roman Literary Culture.* On Ovid as an active agent of Roman imperialism in Tomis, see chapter 8 in Habinek, *Politics of Latin Literature.* It is of course Roman imperialism that Ovid identifies as the potential savior of his poetry.

4. Farrell, "Ovidian *Corpus,*" 138–39.

5. *Epist.* 1.20.13, *Ars Poetica* 345–46.

6. Gibson, "Ovid on Reading," 37 n.61.

Bibliography

Adams, James N. *The Latin Sexual Vocabulary.* London: Duckworth, 1982.

Ahl, Frederick M. "The Rider and the Horse: Politics and Power in Roman Poetry from Horace to Statius." *Aufstieg und Niedergang der römischen Welt* II.32.1 (1984): 40–110.

———. "The Art of Safe Criticism in Greece and Rome." *American Journal of Philology* 105 (1984): 174–208.

———. *Metaformations: Soundplay and Wordplay in Ovid and Other Classical Poets.* Ithaca, N.Y.: Cornell University Press, 1985.

Albis, Robert V. *Poet and Audience in the Argonautica of Apollonius.* Lanham, Md.: Rowman and Littlefield, 1996.

Anderson, William S. "The Orpheus of Virgil and Ovid: *Flebile nescio quid.*" In *Orpheus: The Metamorphoses of a Myth,* edited by J. Warden, 25–50. Toronto: University of Toronto Press, 1982.

———. Review of Stephen Hinds, *The Metamorphosis of Persephone: Ovid and the Self-Conscious Muse* (Cambridge: Cambridge University Press, 1987). *Gnomon* 61.4 (1989): 356–58.

———. "The Artist's Limits in Ovid: Orpheus, Pygmalion, and Daedalus." *Syllecta Classica* 1 (1989): 1–11.

———. *Ovid's* Metamorphoses, *Books 1–5.* Norman: University of Oklahoma Press, 1997.

———. *Ovid's* Metamorphoses, *Books 6–10.* Norman: University of Oklahoma Press, 1997.

Barber, Elizabeth J. W. "The Peplos of Athena." In *Goddess and Polis: The Panathenaic Festival in Ancient Athens,* edited by Jenifer Neils, 103–17. Princeton, N.J.: Princeton University Press, 1992.

Barchiesi, Alessandro. *The Poet and the Prince: Ovid and Augustan Discourse.* Berkeley: University of California Press, 1997.

———. "Endgames: Ovid's *Metamorphoses* 15 and *Fasti* 6." In *Classical Closure: Reading the End in Greek and Latin Literature,* edited by Deborah Roberts,

Francis Dunn, and Don Fowler, 181–208. Princeton, N.J.: Princeton University Press, 1997.

———. *Speaking Volumes: Narrative and Intertext in Ovid and Other Latin Poets.* London: Duckworth, 2001.

———. "Narrative Technique and Narratology in the *Metamorphoses.*" In *The Cambridge Companion to Ovid,* edited by Philip Hardie, 180–99. Cambridge: Cambridge University Press, 2002.

Barkan, Leonard. *The Gods Made Flesh: Metamorphosis and the Pursuit of Paganism.* New Haven, Conn.: Yale University Press, 1986.

Bartholomé, Heinrich. *Ovid und die antike Kunst.* Borna-Leipzig: Robert Noske, 1935.

Bethe, Erich. "Ovid und Nikander." *Hermes* 39 (1904): 1–14.

Bömer, Franz. *P. Ovidius Naso:* Metamorphosen. *Kommentar Buch IV–V.* Heidelberg: Winter, 1976.

———. *P. Ovidius Naso:* Metamorphosen. *Kommentar Buch VI–VII.* Heidelberg: Winter, 1976.

Bourdieu, Pierre. "The Historical Genesis of a Pure Aesthetic." In *The Field of Cultural Production: Essays on Art and Literature,* edited and introduced by Randal Johnson, 254–66. New York: Columbia University Press, 1993.

Boyd, Barbara Weiden, ed. *Brill's Companion to Ovid.* Leiden: Brill, 2002.

Boyle, Anthony J. *The Chaonian Dove: Studies in the* Eclogues, Georgics, *and* Aeneid *of Virgil.* Leiden: Brill, 1986.

Bramble, J. C. "Minor Figures." In *The Cambridge History of Classical Literature II: Latin Literature,* edited by E. J. Kenney, 467–94. Cambridge: Cambridge University Press, 1982.

Braund, Susanna Morton. "*Libertas* or *Licentia?* Freedom and Criticism in Roman Satire." In *Free Speech in Classical Antiquity,* edited by Ineke Sluiter and Ralph M. Rosen, 409–28. Leiden: Brill, 2004.

Bull, Malcolm. *The Mirror of the Gods: How Renaissance Artists Rediscovered the Pagan Gods.* Oxford: Oxford University Press, 2005.

Burton, Joan B. *Theocritus's Urban Mimes: Mobility, Gender, and Patronage.* Berkeley: University of California Press, 1995.

Butrica, James L. "Lygdamus, Nephew of Messalla?" *Liverpool Classical Monthly* 18.4 (1993): 51–53.

Cahoon, Leslie. "The Bed as Battlefield: Erotic Conquest and Military Metaphor in Ovid's *Amores.*" *Transactions of the American Philological Association* 118 (1988): 293–307.

Cameron, Alan. *Callimachus and His Critics.* Princeton, N.J.: Princeton University Press, 1995.

Chrissanthos, Stefan G. "Freedom of Speech and the Roman Republican Army." In *Free Speech in Classical Antiquity,* edited by Ineke Sluiter and Ralph M. Rosen, 341–67. Leiden: Brill, 2004.

Clausen, Wendell V. *A Commentary on Virgil* Eclogues. Oxford: Clarendon Press, 1994.

Coleman, Robert. "Structure and Intention in the *Metamorphoses*." *Classical Quarterly*, n.s., 21 (1971): 461–77.

———, ed. *Vergil:* Eclogues. Cambridge: Cambridge University Press, 1977.

Conte, Gian Biagio. *Latin Literature: A History*. Translated by Joseph B. Solodow. Baltimore, Md.: Johns Hopkins University Press, 1994.

Crabbe, Anna. "Structure and Content in Ovid's *Metamorphoses*." *Aufstieg und Niedergang der römischen Welt* II.31.4 (1981): 2274–327.

Curran, Leo C. "Transformation and Anti-Augustanism in Ovid's *Metamorphoses*." *Arethusa* 5 (1972): 71–91.

———. "Rape and Rape Victims in the *Metamorphoses*." *Arethusa* 11 (1978): 213–41.

Dietrich, Jessica S. "Dead Parrots Society." *American Journal of Philology* 123 (2002): 95–110.

Dover, Kenneth J. *Theocritus: Select Poems*. London: Macmillan, 1971.

Duret, Luc. "Dans l'ombre des plus grands." *Aufstieg und Niedergang der römischen Welt* II.30.3 (1983): 1447–560.

Edmunds, Lowell. *Intertextuality and the Reading of Roman Poetry*. Baltimore, Md.: Johns Hopkins University Press, 2001.

Elsner, Jás, ed. *Art and Text in Roman Culture*. Cambridge: Cambridge University Press, 1996.

———. *Roman Eyes: Visuality and Subjectivity in Art and Text*. Princeton, N.J.: Princeton University Press, 2007.

Evelyn-White, Hugh, tr. *Hesiod, the Homeric Hymns and Homerica*. Cambridge, Mass.: Harvard University Press, 1970.

Fantham, Elaine. *Roman Literary Culture from Cicero to Apuleius*. Baltimore, Md.: Johns Hopkins University Press, 1996.

———. *Ovid Fasti Book IV*. Cambridge: Cambridge University Press, 1998.

Farrell, Joseph. "Dialogue of Genres in Ovid's 'Lovesong of Polyphemus' (*Metamorphoses* 13.719–897)." *American Journal of Philology* 113.2 (1992): 235–68.

———. "The Ovidian *Corpus:* Poetic Body and Poetic Text." In *Ovidian Transformations: Essays on Ovid's* Metamorphoses *and Its Reception*, edited by Philip Hardie, Alessandro Barchiesi, and Stephen Hinds, 127–41. Cambridge: Cambridge Philological Society, 1999.

Feeney, Denis. *The Gods in Epic: Poets and Critics of the Classical Tradition*. Oxford: Oxford University Press, 1991.

———. "*Si licet et fas est:* Ovid's *Fasti* and the Problem of Free Speech under the Principate." In *Roman Poetry and Propaganda in the Age of Augustus*, edited by Anthony Powell, 1–25. London: Bristol Classical Press, 1992.

———. "*Mea Tempora:* Patterning of time in the *Metamorphoses*." In *Ovidian Transformations: Essays on Ovid's* Metamorphoses *and Its Reception*, edited by

Philip Hardie, Alessandro Barchiesi and Stephen Hinds, 13–30. Cambridge: Cambridge Philological Society, 1999.

———. "*Una cum scriptore meo:* Poetry, Principate and the Traditions of Literary History in the Epistle to Augustus." In *Traditions and Contexts in the Poetry of Horace,* edited by Tony Woodman and Denis Feeney, 172–87. Cambridge: Cambridge University Press, 2002.

Fowler, D. P. "Narrate and Describe: The Problem of Ekphrasis." *Journal of Roman Studies* 81 (1991): 25–35.

Fullerton, Mark D. *The Archaistic Style in Roman Statuary.* Leiden: Brill, 1990.

Galinsky, Karl. *Ovid's* Metamorphoses: *An Introduction to the Basic Aspects.* Berkeley: University of California Press, 1975.

———. "Was Ovid a Silver Latin Poet?" *Illinois Classical Studies* 14 (1989): 69–89.

———. *Augustan Culture: An Interpretive Introduction.* Princeton, N.J.: Princeton University Press, 1996.

———. Review of Lothar Spahlinger, Ars latet arte sua. *Untersuchungen zur Poetologie in den Metamorphosen Ovids* (Stuttgart/Leipzig: Teubner, 1996). *Gnomon* 72.4 (2000): 359–61.

Garrison, Daniel H. *Horace: Epodes and Odes.* Norman: University of Oklahoma Press, 1999.

Genette, Gérard. "Frontiers of Narrative." In *Figures of Literary Discourse,* translated by Alan Sheridan, 127–44. New York: Columbia University Press, 1982.

Gibson, Bruce John. "Ovid on Reading: Reading Ovid. Reception in Ovid *Tristia* II." *Journal of Roman Studies* 89 (1999): 19–37.

Goldhill, Simon. "The Naïve and Knowing Eye: Ecphrasis and the Culture of Viewing in the Hellenistic World." In *Art and Text in Ancient Greek Culture,* edited by Simon Goldhill and Robin Osborne, 197–223. Cambridge: Cambridge University Press, 1994.

Gow, A. S. F., and A. F. Scholfield, eds. *Nicander: The Poems and Poetical Fragments.* Cambridge: Cambridge University Press, 1953.

Green, Steven J. *Ovid* Fasti *I: A Commentary.* Leiden: Brill, 2004.

Griffin, Jasper. "Augustus and the Poets: '*Caesar qui cogere posset.*'" In *Caesar Augustus: Seven Aspects,* edited by Fergus Millar and Erich Segal, 189–218. Oxford: Oxford University Press, 1984.

Gugel, Helmut. "Orpheus' Gang in die Unterwelt in den Metamorphosen Ovids (*Met.* X, 1–71)." *Ziva Antika* 22 (1972): 39–59.

Habinek, Thomas. *The Politics of Latin Literature: Writing, Identity, and Empire in Ancient Rome.* Princeton, N.J.: Princeton University Press, 1998.

———. *The World of Roman Song: From Ritualized Speech to Social Order.* Baltimore, Md.: Johns Hopkins University Press, 2005.

Hardie, Philip. *Virgil's* Aeneid: Cosmos *and* Imperium. Oxford: Clarendon Press, 1986.

———. "Augustan Poets and the Mutability of Rome." In *Roman Poetry and Propaganda in the Age of Augustus*, edited by Anthony Powell, 59–82. London: Bristol Classical Press, 1992.

———. *Ovid's Poetics of Illusion*. Cambridge: Cambridge University Press, 2002.

———, ed. *The Cambridge Companion to Ovid*. Cambridge: Cambridge University Press, 2002.

———. "Ovid and Early Imperial Literature." In *The Cambridge Companion to Ovid*, edited by Philip Hardie, 34–45. Cambridge: Cambridge University Press, 2002.

Hardie, Philip, Alessandro Barchiesi, and Stephen Hinds, eds. *Ovidian Transformations: Essays on Ovid's* Metamorphoses *and Its Reception*. Cambridge: Cambridge Philological Society, 1999.

Harries, Byron. "Causation and the Authority of the Poet in Ovid's *Fasti*." *Classical Quarterly* 39.1 (1989): 164–85.

———. "The Spinner and the Poet: Arachne in Ovid's *Metamorphoses*." *Proceedings of the Cambridge Philological Society*, n.s., 36 (1990): 64–82.

Heckel, Hartwig. "A Genius on Genius: Ovid, Orpheus, Arachne." *Classica Cracoviensia* 5 (2000): 225–49.

Heffernan, James A. W. *Museum of Words: The Poetics of Ekphrasis from Homer to Ashbery*. Chicago: University of Chicago Press, 1993.

Heinze, Richard. "Ovids elegische Erzählung." Berichte der Sächsischen Akademie zu Leipzig, Philologisch-historiche Klasse 71.7. Leipzig. Reprinted in *Vom Geist des Römertums*, R. Heinze, 308–403. Stuttgart: B.G. Teubner, 1960.

Hill, D. E. "From Orpheus to Ass's Ears: Ovid, *Metamorphoses* 10.1–11.193." In *Author and Audience in Latin Literature*, edited by Tony Woodman and Jonathan Powell, 124–37. Cambridge: Cambridge University Press, 1992.

Hinds, Stephen. "Generalizing about Ovid." *Ramus* 16 (1987): 4–31.

———. *The Metamorphosis of Persephone: Ovid and the Self-Conscious Muse*. Cambridge: Cambridge University Press, 1987.

———. "*Arma* in Ovid's *Fasti* Part 2: Genre, Romulean Rome and Augustan Ideology." *Arethusa* 25 (1992): 113–53.

———. *Allusion and Intertext: Dynamics of Appropriation in Roman Poetry*. Cambridge: Cambridge University Press, 1998.

———. "Landscape with Figures: Aesthetics of Place in the *Metamorphoses* and Its Tradition." In *The Cambridge Companion to Ovid*, edited by Philip Hardie, 122–49. Cambridge: Cambridge University Press, 2002.

Hofmann, H. "Ovid's *Metamorphoses: Carmen perpetuum, carmen deductum*." *Papers of the Liverpool Latin Seminar* 5 (1985): 223–41.

Hollander, John. "The Poetics of *Ekphrasis*." *Word and Image* 4.1 (1988): 209–19.

Holleman, A. W. J. "Ovid and Politics." *Historia* 20 (1971): 458–66.

Holzberg, Niklas. "*Ter quinque volumina* as *carmen perpetuum*: The Division into Books in Ovid's *Metamorphoses*." *Materiali e discussioni per l'analisi dei testi classici* 40 (1998): 77–98.

Hunter, Richard L. *The* Argonautica *of Apollonius: Literary Studies.* Cambridge: Cambridge University Press, 1993.

Janan, Micaela. "The Book of Good Love? Design vs. Desire in *Metamorphoses* 10." *Ramus* 17 (1988): 110–37.

———. "'There beneath the Roman Ruin where the purple flowers grow': Ovid's Minyeides and the Feminine Imagination." *American Journal of Philology* 115.3 (1994) 427–48.

Jeffreys, R. "The Date of Messalla's Death." *Classical Quarterly* 35 (1985): 140–48.

Jesnick, Ilona J. *The Image of Orpheus in Roman Mosaic.* Oxford: Oxford University Press, 1997.

Johnson, Patricia J. "Constructions of Venus in Ovid's *Metamorphoses* V." *Arethusa* 29.1 (1996): 125–49.

———. "Ovid and Poetic *Facundia.*" *Latomus: Studies in Latin Literature and Roman History VIII* 239 (1997): 231–44.

Johnson, Patricia J., and Martha Malamud. "Ovid's *Musomachia.*" *Pacific Coast Philology* 23 (1988): 30–38.

Johnson, W. R. *Darkness Visible: A Study of Vergil's* Aeneid. Berkeley: University of California Press, 1976.

Joplin, Patricia K. "The Voice of the Shuttle Is Ours." *Stanford Literature Review* 1 (1984): 25–53.

Kannicht, Richard, ed., *Euripides, Helena. Vol. II, Kommentar.* Heidelberg: Winter, 1969.

Keith, Alison. "Versions of Epic Masculinity in Ovid's *Metamorphoses.*" In *Ovidian Transformations: Essays on Ovid's* Metamorphoses *and Its Reception,* edited by Philip Hardie, Alessandro Barchiesi, and Stephen Hinds, 214–39. Cambridge: Cambridge Philological Society, 1999.

———. "Sources and Genres in Ovid's *Metamorphoses* 1–5." In *Brill's Companion to Ovid,* edited by Barbara Weiden Boyd, 235–69. Leiden: Brill, 2002.

Kennedy, Duncan F. "'Augustan' and 'Anti-Augustan': Reflections on Terms of Reference." In *Roman Poetry and Propaganda in the Age of Augustus,* edited by Anthony Powell, 26–58. London: Bristol Classical Press, 1992.

Kenney, E. J. "Ovid." In *The Cambridge History of Classical Literature II: Latin Literature,* edited by E. J. Kenney, 420–57. Cambridge: Cambridge University Press, 1982.

———, ed. *Ovid* Heroides *XVI–XXI.* Cambridge: Cambridge University Press, 1996.

Kern, Otto. *Orphicorum Fragmenta.* Berlin: Weidmann, 1922.

Knox, Peter. *Ovid's* Metamorphoses *and the Traditions of Augustan Poetry.* Cambridge, Mass.: Harvard University Press, 1986.

———, ed. *Ovid* Heroides, *Select Epistles.* Cambridge: Cambridge University Press, 1995.

———. "The Poet and the Second Prince: Ovid in the Age of Tiberius." *Memoirs of the American Academy in Rome* 49 (2004): 1–20.

Krieger, Murray. *Ekphrasis: The Illusion of the Natural Sign.* Baltimore, Md.: Johns Hopkins University Press, 1991.

Lafaye, Georges. *Les Métamorphoses d'Ovide et leurs modèles Grecs.* Paris: F. Alcan, 1904.

Laird, Andrew. "Sounding Out Ecphrasis: Art and Text in Catullus 64." *Journal of Roman Studies* 83 (1993): 18–30.

Lamberton, Robert. *Hesiod.* New Haven, Conn.: Yale University Press, 1988.

———. "Plutarch, Hesiod and the Mouseia of Thespiai." *Illinois Classical Studies* 13.2 (1988): 491–504.

Lateiner, Donald. "Mythic and Non-Mythic Artists in Ovid's Metamorphoses." *Ramus* 13 (1984): 1–30.

Leach, Eleanor Winsor. "Ekphrasis and the Theme of Artistic Failure in Ovid's *Metamorphoses.*" *Ramus* 3 (1974): 102–42.

———. *The Rhetoric of Space: Literary and Artistic Representations of Landscape in Republican and Augustan Rome.* Princeton, N.J.: Princeton University Press, 1988.

Lee, M. Owen. *Virgil as Orpheus: A Study of the* Georgics. Albany: State University of New York Press, 1996.

Lessing, Gotthold Ephraim. *Laocoön: An Essay on the Limits of Painting and Poetry,* translated by Edward A. McCormick. Baltimore, Md.: Johns Hopkins University Press, 1984.

Levene, David S., and Damien P. Nelis, eds. *Clio and the Poets: Augustan Poetry and the Traditions of Ancient Historiography.* Leiden: Brill, 2002.

Lindheim, Sara H. *Mail and Female: Epistolary Narrative and Desire in Ovid's* Heroides. Madison: University of Wisconsin Press, 2003.

Ludwig, Walter. *Struktur und Einheit der Metamorphosen Ovids.* Berlin: De Gruyter, 1965.

Lyne, R. O. A. M. *Ciris.* Cambridge: Cambridge University Press, 1978.

———. *Horace: Behind the Public Poetry.* New Haven, Conn.: Yale University Press, 1995.

Makowski, John F. "Bisexual Orpheus: Pederasty and Parody in Ovid." *Classical Journal* 92.1 (1996): 25–38.

Mansfield, John M. "The Robe of Athena and the Panathenaic 'Peplos.'" Ph.D. dissertation, University of California at Berkeley, 1985.

Markus, Donka D. "Performing the Book: The Recital of Epic in First-Century C.E. Rome." *Classical Antiquity* 19.1 (2000): 138–79.

McHugh, Mary R. "Historiography and Freedom of Speech: The Case of Cremutius Cordus." In *Free Speech in Classical Antiquity,* edited by Ineke Sluiter and Ralph M. Rosen, 391–408. Leiden: Brill, 2004.

McNeill, Randall L. B. *Horace: Image, Identity and Audience.* Baltimore, Md.: Johns Hopkins University Press, 2001.

Myers, K. Sara. *Ovid's Causes: Cosmogony and Aetiology in the* Metamorphoses. Ann Arbor: University of Michigan Press, 1994.

———. "The Metamorphosis of a Poet: Recent Work on Ovid." *Journal of Roman Studies* 89 (1999): 190–204.

Nagle, Betty Rose. "Two Miniature *Carmina Perpetua* in the *Metamorphoses:* Calliope and Orpheus." *Grazer Beitrage* 15 (1988): 99–125.

Navarro Antolín, Fernando, ed. *Lygdamus: Corpus Tibullianum III.1–6. Lygdami Elegiarum Liber.* Leiden: Brill, 1996.

Neils, Jenifer, ed. *Goddess and Polis: The Panathenaic Festival in Ancient Athens.* Princeton, N.J.: Princeton University Press, 1992.

Nelis, Damien P. "Demodocus and the Song of Orpheus: Ap. Rhod. *Arg.* 1.496–511." *Museum Helveticum* 49.3 (1992): 153–70.

Neumeister, C. "Orpheus und Eurydike: Eine Vergil-Parodie Ovids (Ov. *Met.* X 1–XI 66 und Verg. *Georg.* IV 457–527)." *Würzburger Jahrbücher für die Altertumswissenschaft* 12 (1986): 169–81.

Newlands, Carole. "Ovid's Narrator in the *Fasti.*" *Arethusa* 25 (1992) 33–54.

———. *Playing with Time: Ovid and the* Fasti. Ithaca, N.Y.: Cornell University Press, 1995.

O'Hara, James J. "They Might Be Giants: Inconsistency and Indeterminancy in Vergil's War in Italy." *Colby Quarterly* 30.3 (1994): 206–32.

Oliensis, Ellen. "The Power of Image-Makers: Representation and Revenge in Ovid *Metamorphoses* 6 and *Tristia* 4." *Classical Antiquity* 23.2 (2004): 285–321.

Otis, Brooks. "Ovid and the Augustans." *Transactions of the American Philological Association* 69 (1938): 188–229.

———. *Ovid as an Epic Poet.* 2nd ed. Cambridge: Cambridge University Press, 1970.

———. *Virgil: A Study in Civilized Poetry.* Oxford: Oxford University Press, 1964.

Pagán, Victoria. "Speaking before Superiors: Orpheus in Vergil and Ovid." In *Free Speech in Classical Antiquity,* edited by Ineke Sluiter and Ralph M. Rosen, 369–89. Leiden: Brill, 2004.

Panyagua, Enrique R. "La Figure de Orfeo en el Arte Griego y Romano." *Helmantica* 18.56 (1967): 173–239.

———. "Catalogo de Representaciones de Orfeo en el Arte Antiguo Parte I." *Helmantica* 23 (1972): 83–135.

———. "Catalogo de Representaciones de Orfeo en el Arte Antiguo Parte III." *Helmantica* 24.75 (1973): 433–98.

Papathomopoulos, Manolis, ed. *Antoninus Liberalis, Les* Métamorphoses. Paris: Les Belles Lettres, 1968.

Pierini, Rita Degl'Innocenti. "Due Note sul Mito di Scilla (in Ovidio e nella *Ciris*)." *Atene e Roma* 40.2–3 (1975): 72–77.

Pöschl, Viktor. "Der Katalog der Bäume in Ovids *Metamorphosen.*" In *Medium Aevum Vivum: Festschrift für Walter Bulst,* edited by H. R. Jauss and D. Schaller, 13–21. Heidelberg: Winter, 1960.

Powell, Anton, ed. *Roman Poetry and Propaganda in the Age of Augustus.* London: Bristol Classical Press, 1992.

Primmer, Adolf. "Das Lied des Orpheus in Ovids *Metamorphosen.*" *Sprachkunst* 10 (1979): 123–37.

Putnam, Michael C. J. *Artifices of Eternity: Horace's Fourth Book of Odes.* Ithaca, N.Y.: Cornell University Press, 1986.

———. *Virgil's* Aeneid: *Interpretation and Influence.* Chapel Hill: University of North Carolina Press, 1995.

———. *Virgil's Epic Designs: Ekphrasis in the* Aeneid. New Haven, Conn.: Yale University Press, 1998.

———. *Horace's* Carmen Saeculare: *Ritual Magic and the Poet's Art.* New Haven, Conn.: Yale University Press, 2000.

Raaflaub, Kurt A., and Loren J. Samons II. "Opposition to Augustus." In *Between Republic and Empire: Interpretations of Augustus and His Principate,* edited by Kurt A. Raaflaub and Mark Toher, 417–54. Berkeley: University of California Press, 1990.

Raeburn, David, tr., *Ovid.* Metamorphoses. London: Penguin Books, 2004.

Reinach, Salomon. *Répetoire de Peintures Grecques et Romaines (RPGR) avec 2720 Gravures.* Roma: "L'Erma" di Bretschneider, 1970.

Rhorer, Catherine C. "Red and White in Ovid's *Metamorphoses:* The Mulberry Tree in the Tale of Pyramus and Thisbe." *Ramus* 9 (1980): 79–88.

Richlin, Amy. "Reading Ovid's Rapes." In *Pornography and Representation in Greece and Rome,* edited by Amy Richlin, 158–79. Oxford: Oxford University Press, 1992.

Ridgway, Brunilde S. "Images of Athena on the Acropolis." In *Goddess and Polis: The Panathenaic Festival in Ancient Athens,* edited by Jenifer Neils, 119–42. Princeton, N.J.: Princeton University Press, 1992.

Roberts, Deborah, Francis Dunn, and Don Fowler, eds. *Classical Closure: Reading the End in Greek and Latin Literature.* Princeton, N.J.: Princeton University Press, 1997.

Rohde, Erwin. *Der Griechische Roman und seine Vorläufer.* Hildesheim: Olms Verlag, 1974.

Rosati, Gianpiero. "Form in Motion: Weaving the Text in the *Metamorphoses.*" In *Ovidian Transformations: Essays on the* Metamorphoses *and Its Reception,* edited by Philip Hardie, Alessandro Barchiesi, and Stephen Hinds, 240–53. Cambridge: Cambridge Philological Society, 1999.

———. "Narrative Techniques and Narrative Structures in the *Metamorphoses.*" In *Brill's Companion to Ovid,* edited by Barbara Weiden Boyd, 271–304. Leiden: Brill, 2002.

Ross, David O. *Vergil's Elements: Physics and Poetry in the* Georgics. Princeton, N.J.: Princeton University Press, 1987.

Sansone, David. "Orpheus and Eurydice in the Fifth Century." *Classica et Mediaevalia* 36 (1985): 53–64.

Scheid, John, and Jesper Svenbro. *The Craft of Zeus: Myths of Weaving and Fabric,* translated by Carol Volk. Cambridge, Mass.: Harvard University Press, 1996.

Scully, Stephen. "Refining Fire in *Aeneid* 8." *Vergilius* 46 (2000): 97–113.

Segal, Charles. "Myth and Philosophy in the *Metamorphoses:* Ovid's Augustanism and the Augustan Conclusion of Book XV." *American Journal of Philology* 90.3 (1969): 257–92.

———. *Landscape in Ovid's* Metamorphoses: *A Study in the Transformation of a Literary Symbol.* Hermes Zeitschrift für Klassische Philologie Einzelschriften 23. Wiesbaden: Franz Steiner Verlag, 1969.

———. "Ovid's Orpheus and Augustan Ideology." *Transactions of the American Philological Association* 103 (1972): 473–94.

———. *Orpheus: The Myth of the Poet.* Baltimore, Md.: Johns Hopkins University Press, 1989.

———. "Ovid's Metamorphic Bodies: Art, Gender and Violence in the *Metamorphoses.*" *Arion* 5.3 (1998): 9–41.

———. "Ovid's Arcadia and the Characterization of Jupiter in the *Metamorphoses.*" In *Ovid: Werk und Wirkung: Festgabe für Michael von Albrecht zum 65. Geburtstag Vol. I,* 401–12. Frankfurt am Main: Lang, 1998.

Shackleton-Bailey, D. R., ed. and tr. *Martial: Epigrams.* Vol. 2. Cambridge, Mass.: Harvard University Press, 1993.

Sharrock, Alison. "Womanufacture." *Journal of Roman Studies* 81 (1991): 36–49.

———. "Representing Metamorphosis." In *Art and Text in Roman Culture,* edited by Jás Elsner, 103–30. Cambridge: Cambridge University Press, 1996.

———. "Gender and Sexuality." In *The Cambridge Companion to Ovid,* edited by Philip Hardie, 95–107. Cambridge: Cambridge University Press, 2002.

Skutsch, Franz. *Aus Vergils Frühzeit.* Aalen: Scientia Verlag, 1982.

Sluiter, Ineke, and Ralph M. Rosen, eds. *Free Speech in Classical Antiquity.* Leiden: Brill, 2004.

Smith, Mack. *Literary Realism and the Ekphrastic Tradition.* University Park: Pennsylvania State University Press, 1995.

Smith, R. Alden. *Poetic Illusion and Poetic Embrace in Ovid and Virgil.* Ann Arbor: University of Michigan Press, 1997.

Solodow, Joseph B. *The World of Ovid's* Metamorphoses. Chapel Hill: University of North Carolina Press, 1988.

Stephens, Wade C. "Cupid and Venus in Ovid's *Metamorphoses.*" *Transactions of the American Philological Association* 89 (1958): 286–300.

Stern, Henri. "Les Débuts de l'Iconographie d'Orphée Charmant les Animaux." In *Mélanges de numismatique, d'archéologie et d'histoire offerts à Jean Lafaurie,* edited by Pierre Bastien, 157–64. Paris: Société française de numismatique, 1980.

Suits, T. A. "The Iambic Character of Propertius 1.4." *Philologus* 120 (1976): 86–91.

Syme, Sir Ronald. *The Roman Revolution.* Oxford: Oxford University Press, 1951.

———. *History in Ovid.* Oxford: Oxford University Press, 1978.

Talvacchia, Bette. *Taking Positions: On the Erotic in Renaissance Culture.* Princeton, N.J.: Princeton University Press, 1999.

Tarrant, Richard. "Ovid and Ancient Literary History." In *The Cambridge Companion to Ovid,* edited by Philip Hardie, 13–33. Cambridge: Cambridge University Press, 2002.

Thomas, Richard F. "Callimachus, the Victoria Berenices, and Roman Poetry." *Classical Quarterly,* n.s., 33 (1983): 92–113.

———. "Virgil's Ecphrastic Centerpieces." *Harvard Studies in Classical Philology* 87 (1983): 175–84.

———, ed. *Virgil:* Georgics *Vol. 1, Books I–II.* Cambridge: Cambridge University Press, 1988.

———, ed. *Virgil:* Georgics *Vol. 2, Books III–IV.* Cambridge: Cambridge University Press, 1988.

Tissol, Garth. "Polyphemus and His Audiences: Narrative and Power in Ovid's *Metamorphoses.*" *Syllecta Classica* 2 (1990) 45–58.

———. "The House of Fame: Roman History and Augustan Politics in *Metamorphoses* 11–15." In *Brill's Companion to Ovid,* edited by Barbara Weiden Boyd, 305–35. Leiden: Brill, 2002.

Tupet, Anne Marie. "La magie dans la métamorphose d'Arachné (Ovide, *Met.,* 6,135–145)." In *Journeés Ovidiennes de Parménie: Actes du Colloque sur Ovide (24–26 juin 1983),* edited by Jean M. Frécaut and Danielle Porte, 215–28. Brussells: Latomus, 1985.

Vasaly, Ann. "The Structure of Livy's First Pentad and the Augustan Poetry Book." In *Clio and the Poets: Augustan Poetry and the Traditions of Ancient Historiography,* edited by David S. Levene and Damien P. Nelis, 275–90. Leiden: Brill, 2002.

Viarre, Simone. *l'Image et la pensée dans les* "Métamorphoses" *d'Ovide.* Paris: Presses universitaires de France, 1964.

Vincent, Michael. "Between Ovid and Barthes: *Ekphrasis,* Orality, Textuality in Ovid's 'Arachne.'" *Arethusa* 27 (1994): 361–86.

von Albrecht, Michael. "l'Episode d'Arachné dans les *Métamorphoses* d'Ovide." *Révue des études latines* 57 (1979): 267–77.

Wallace-Hadrill, Andrew. "Time for Augustus: Ovid, Augustus and the *Fasti.*" In *Homo Viator: Classical Essays for John Bramble,* edited by Michael Whitby, Philip Hardie and Mary Whitby, 221–30. London: Bristol Classical Press, 1987.

Warden, J., ed. *Orpheus: Metamorphoses of a Myth.* Toronto: University of Toronto Press, 1982.

Weinberg, Gladys D., and Saul S. Weinberg. "Arachne of Lydia at Corinth." In *The Aegean and the Near East: Studies Presented to Hetty Goldman,* edited by Saul S. Weinberg, 262–67. Locust Valley, N.Y.: J. J. Augustin, 1956.

West, Martin L. *The Orphic Poems.* Oxford: Clarendon Press, 1983.

Wheeler, Stephen M. "*Imago Mundi:* Another View of the Creation in Ovid's *Metamorphoses.*" *American Journal of Philology* 116.1 (1995): 95–121.

———. *A Discourse of Wonders: Audience and Performance in Ovid's* Metamorphoses. Philadelphia: University of Pennsylvania Press, 1999.

Wilkinson, L. P. *Ovid Recalled.* Cambridge: Cambridge University Press, 1955.

Williams, Gordon. *Change and Decline: Roman Literature in the Early Empire.* Berkeley: University of California Press, 1978.

Woodman, Tony, and Denis Feeney, eds. *Traditions and Contexts in the Poetry of Horace.* Cambridge: Cambridge University Press, 2002.

Woodman, Tony, and Jonathan Powell. *Author and Audience in Latin Literature.* Cambridge: Cambridge University Press, 1992.

Zeitlin, Froma I. *Under the Sign of the Shield: Semiotics and Aeschylus'* Seven against Thebes. Rome: Edizioni dell'Ateneo, 1982.

———. "The Artful Eye: Vision, Ecphrasis and Spectacle in Euripidean Theatre." In *Art and Text in Ancient Greek Culture,* edited by Simon Goldhill and Robin Osborne, 138–96. Cambridge: Cambridge University Press, 1994.

Zissos, Andrew. "The Rape of Proserpina in Ovid *Met.* 5.341–661: Internal Audience and Narrative Distortion." *Phoenix* 53 (1999): 97–113.

Index

Note: This general index includes subjects, names, and words discussed in the text. Specific textual references can be located using the *index locorum* that follows.

Index Locorum

WISCONSIN STUDIES IN CLASSICS

General Editors
William Aylward, Nicholas D. Cahill, and Patricia A. Rosenmeyer

---

E. A. THOMPSON
Romans and Barbarians: The Decline of the Western Empire

JENNIFER TOLBERT ROBERTS
Accountability in Athenian Government

H. I. MARROU
A History of Education in Antiquity
Histoire de l'Education dans l'Antiquité, translated by George Lamb

ERIKA SIMON
Festivals of Attica: An Archaeological Commentary

G. MICHAEL WOLOCH
Roman Cities: Les villes romaines by Pierre Grimal, translated and edited by G. Michael Woloch, together with A Descriptive Catalogue of Roman Cities by G. Michael Woloch

WARREN G. MOON, editor
Ancient Greek Art and Iconography

KATHERINE DOHAN MORROW
Greek Footwear and the Dating of Sculpture

JOHN KEVIN NEWMAN
The Classical Epic Tradition

JEANNY VORYS CANBY, EDITH PORADA, BRUNILDE SISMONDO RIDGWAY, and TAMARA STECH, editors
Ancient Anatolia: Aspects of Change and Cultural Development

ANN NORRIS MICHELINI
Euripides and the Tragic Tradition

WENDY J. RASCHKE, editor
The Archaeology of the Olympics: The Olympics and Other Festivals in Antiquity

PAUL PLASS
Wit and the Writing of History: The Rhetoric of Historiography in Imperial Rome

BARBARA HUGHES FOWLER
The Hellenistic Aesthetic

F. M. CLOVER and R. S. HUMPHREYS, editors
Tradition and Innovation in Late Antiquity

BRUNILDE SISMONDO RIDGWAY
Hellenistic Sculpture I: The Styles of ca. 331–200 B.C.

BARBARA HUGHES FOWLER, editor and translator
Hellenistic Poetry: An Anthology

KATHRYN J. GUTZWILLER
Theocritus' Pastoral Analogies: The Formation of a Genre

VIMALA BEGLEY and RICHARD DANIEL DE PUMA, editors
Rome and India: The Ancient Sea Trade

RUDOLF BLUM
HANS H. WELLISCH, translator
Kallimachos: The Alexandrian Library and the Origins of Bibliography

DAVID CASTRIOTA
Myth, Ethos, and Actuality: Official Art in Fifth Century B.C. Athens

BARBARA HUGHES FOWLER, editor and translator
Archaic Greek Poetry: An Anthology

JOHN H. OAKLEY and REBECCA H. SINOS
The Wedding in Ancient Athens

RICHARD DANIEL DE PUMA and JOCELYN PENNY SMALL, editors
Murlo and the Etruscans: Art and Society in Ancient Etruria

JUDITH LYNN SEBESTA and LARISSA BONFANTE, editors
The World of Roman Costume

JENNIFER LARSON
Greek Heroine Cults

WARREN G. MOON, editor
Polykleitos, the Doryphoros, and Tradition

PAUL PLASS
The Game of Death in Ancient Rome: Arena Sport and Political Suicide

MARGARET S. DROWER
Flinders Petrie: A Life in Archaeology

SUSAN B. MATHESON
Polygnotos and Vase Painting in Classical Athens

JENIFER NEILS, editor
Worshipping Athena: Panathenaia and Parthenon

PAMELA A. WEBB
Hellenistic Architectural Sculpture: Figural Motifs in Western Anatolia and the Aegean Islands

BRUNILDE SISMONDO RIDGWAY
Fourth-Century Styles in Greek Sculpture

LUCY GOODISON and CHRISTINE MORRIS, editors
Ancient Goddesses: The Myths and the Evidence

JO-MARIE CLAASSEN
Displaced Persons: The Literature of Exile from Cicero to Boethius

BRUNILDE SISMONDO RIDGWAY
Hellenistic Sculpture II: The Styles of ca. 200–100 B.C.

PAT GETZ-GENTLE
Personal Styles in Early Cycladic Sculpture

CATULLUS
DAVID MULROY, translator and commentator
The Complete Poetry of Catullus

BRUNILDE SISMONDO RIDGWAY
Hellenistic Sculpture III: The Styles of ca. 100–31 B.C.

ANGELIKI KOSMOPOULOU
The Iconography of Sculptured Statue Bases in the Archaic and Classical Periods

SARA H. LINDHEIM
Mail and Female: Epistolary Narrative and Desire in Ovid's Heroides

GRAHAM ZANKER
Modes of Viewing in Hellenistic Poetry and Art

ALEXANDRA ANN CARPINO
Discs of Splendor: The Relief Mirrors of the Etruscans

TIMOTHY S. JOHNSON
A Symposion of Praise: Horace Returns to Lyric in Odes *IV*

JEAN-RENÉ JANNOT
Religion in Ancient Etruria
Devins, Dieux et Démons: Regards sur la religion de l'Etrurie antique, translated by Jane K. Whitehead

CATHERINE SCHLEGEL
Satire and the Threat of Speech: Horace's Satires, *Book 1*

CHRISTOPHER A. FARAONE and LAURA K. MCCLURE, editors
Prostitutes and Courtesans in the Ancient World

PLAUTUS
JOHN HENDERSON, translator and commentator
Asinaria: The One about the Asses

PATRICE D. RANKINE
Ulysses in Black: Ralph Ellison, Classicism, and African American Literature

PAUL REHAK
JOHN G. YOUNGER, editor
Imperium and Cosmos: Augustus and the Northern Campus Martius

PATRICIA J. JOHNSON
Ovid before Exile: Art and Punishment in the Metamorphoses

VERED LEV KENAAN

Pandora's Senses: The Feminine Character of the Ancient Text